MAPHAEUS VEGIUS

AND HIS
THIRTEENTH BOOK
OF THE AENEID

Edited with Introduction,
Bibliography and Commentary by
Anna Cox Brinton

Bristol Classical Press

First published in 1930 by Stanford University Press

This edition published in 2002 by
Bristol Classical Press
an imprint of
Gerald Duckworth & Co. Ltd
61 Frith Street
London W1D 3JL
e-mail: inquiries@duckworth-publishers.co.uk
Website: www.ducknet.co.uk

A catalogue record for this book is available
from the British Library

ISBN 1-85399-629-7

BCP Classic Commentaries on Latin and Greek Texts
Current and forthcoming titles:

Aristophanes: Ecclesiazusae, R. Ussher
Calpurnius Siculus: The Eclogues, C. Keene
Cicero: De Oratore I-III, A.S. Wilkins
Empedocles: The Extant Fragments, M. Wright
Euripides: Alcestis, A. Dale
Euripides: Cyclops, R. Seaford
Euripides: Helen, A. Dale
Euripides: Iphigenia in Tauris, M. Platnauer
Euripides: Troades, K. Lee
Herodas: The Mimes and Fragments, W. Headlam
Herodotus: Book II, W.G. Waddell
Maphaeus Vegius & his Thirteenth Book of the Aeneid, A. Cox Brinton
Nicander: Poems & Poetical Fragments, A. Gow & A. Scholfield
Persius: Satires, J. Conington & H. Nettleship
Plutarch: Alexander (commentary only), J. Hamilton & P. Stadter
Seneca the Elder: Suasoriae, W. Edward
Statius: Silvae IV, K. Coleman
Tacitus: Dialogus, W. Peterson
Tacitus: Germania, J. Anderson
The Poems of Cicero, W. Ewbank
Virgil: Aeneid III, R. Williams

V   THE WEDDING FEAST OF AENEAS AND LAVINIA

PREFACE

The present vivid intereſt in Italian humanism, and that perennial admiration for Virgil which makes his scholars in the twentieth century no ſtrangers to his lovers in the fifteenth, prompts the publication of this ſtudy of the moſt famous and moſt widely read sequel to the *Aeneid*.

The answers to the two queſtions "Why was 'The Thirteenth Book of the *Aeneid*' written?" and "Why was it read and enjoyed all over Europe for more than two hundred years?" throw light on Virgil's spiritual sway over European thought. This hitherto unwritten chapter is presented as a contribution to the hiſtory of Virgil's influence at the two-thousandth anniversary of his birth, when all the world is preparing to make grateful acknowledgment of the legacy of light and leading of this beſt-beloved of Roman poets.

Interpretation of the *Aeneid* is a barometer which regiſters changes in the thought-climate of Weſtern civilization. The Middle Ages knew Virgil as a man of myſtery, a magician; modern scholarship analyzes him as artiſt and philosopher; but the Renaissance adored him as author of a divine allegory, a pilgrim's progress of heroic souls. To Chriſtian enthusiasm in the fifteenth century, accuſtomed as it was to the dogma of resurrećtion and to the canonization of saints, the *Aeneid* ſtopped short of a final emphatic ſtatement of its glorious climax. Maphaeus Vegius' "Thirteenth Book" was the audacious effort of ardent youth to bring Virgil's narrative to its own sublime conclusion. The pleasant Virgilian cadences of the young Italian poet who followed his ancient maſter *"non passibus aequis,"* but with love, awakened a subtle sympathy from readers in many lands to whom the world-transforming invention of the printing-press brought the *Aeneid* as well as the Bible. More than one hundred and eighty editions of Virgil appeared before 1500, that is, within the firſt fifty years after the introdućtion of the art of printing. The following century was almoſt as prolific of new editions. Until about 1650, Vegius' "Supplement" usually accompanied the *Aeneid*.

Maphaeus Vegius' "Thirteenth Book" claims as its *editio princeps* the Virgil of 1471, published in Venice by Adam de Ambergau. Of this small and rare edition Copinger has been able to identify only four copies. I have followed this text throughout. The spelling has been modified to conform to modern usage. The punctuation is my own. The beautiful round Roman types of the handsome Venetian original are illustrated by a photograph of the opening lines of the poem. This facsimile and the series of Sebastian Brant's spirited woodcuts (Strassburg, 1502) which illustrate the text were photographed in the British Museum.

The quaint English version with its terse insets, which is printed on alternate pages with the Latin text, is by Thomas Twyne, M.D., who completed the *Virgil* left unfinished by Dr. Thomas Phaer at his death in 1560. *The Whole XIII Bookes of the Aeneidos of Virgil* by Twyne and Phaer was first published in London in 1584. The facsimile title page photographed by the Henry E. Huntington Library appears following page 50.

Bishop Gavin Douglas' Scotch translation follows. It is introduced by a whimsical and delightful "Proloug of the Threttene Buik of Eneados ekit to Virgill be Mapheus Vegius." *The XIII Bukes of Eneados of the famose poete Virgill translatet out of Latyne verses into Scottish metir, bi the Reverend Father in God, Mayster Gawin Douglas Bishop of Dunkel and unkil to the Erle of Angus, Euery buke hauing hys perticular Prologe* was completed in 1513. Its earliest publication is dated London, 1553. This translation has special significance because it is the most important literary monument of ancient Scottish speech.

Two biographical and critical monographs, printed at Lodi in Lombardy in 1896 and 1909, respectively, supply valuable summaries of the life and work of Vegius. They are entitled *La vita di Maffeo Vegio, unamista lodigiano,* by Mario Minoia, and *Maffeo Vegio,* by Luigi Raffaele. The profile of Maphaeus Vegius which appears on the cover of this volume is adapted from a portrait in the town library of Lodi, published on page 76 of the latter. Liverani's edition of the "Thirteenth Book," Livorno, 1897, has also been of service.

Obligations to standard works are recorded in the notes.

I wish to express my thanks to the professors of Classical Literature at Stanford University, H. Rushton Fairclough, Augustus T. Murray, B. O. Foster, and Jefferson Elmore, who, as teachers, colleagues, and friends have aided my study. Professor Fairclough has taken especial interest in the present monograph on account of his own devotion to Virgil. Professor Foster made helpful suggestions in the early stages of this work. Miss Flora B. Ludington of the staff of the Mills College Library has given useful counsel in regard to bibliographical references.

ANNA COX BRINTON

MILLS COLLEGE
January 30, 1930

CONTENTS

ILLUSTRATIONS

INTRODUCTION

Comparetti's magic tale of Virgil in the Middle Ages[1] describes the metamorphosis of the exponent of Rome's imperial ideal into a wizard of popular legend and traces his gradual literary transformation into the prophetic guide of Christian souls. This astonishing narrative will some day be followed by the no less romantic story of Virgil in the Renaissance. The ascendancy of the *Aeneid* was long and brilliant, for Virgil was, in a unique sense, master and model of all epic poets from Petrarch to Milton.

A delightful and almost fantastic chapter in the romance of Virgil's influence concerns Maphaeus Vegius' "Thirteenth Book of the *Aeneid*," a canto of six hundred and thirty lines, written at Pavia in 1428 by a lad of twenty-one. This audacious composition early had the strange fortune, as the piquant Virgilian critic, Dr. Henry, aptly puts it, to become "established as an eke or co-tenant under the same roof with the *Aeneid*,"[2] where it remained an almost constant resident for a century and a half after the invention of printing. Later it became, as it were, a visitor, and, in the eighteenth century, only an occasional guest in Virgil's house. Its final appearance at the close of the *Aeneid* occurred in Lemaire's *Bibliotheca classica*, Paris, 1820.

As early as 1500 Iodocus Badius Ascensius had enriched Maphaeus Vegius' "Thirteenth Book" with a copious commentary. Two years later Sebastian Brant embellished it with six inimitable woodcuts. It was many times translated, and in the eighteenth century it was even parodied.

Maphaeus Vegius was not alone in his aspiration to complete the tale of Aeneas' fortunes.[3] Pier Candido Decembrio, the illustrious

---

[1] D. Comparetti, *Virgil in the Middle Ages*, translated by E. F. M. Benecke, London, 1895.

[2] J. Henry, *Aeneidea* (Dublin, 1878), I, Introduction, page 60.

[3] See: (1) *Vierteljahrsschrift für Kultur und Litteratur der Renaissance*, Berlin, 1886; (2) C. Borinski, *Das Epos der Renaissance*; (3) *Giornale storico della letteratura italiana* (1885), VI, 472.

translator of Appian and Plato, whose features are pictured for posterity in Pisanello's distinguished medallion, also ventured in his youth to compose a supplement to the *Aeneid*, but he says that he laid the manuscript away among his papers and did not give it to the world. It has, however, survived, at least in part, and a considerable passage is quoted by Saxius in his laborious chronicle of the literature of Milan.[4]

In 1483 the anonymous author of the "Analysis of the *Aeneid*" wrote a continuation to Virgil's Twelfth Book. Joseph Forestus[5] and C. S. de Novavilla,[6] in the sixteenth and seventeenth centuries, respectively, devised additional conclusions to the epic. In the nineteenth century an English translator of Virgil named Seymour Burt,[7] not satisfied with translating Vegius' supplement, even had the temerity to propose a fourteenth book evolved from the early chapters of Livy's history. So far afield had his admirers strayed from a true understanding of the structural completeness of Virgil's epic and a just appreciation of its tragic close.

Maphaeus Vegius' "Thirteenth Book of the *Aeneid*" was the only one of these sequels which became famous. To Vegius, Virgil's epic was above all an allegory of the soul. For this reason he could ill spare what was to him the climax of its narrative—the crossing of the river where the mortal garment was left behind and the swift ascent through regions of air to a place of glory among the stars. Aeneas' westward voyage, his war in Italy, his marriage, and his apotheosis all lent themselves to symbolic interpretation.

Vegius' "Thirteenth Book" opens with the same dramatic picture with which Virgil's twelfth book closes. It proceeds to relate how Aeneas, now master of Italy, since he has slain Turnus in single combat, receives the Rutuli in surrender. The captains strike their

[4] J. A. Saxius, *Historia literaria typographica mediolanensis*, Milan, 1745; also *Giornale storico della letteratura italiana* (1893), XXII, 433.

[5] *Virgilius*, edited by C. G. Heyne, supplemented by N. E. Lemaire (Paris, 1820), pages 408 ff.

[6] C. S. de Novavilla or Villanova, *Supplementum ad Aeneida seu Aeneidos liber decimus tertius*, Paris, 1698.

[7] See below, page 39.

spears into the earth and lay down their shields. Though ſtricken with grief, they prefer submission to further ſtruggle. Meanwhile the Trojans bury their dead and make sacrifice to the gods. Aeneas exhorts his comrades to continued perseverance. The Latins lament their hero Turnus, whose body is sent home by night with a ſtately funeral train. When the sad procession reaches Ardea, the city is in flames, and old king Daunus, beset with harrowing grief at home, is confronted with the loss of his only son in war. In the midſt of all this sorrow heaped on sorrow, the spirit of the ancient city of Ardea, in the form of the bird Ardea, rises Phoenix-like from the burning embers. On the following day Latinus sends an embassy to Aeneas confirming peace and promising his daughter in marriage. Aeneas and the Trojans journey to Laurentum with pomp and circumſtance. The kings meet, Lavinia is betrothed, and rich Trojan gifts are beſtowed upon Latinus and his daughter. After nine days of dancing, feaſting, and rehearsing adventures, Aeneas marks out his new city with the plow. A flame of fire like a saint's aureole glows about the bride Lavinia's brow, and blessed Venus appears to confirm and expound the omen. Latinus finishes his days and goes to his reward. Aeneas rules on in holy peace for the space of three years. Finally, by Jupiter's decree, his spirit is translated to the ſtars.

Vegius' ſtyle is fluent and easy; his language and meter are characteriſtic of the early quattrocento, when eloquence was more highly prized and more enthusiaſtically cultivated than accurate adherence to the literary canons of Auguſtan Rome. He did not revise his juvenilia in later life as "good old Mantuan"[8] revised his famous *Eclogues*, but preferred to have his reputation reſt upon more serious and mature prose works. His heroic poems, all of which were composed during his early years, show the faults as well as the freshness of youth eager to emulate great poets.[9] The words and phrases of his maſter, Maro, whom he reverenced as a god upon earth,[10] were always ringing in his

[8] W. P. Mustard, *Eclogues of Mantuan*, Baltimore (1911), page 35.

[9] Maphaeus Vegius, *Aſtyanax*, Pavia, 1430; *Velleris aurei libri quattuor*, Pavia, 1431.

[10] Maphaeus Vegius, *De perseverantia religionis*, I, 1: "Quem alterum in terris Deum esse arbitrabar."

[3]

ears, and it was second nature for Vegius to infuse Virgilian cadences
into his own verse. This he did by adaptation and allusion rather than
by the method of direct transference which characterizes the true cento,
that "pseudo poetry—which pleases the learned by its ingenuity and
deceives the unlearned by its affected stateliness."[11]

The "Thirteenth Book" is shorter by seventy-five lines than Book
IV, which is the shortest book of the *Aeneid*. It contains eight similes,
an average number for the same number of lines in Virgil. Julius
Caesar Scaliger writes in his *Poetices*, which is one of the first modern
attempts at a systematic treatment of poetry and poets, that, in his
opinion, the first two similes of Vegius are as good or better than those
of Lucan and Statius.[12] The imitative element is less pronounced in
Vegius' figures than in his narrative. The second simile is, however,
composed entirely upon a Virgilian model. The first and fifth show
Virgil's influence, though in each the point of comparison is different
from his. The other five have only a faint resemblance to similes in
the *Aeneid*. The last portrays a characteristically Italian agricultural
scene in which peasants who have been housebound by a siege of rain
are rejoicing in the return of fair weather. The description is well
expressed and has real poetic merit.

The greatest flaw in the composition of the "Thirteenth Book" is
an excess of speeches; these were introduced, no doubt, to increase
dramatic effectiveness, but they far overshoot their mark. There are
no less than thirteen harangues, laments, addresses, appeals, and
prayers, ranging in length from four to forty-two lines. An age in
which public eloquence was prized above every other literary accom-
plishment fell naturally into this error of taste.

The plot is based on the latter half of the *Aeneid*, with hints from
the early chapters of Livy's history. Two conspicuous episodes, the
burning of Ardea and the death of Aeneas, are adapted from the *Meta-
morphoses* of Ovid.[13]

---

[11] James Rendell Harris, *The Homeric Centones and the Acts of Pilate*, Lon-
don, 1898.

[12] J. C. Scaliger, *Poetices libri septem* (Heidelberg, 1581, second edition),
page 783.

[13] *Metamorphoses*, XIV, 573–581, 581–608.

His own contemporaries were Vegius' enthusiastic admirers. The facility and youthful high spirit of his verse and his frank appropriation of the measures and phrases of the idolized ancients made him a general favorite. Quattrocentists found no inappropriateness in applying to him epithets such as *"alter Maro"*[14] and *"alter Parthenias"*[15] and the adjectives *"doctissimus"*[16] and *"altiloquus."*[17]

MAPHAEUS VEGIUS, POET AND ESSAYIST

Maphaeus Vegius was born in the Lombard town of Lodi in 1407,[18] the very year in which his more famous friend, the learned and audacious critic, Lorenzo Valla, was born in Rome; and he died at Rome in 1458, one year after Valla's death. His life covered a brilliant half-century in which Italy set the intellectual pace for Western Europe. Party strife no longer engrossed the entire attention of able men, and flourishing trade brought wealth and a standard of living favorable to the arts. The Papacy became permanently re-established in Rome after the vicissitudes of the "Babylonian Captivity"; the "Great Schism" came to an end; important cosmopolitan councils, which brought Eastern and Western Christendom together, definitely increased the prestige of the Roman See. City tyrants and princes of the Church vied with one another as patrons of art and of the scholarly industry that was unearthing legacies from antiquity. Literature had, since Petrarch, passed to its autumn, a season of erudition and research; but the plastic and pictorial arts were in the heydey of springtime. The early decades of the century witnessed the spiritual quickening of the Franciscan Revival and of its northern counterpart, the mission of John Huss. Travel and exploration were rapidly revising Ptolemaic conceptions of geography. Among all the varied achievements of this exuberant

---

[14] G. Mancini, *Lorenzo Valla* (Florence, 1891), page 48.

[15] Arundel Manuscripts 82 and 193, British Museum.

[16] Antonio d'Asti, *In rerum italicarum scriptores*, XIV, 1013.

[17] *Carmina poetarum italorum*, VII, 519.

[18] The fifth centenary of their poet's birth was celebrated by the citizens of Lodi in 1907.

era of discovery, none was more remarkable than the new curriculum
of study and physical exercise developed for the education of youth
in the schools of the humanists.

An intimate record of even average experience in such a century
has more than average interest, and Maphaeus Vegius, in his early
poems and in the biographical passages of his historical and moral
essays, vividly pictures the activities and enthusiasms of a talented
and precocious child of this brilliant epoch. His accounts are incidental
and fragmentary, but they have more significance than the barren
framework of fact supplied by his fifteenth- and sixteenth-century
biographers.

Family and childhood.—Maphaeus Vegius came of a substantial
family. His father, Bellortus Vegius, and his mother, Caterina Lan-
teria, were "distinguished for noble lineage and both of them admi-
rable for moral excellence."[19] He had at least two brothers and two
sisters and was himself the second son.

Contrary to the usual practice among women of position, Caterina
esteemed it a privilege and duty to suckle her own babes when she
could; but for the elder boys considerations of health required her to
secure a nurse. Maphaeus' foster-mother was modest and bashful, with
a disposition as gentle as her countenance. Her eyes were always down-
cast in the fashion admired during the Renaissance.[20] Maphaeus looked
back in after years to the influence of his nurse as wholly good.[21] He did
not fare so well, however, at the hands of the other servants.[22] Their
tales of ghosts and goblins instilled such terror in his baby mind that he
was hardly able to shake off the impression even when he was a big
boy in his teens.

His elder brother, Laurence,[23] a child of rare promise and gentle
nature whom Maphaeus dearly loved, was an invalid from childhood

---

[19]Anonymous life prefaced to Vegius' works, published at Lodi [?], 1613.

[20] Leonardo da Vinci, *A Treatise on Painting*, translated by J. F. Rigaud, Lon-
don, 1906.

[21] Maphaeus Vegius, *De educatione liberorum*, I, 5.

[22] *Ibid.*, I, 11.

[23] *Ibid.*, I, 6.

and died early. To a second brother, Eustace, he inscribed his first prose work, the dialogue *Philalethes*, which, with another entitled *De felicitate et miseria*, passed for some time as a work of Lucian. It was a happy dedication, for Eustace was a man whose character and love of learning made him, like a second Philalethes, fit to welcome Truth, wounded and bleeding from the violence of an unscrupulous age. In concluding his preface, Maphaeus remarks that, as others give their brothers jewels and furniture, things perishable, he dedicates to Eustace his quest for Truth, which is eternal. His sisters, Elizabeth and Monica,[24] were much younger. Maphaeus says that he brought them up himself. It was with paternal satisfaction that he received the news that they had both taken the veil. Toward the end of his life he dedicated to them a tract entitled *De perseverantia religionis*. These pages, full of learned quotation and allusion, presuppose a breadth of familiarity with sacred and profane authors far exceeding that recommended for girls in his own treatise on education.

Bellortus Vegius was genuinely interested in his sons' progress, and afforded them excellent opportunities for healthy rural life and for elaborate schooling.[25] Country rambles supplied Maphaeus with material which he soon put to use in the prolific epigrams of his adolescent years and in illustrations for his maturer poetry.

A pretty simile in the "Thirteenth Book" (lines 445–449), which describes Italian farmers congratulating one another when a long siege of rain is finally lifted, may well have come from this source. Homely wit was likewise bred of rustic experience. On one occasion little Maphaeus met a shepherd driving his flock in the depth of winter. His feet were bare and his cloak was scanty. The boy asked him how he bore the cold so well, to which the peasant answered: "Do you think, my son, that you would be cold if you had on all the clothes you own?" Maphaeus shook his head. "Then don't be surprised," said he, "that I am not cold. I always wear all the clothes I have."[26]

[24] Maphaeus Vegius, *De perseverantia religionis*, I, 1.

[25] Maphaeus Vegius, *De educatione liberorum*, I, 4; II, 9; III, 2, and the anonymous *Life* prefixed to the Basle edition of Vegius' works.

[26] Maphaeus Vegius, *De educatione liberorum*, I, 6.

His education.—At seven[27] Maphaeus was sent to school in Milan[28] to a *"plagosus Orbilius,"* who, like some more recent teachers, showed a very different face to his pupils' parents from that which characterized him at the desk. Happily the boy was soon transferred to a dear old man whose genuine love of literature made up for lack of profound learning. Under his gentle tutelage, Maphaeus read omnivorously of his own free will from Virgil and Ovid and spared no pains to understand their meaning. Every day he learned by heart some passage for sheer love of it.

These were the years of the Franciscan Revival,[29] when its most famous preacher, Fra Bernardino of Siena, came to Milan. On feast days the teacher would say to his favorite pupils, of whom Maphaeus was one, "Sons, let us go to hear the good little brother who wears such poor and threadbare garments, but whose speech is so rich in grace, whose eloquence is so brilliant, who has such an apt turn for teaching and such majesty of expression and thought."[30]

The boys relied upon their teacher's judgment, since they were too young to form their own, and listened with the closest attention, though they could not fully comprehend the "heaven-inspired discourse." The memory of these sermons was still fresh after thirty years, when, at the Pope's jubilee in 1450, Bernardino of Siena and Joan of Arc were first proposed for canonization. Maphaeus Vegius wrote one of the biographical appreciations of the great Franciscan preacher for this spectacular occasion. Aeneas Silvius Piccolomini, afterward Pope Pius II, also heard the famous friar in childhood. He describes him[31] as always "jolly and merry; never was his face sad unless he was distressed over some public wrong." Sienese gaiety joined to Franciscan playfulness commended his stern message of reform.

[27] Maphaeus Vegius *De educatione liberorum*, II, 2.

[28] *Ibid.*, II, 9; II, 19.

[29] Lucas Wadding, *Annales minorum*, Naples, 1731–1860.

[30] Maphaeus Vegius, *Vita sancti Bernardini, acta sanctorum*, Maii V, 88.

[31] Aeneas Silvius, *De viris illustribus, De Benardino Senensi.* Stuttgart, *Literarische Vereinbibliotek*, 1843.

At fifteen a *"furor poeticus"* seized young Vegius, and he began to compose his *Pompeiana,* elegies and epigrams on country life.[32] In these he followed a fashionable literary type which had a distinct affinity with Roman epigram but was also colored by medieval sarcastic verse. The poems contain some picturesque and tender passages,[33] but more that seem spiteful or vulgar to modern taste.

Bellortus Vegius broke in upon these youthful fancies and commanded his son to leave off frivolity and devote himself to dialectic.[34] The boy obeyed, though he found the study nothing short of "pestiferous." Maphaeus was destined eventually for the law, a pursuit even more distasteful to him than the study of dialectic. To quote his own language, "it was easier for Orpheus to withhold his gaze from Eurydice than for him to persist in the neglect of his beloved poets."

Pavia.—A happy change of fortune took him at nineteen to Pavia,[35] where the University was rapidly becoming a distinguished seat of the new learning. He found himself among congenial friends and was free to devote himself to poetry. Here, too, he studied Greek.[36]

It was in these agreeable surroundings, when Vegius was a youth of twenty-one, that he wrote his "Thirteenth Book of the *Aeneid.*" He knew almost by heart the epic of his beloved Virgil, to whom he offered this tribute in eager, youthful homage. The original caption was *A Supplement to the Twelfth Book of the Aeneid.* It bore the date, Pavia, October 4, 1428.[37]

University days afforded no more memorable experience to Maphaeus Vegius than his intimacy with Lorenzo Valla,[38] one of the most

[32] Maphaeus Vegius, *Pompeiana,* 1423; J. P. Nicéron, *Memoires;* G. Ghilini, *Teatro.*

[33] L. Raffaele, *Maffeo Vegio* (Bologna, 1909), pages 5–14.

[34] J. A. Saxius, *Historia literaria typographica mediolanensis,* letter to Bartolomeo de la Capra, page 405.

[35] M. Minoia, *La vita di Maffeo Vegio* (Lodi, 1896), chapter ii; L. Raffaele, *Maffeo Vegio* (Bologna, 1909), page 15.

[36] Vespasiano da Bisticci, *Vite* (Florence, 1859), "*Vita di Maffeo Veggio.*"

[37] See list of works, pages 145–146.

[38] A. Mancini, *Vita di Lorenzo Valla* (Florence, 1891), page 37.

original, as well as one of the moſt critical minds of that generation. The publication of Valla's observations on the text of Isaiah ranked him at once as the foremoſt Biblical scholar of the time. It was he who exposed the Donation of Conſtantine and the pseudo-Isadorian Decretals.[39] Their friends said that Vegius exercised a salutary reſtraint on the fiery young radical. Many years later they renewed their intimacy in Rome as papal secretaries.

In 1431 the plague broke up town life. Vegius fled to Lodi[40] to a charming retreat, described by Valla as a cottage with a lovely orchard near a Gregorian portico. To these charms were added a cook and several servitors. But Vegius pined for his gay companions, and, like Ovid in his exile, found consolation in tearful elegy.

Florence.—When the danger was paſt we find him again in Pavia and later in Milan, where he vainly aspired to a laureate's crown from the powerful Visconti.[41] Finally, he was off to seek his fortune among the firſt men of that age in Florence. His literary passports gained him immediate access to the brilliant galaxy of writers attached to the Medicean and papal courts. Their paſtime was exchange of verses, and Vegius was not a whit behind the reſt. He forthwith dedicated two books of diſtichs to Carlo Marsuppini, the leading poet of that learned circle, an attention which the Cardinal acknowledged in a series of epigrams. To Leonardo Bruni, Vegius inscribed two books of epigrams. The aged hiſtorian responded with helpful criticism.

The Curia was then in Florence and, through the good offices of his friends, Vegius obtained preferment under the hardheaded pope, Eugenius IV. For half a dozen years he served as abbreviator, and was then promoted to the rank of datary. He traveled with the papal court to Bologna, to Ferrara, and back again to Florence, marking his ſtay in the various cities by epitaphs on the great men, ecclesiaſtical, scientific,

---

[39] C. B. Coleman, *Lorenzo Valla on the Donation of Conſtantine*, Yale University Press, 1922.

[40] *Carmina poetarum italorum*, II, 9 and 10; see also a letter of Vegius dated 1433, J. A. Saxius, *Hiſtoria literaria typographica mediolanensis* (Milan, 1745).

[41] Maphaeus Vegius, *Convivium Deorum*, 1430; also *Ad Philippum Mariam Angelum ducem mediolanensium*. See liſt of works, pages 145–146.

and literary, who died within those years.[42] Vegius' time was largely absorbed by a tedious routine of pontifical correspondence. His amusement in leisure hours remained the composition of verse.

Rome.—The year 1443 marks the final return of the papacy to Rome, where Vegius spent the remaining fifteen years of his life. Here he was again associated with Lorenzo Valla, who introduces one of his dialogues[43] with a description of a Christmas excursion to the Sacro Speco at Subiaco and thence to Monte Cassino. Pietro di Noceto, trusted minister of Nicholas V, Maphaeus Vegius, Flavius Blondus, and Valla himself made up the party. Noceto fell in with hunters, in whose company he ranged the wooded hills below the monastery, while the savants took occasion to examine old books in the library.

In December of his first year in Rome, Vegius was appointed Canon of the Basilica of Saint Peter,[44] an office which he held until his death. A report was current in the fifteenth century that he became an Augustinian friar.[45] Luigi Raffaele[46] successfully refutes this statement, which was a natural supposition in view of Vegius' well-known devotion to Saint Monica and her son.

Authorship.—Vegius' life as a popular writer may be divided neatly into two periods of fifteen years each. In the first, like most young men of parts in the early fifteenth century, he wrote pagan poetry; in the second, which was the more prolific of the two, his dialogues, essays, epistles, psalms, hymns, and liturgies recall the great religious subjects that glow before our eyes in quattrocento frescoes. Flavoring all the copious writing of this very industrious author is a kind of Maronian essence, which does not lose its savor even after Augustine succeeded Virgil as his patron saint. The Puritan habit of discoursing in Biblical language is the closest literary parallel to Ma-

[42] *Carmina poetarum italorum*, X, 305 ff.

[43] Aeneas Silvius Piccolomini, *Tractatus*, 1453.

[44] *Regesta Laterana*, 399, Bull of Eugenius IV, naming Vegius Canon of Saint Peter's.

[45] Vespasiano da Bisticci, *Vite* (Florence, 1859), "*Vita di Maffeo Veggio.*"

[46] L. Raffaele, *Maffeo Vegio* (Bologna, 1909), Correspondence quoted on pages 44 ff.

phaeus Vegius' habit of employing the words and phrases of his adored master, Virgil.

In Rome, Vegius concentrated his attention on philosophical and ecclesiastical studies. Saint Augustine was now the unrivaled master of his heart. It was natural for humanists to feel a special kinship to the learned Bishop of Hippo; like themselves, he had come to Christianity "through the door of the classics." In Vegius' case there may also have been an inherited reverence. His parents had named their daughters after Augustine's mother Monica and her sister Elizabeth. Vegius expressly states that it was through the influence of his two sisters that he took holy orders, a decision which was a surprise, he says, even to himself.[47] As a boy he had followed Saint Augustine's steps in Northern Italy. It was at Milan that the ardent young African student had embraced Latin Christianity, and his relics were enshrined in Pavia.

In 1455 Vegius built a chapel[48] in honor of Saint Monica, whose bones had been translated from Ostia and received in Rome with great pomp in 1430. He commissioned Isaia di Pippo di Gante·da Pisa, who had carved the tomb of Eugenius IV and who may have wrought the grave slab of Fra Angelico, to design and execute the monument for which he composed an inscription in elegiac couplets. He also prepared an account of her life in three books, to which he added sacred offices in her name and in that of her son. The titles of eight of his compositions bear witness to his special veneration of the mother Monica and her son Augustine. They are: *Vita et officium B. Monicae; Officium translationis B. Monicae; De vita et obitu B. Monicae ex verbis S. Augustini; Laudatio B. Monicae; Salutatio B. Monicae; In Sanctam Monicam; Officium conversionis B. Augustini; Vita et officium B. Augustini.*

Maphaeus Vegius' love of ancient literature plays almost as distinct a rôle in the period of his prose writing as in his earlier works in verse.[49] His quotations are amazingly profuse and cover an astonish-

---

[47] Maphaeus Vegius, *De perseverantia religionis*, I, 1.

[48] G. S. Davies, *The Sculptured Tombs of the Fifteenth Century in Rome* (London, 1910), page 70; C. Janning, *Acta sanctorum* (Rome, 1867), Junii VII, 58.

[49] Maphaeus Vegius, *De perseverantia religionis*, V, 5.

ing range. In a single chapter on prayer,[50] in the tract dedicated to his two cloistered sisters, he quotes from saints and doctors, Bernard, Basil, Chrysostom, Ambrose, Cyprian, Jerome, Climax, Cassian, Porphyry, and Eusebius; from the Old Testament books, Exodus, Psalms, Daniel, and Isaiah; from the Gospels of Matthew, Luke, and John; from Apollonius of Tyana and Hermes Trismegistus. He finally caps his argument with a passage from the Greek dramatist Menander and with the famous conclusion of the second satire of the Roman poet Persius. In his treatise on education, which was composed at this time,[51] he makes a sound knowledge of the Latin language and a liberal familiarity with pagan literature, supplemented by a generous admixture of scriptural and ecclesiastical reading, the basis of learning and culture.[52] Vegius differed from other educationalists of the century in his stronger insistence on religious training. His suggestions for the instruction of girls show less advance from medieval prejudices than his curriculum for boys. Modesty of the crystalline type portrayed in Fra Angelico's virgins can, he thinks, be secured by limited reading, little exercise, few baths, much attention to household arts, and extensive contemplation of such models of feminine fortitude and virtue as Saint Monica and her sister Elizabeth.[53]

De educatione liberorum et eorum claris moribus assumes an important place in the prolific pedagogic output of the fifteenth century because of its detailed completeness and because of the adequate impression that it gives of the extent to which the ideals of progressive educational liberals were assimilated by moderate religious conservatives. To the re-applied slogans of antiquity, "a sound mind in a sound body" and "reverence for the age of childhood," is added a moral emphasis from the intervening Christian centuries.[54] Physical vigor and mental power are to be tempered and made significant by

[50] *Ibid.*, V, 2.

[51] Rome, 1444. See chronological list of the writings of Maphaeus Vegius, on pages 145 and 146.

[52] Maphaeus Vegius, *De educatione liberorum*, II, 18–20.

[53] *Ibid.*, III, 12–15.

[54] *Ibid.*, IV.

Christian virtue. After the invention of printing this essay was translated into French. It had a great vogue and was ascribed to the erratic scholar Francesco Filelfo[55] (1398–1481), whose Greek studies and Latin eloquence added luster to Florentine humanism, though pride and bad temper embittered his relations with his more amiable contemporaries.

During the whole of Vegius' Roman experience the papal city was astir with rebuilding. The enterprise of Nicholas V[56] surpassed even that of Leo IV, and deserves to be ranked with the prodigious projects of that greatest of city-planners, Julius Caesar. In the course of excavation and construction many antique treasures came to light. It occurred to Maphaeus Vegius to do, in a small way, for Christian Rome what Flavius Blondus was doing for the Pagan City in his monumental treatise entitled *Roma instaurata*. The result of our author's *"promenades archéologiques"* is a history of the old Basilica of Saint Peter. Among other inscriptions which he rescued from destruction is the epitaph of the medieval poetess Proba of the Anician family whose long-lived Virgilian cento on Old Testament history may still be read. Her use of Virgil's words was even more fantastic than Vegius' own. Comparetti remarks, with Proba in mind, that in the sixth century Virgil's chief office was to teach children in the schools and so provide them with a "means of emphasizing their childishness when they grew up."[57] Proba worshiped the letter of Virgil's language; Vegius, who was, in a certain sense, her successor after a thousand years, paid homage to its spirit.

The archaeological treatise *De rebus antiquis memorabilibus Basilicae Sancti Petri Romae* was Vegius' last work. It entitles its author to be ranked as the founder of the study of Christian archaeology.[58] He had begun his career as a scholar in the ardent study of Rome's

---

[55] J. P. Nicéron, *Memoires* (Paris, 1734), Volume XXVI.

[56] A. S. Cox (Brinton), "Nicholas V, a Restorer of the Papal City," *Art and Archaeology*, July, 1918.

[57] D. Comparetti, *Virgil in the Middle Ages*, translated by E. F. M. Benecke (London, 1895), page 54. See also Aschbach, *Die Anicier und die romische Dichterin Proba* (Vienna, 1870), pages 54 ff.

[58] J. B. de Rossi, *Inscriptiones christianae* (Rome, 1857–1888), chapter ii.

pagan poets; he concluded it with earnest and original investigation of the early monuments of her Christian Church. He died in 1458 and was buried in the chapel which he had dedicated to Saint Monica. The marble slab bearing his name and effigy has disappeared. An interesting eulogy from among several composed in his honor appears in the edition of his works published at Milan in 1613. It was written by the younger Carlo Aretino about his father's friend:

HIC, MAPHAEE, IACES INIMICA MORTE SOLUTUS
QUEM SIBI PRAEREPTUM LINGUA LATINA DOLET.
NON LASCIVUS ERAS, QUALES SUNT SAEPE POETAE,
MENS TIBI CUM CASTO CORPORE SANCTA FUIT.
EDITA TESTANTUR CENTENA VOLUMINA PER TE,
INGENII FUERINT FLUMINA QUANTA TUI,
URBS TE LAUDENSIS VEGIORUM E SANGUINE CLARO
EDIDIT, EXSTINCTUM ROMA VETUSTA TENET.[59]

Friends and patrons.—Maphaeus Vegius' friends and patrons were literary men, but what person of position in the early fifteenth century was not a writer or a fighter? Talent was common, and fashion decreed that aspirants to public notice, if they did not wield the sword, should

. . . . call for pen and ink to show their wit,
For those who cannot write and those who can
All rhyme and scrawl and scribble to a man.

A list of his associates in Pavia, Florence, and Rome includes the ablest humanists of the time. In public life these men were administrators of Church and State; in private life they were scholars. They brought to light the legacy of antiquity, they originated historical criticism, they were precursors of modern science. Fresh knowledge and appreciation of the great personalities of Greece and Rome stimulated new enthusiasm for individual distinction. Ways opened in all directions for spontaneous, inwardly inspired thought, investigation, and action. By official appointments, the curia and the Italian city-states paid homage to the culture derived from learning and eloquence.

[59] *Opera Vegii* (Lodi [?], 1613), Part II, page 72.

Under this stimulating patronage the humanists produced an enormous body of writing in prose and verse. Their fame was instantaneous and widespread. The impermanence of their reputation, as compared with that of painters and sculptors of the early Renaissance, is due to the fact that Europe promptly absorbed and bettered their literary achievement, while the charm of quattrocento painting has remained unparalleled. In one notable respect, however, these men deserve our special thanks. The pagan poets of the Renaissance preceded the pagan painters and for them turned a searchlight on antiquity, disclosing loveliness unguessed-at for a thousand years. If Italian poets and mythologists had not revealed gods and heroes in a radiance as familiar and appealing as that with which the Church had illumined Christian legend, Botticelli could not have followed his early Madonnas with the lovely "Primavera" nor his famous "Adoration" with "Pallas and the Centaur." Poets brought pagan beauty to light, then painters caught the vision and left behind them a record, undimmed by five hundred years, of that first radiant impression.[60] The poets were, for the most part, aristocrats and the painters were guildsmen and burghers; but the comparative merit of their accomplishment is correctly gauged by the relative popularity in our own day of Paulus Jovius' *Eulogies of Learned Men* and Vasari's *Lives of the Painters and Sculptors*.

The fifteenth century was an age of travel, when scholars migrated from court to court, from Naples to Milan, from Ferrara to Florence. As Rome regained her ancient prestige under Nicholas V and his successors, they contributed their fame to enhance the brilliance of the papal city. They visited Constantinople in search of Greek manuscripts and Northern Europe on diplomatic errands. Much of their voluminous correspondence has survived in manuscript or in ponderous black-letter volumes. Positive in their loves, but still more definite and voluble in their hates, each man's intellectual career dominated his human experience. We know the features of the more distinguished humanists from their portraits on medallions and from the sculptured effigies upon their tombs. High-souled and exquisite, they added a new type to European patterns of manhood. Pagan thought lured

---

[60] Walter Pater, *The Renaissance*, London, 1900, page 59.

them with its iridescent charm to strip off the shackles of asceticism and become modern men. But fifteen centuries of Christianity could not be ignored. Many humanists, like Traversari and Vegius, captivated in youth by the new freedom, came to realize as they grew older that it was more significant to interpret the new knowledge in terms of Christianity than to revive an unaltered paganism. Their writings glow with the same pure flame of Christian emotion that illumined the Madonnas of Fra Angelico and the della Robbias.

Vegius' early patrons were students and ecclesiastics in and near his native town who recognized the boy's precocity and provided him opportunities to read the books he loved. In 1421, his own bishop, Gerardo Landriani, made an important literary discovery that set all Lodi on fire with enthusiasm. Among dusty documents in an old chest in the cathedral, he came upon a manuscript of the rhetorical works of Cicero. The *Brutus* was entirely new to the world of scholars. *De Oratore* and the *Orator* were previously known only from imperfect copies. News of the recovery of these important treatises traveled to the very outposts of civilization with remarkable rapidity considering the difficulties of travel in this period. Poggio Bracciolini, the indefatigable discoverer of ancient manuscripts, who had added no less than fifteen authors to those who were known and read from century to century through the Middle Ages, was visiting in Britain, but tidings of the new find quickly reached him, as they did Aurispa in Constantinople. So thrilling an event could not fail to stir the heart of our fourteen-year-old humanist, Maphaeus Vegius, who composed an epigram to celebrate it. More than twenty years later, he dedicated his dialogue *De felicitate et miseria* to this same fellowtownsman, now Cardinal Landriani.

In spite of much court poetry written during the next decade, notably a *Convivium Deorum* and a *Carmen heroicum ad Philippum Mariam Angelum Ducem Mediolanensium* and some outrageous flattery of the Visconti, Maphaeus gained no preferment with the ducal family. Bartolomeo de la Capra, the archbishop of Milan, was, however, a frank friend and critic. He praised Maphaeus for his facile pen, while he blamed the wanton subjects of many of his early poems. To him young Vegius dedicated his *Vocabolista*, a glossary of legal terms.[61] De la Capra was, like Vegius, a lover of Virgil. Aeneas Silvius Piccolomini describes him as "learned in the highest degree, but more given to poetry than to other fields of knowledge. Virgil he had ever before him and he wrote elegant verse."[62]

At Pavia, Vegius himself appears in the rôle of patron to a younger writer named Antonio d' Asti, who expressed his warm appreciation of his poet friend by an enthusiastic eulogy in a poem entitled *De varietate Fortunae.*

Within the next few years Vegius dedicated a book of elegies to Lanzarotto Crotti, governor of the Castle of Pavia, whose brother, Luigi, was ducal secretary and, in that capacity, had jurisdiction over the library of a thousand or more volumes, which included, in addition to medieval ecclesiastical writings, the works of Homer, Plato, and Aristotle in Greek, and, among Roman authors, Terence, Cicero, Sallust, Virgil, Horace, Ovid, Lucan, Statius, Pliny, Persius, Juvenal, Seneca, Suetonius, Valerius Maximus, and Claudian. Young Vegius doubtless had access to these books.[63]

A large and representative group of humanists sojourned from time to time in Pavia, where the University was yearly increasing in importance as a center of the new learning. In these stimulating surroundings, Vegius remained almost continuously from the age of twenty to that of thirty. He was on excellent terms with all the great men who graced the new academy. He numbered among his friends the pioneer archaeologist of the Renaissance, Cyriaco of Ancona, who has been cleverly styled the Schliemann of his time. No doubt Cyriaco and Flavius Blondus are to a certain degree responsible for the taste for antiquities which resulted in Vegius' last work, *De rebus antiquis memorabilibus basilicae Sancti Petri.*

Antonio Beccadelli, soon to become the most notorious poet of his generation, who in his merry old age founded the literary academy at

[61] Correspondence between Vegius and De la Capra, in J. A. Saxius, *Historia literaria typographica mediolanensis* (Milan, 1745).

[62] Aeneas Silvius Piccolomini, *De viris illustribus,* Stuttgart, *Literarische Vereinsbibliotek* (1843), Volume I.

[63] G. d'Adda, *Indagini sulla libreria visconteo sforzesca nel castello di Pavia,* Milan, 1875. Cited by M. Minoia in *La vita di Maffeo Vegio,* Lodi, 1898.

Naples, had frequent association with Vegius in Pavia. On one occasion he sent their mutual friend, the poet Cambio Zambeccari, a manuscript of Virgil's poems. The accuracy of the copy was attested both by himself and Vegius, whom he styled "*poetam haud reüciendum.*" He wrote to another friend that Maphaeus could attain distinction if only he would guard against his over-great ease of composition—"*Modo sibi tantum non indulgeat.*"[64]

In spite of a brief passage at arms over their respective supplements to the *Aeneid*,[65] Pier Candido Decembrio, Latin secretary to the Duke of Milan, was Vegius' friend. The dedications of Decembrio's books illustrate how cosmopolitan was the acquaintanceship of individual Italian scholars. His Latin version of the fifth book of Plato's *Republic* was inscribed to Duke Humphrey of Gloucester, a literal rendering of books one to four of the *Iliad* to John II of Castile, and a translation of Appian's *Civil Wars* to Alfonso, King of Naples.

A special favorite of Maphaeus Vegius was the lovesick poet, Marrasius of Sicily, who almost forgot his desolation in pleasure at reading Vegius' consolatory elegy written in the person of his cruel but lovely lady, Angelina Piccolomini.

Antonio da Rho, a friar minor, was Beccadelli's hardly less scandalous literary enemy. After teaching at Pavia, he succeeded Gasparino Barzizza in the chair of rhetoric at Milan. Nothing could be more extravagant than his praise of Vegius in several letters that have survived.

Reference has already been made to the friendship of Vegius and Valla. In a dialogue, *De vero bono*, which belongs to Valla's youth, he puts the gentle arguments of Epicurus in the mouth of Vegius.[66] A long letter is extant in which Vegius pleads with his hot-headed friend to be tolerant of criticism.[67] Finally, a literary quarrel, in which Valla was one of the main figures, broke up the first circle of humanists in Pavia.

[64] M. Minoia, *La vita di Maffeo Vegio* (Lodi, 1896), pages 39 f.

[65] L. Raffaele, *Maffeo Vegio* (Bologna, 1909), pages 21 f.

[66] Printed at Louvain, 1483, and at Basle, 1519 and 1540, with some alterations.

[67] Barozzi and Sabbadini, *Studi sul Panormita e sul Valla* (Florence, 1891), page 89.

Of his papal patrons, Eugenius IV and Nicholas V, Vegius writes in terms of enthusiastic devotion in his essay on the antiquities of Saint Peter's and in various other places. Three of his longer poems were dedicated to Eugenius.[68] An honorary epitaph celebrates Nicholas as *"aemulus Numae"* and *"alter Augustus."*[69] The first epithet refers to his mild measures toward the Turks, the second to his patronage of learning. Though Nicholas saw no way to avert the fall of Constantinople, he did know how to rescue its manuscripts, and he evolved a magnificent plan for making them available through translation to scholars of the West. The climax of Vegius' epitaph is a distich on the healing of the Great Schism.

> Qui scissum ecclesiae Pastor compegit ovile
> At sua errantes claustra reduxit oves.

Aeneas Silvius Piccolomini was another ecclesiastical patron. His quick, allusive repartee, *"Sum Pius Aeneas,"* to the cardinal who asked at his election what pontifical name he desired to assume, illustrates how his thought was tinctured with Virgilian phraseology. Vegius is not infrequently mentioned in Aeneas Silvius' extensive correspondence. A curious letter, number 108, addressed to Procopius of Rabenstein, describes Vegius in the rôle of guide to the strange, noteworthy sights of Fortune's realm. A still more novel *jeu d'esprit* is the dialogue[70] in which Bernardino of Siena conducts Aeneas Silvius to the kingdom of the dead where he sees Saint John the Evangelist, the Prophet Elijah, Constantine the Great, Valla the humanist, Vegius the poet, and even the Almighty himself.

During the council at Ferrara, a friendship was formed between Vegius and Guarino of Verona (1374–1460), the distinguished preceptor to the son and heir of Marquis Niccolo d'Este. From his famous school, says Bartolomeo Facio, came more scholars "than warriors out

---

[68] Maphaeus Vegius, *Antoniados libri quattuor*, Bologna, 1433; *De vita et obitu beati Caelistini Quinti papae*, Rome, 1445; *De vita et obitu beatae Monicae*, Rome, 1453–1458.

[69] *Carmina poetarum italorum*, X, 309.

[70] William Boulting, *Aeneas Silvius* (London, 1908), page 216; Acneas Silvius, *Dialogi*, Rome, 1453.

of the Trojan horse." He was the first Italian humanist to travel in the East and study at Byzantium. Because of his wide acquaintance in Italy and the Levant, and because of his proficiency in Greek and Latin eloquence, Guarino was selected to interpret between the Eastern and Western bishops at the Council which formally ended the Great Schism. Vegius was then serving as a papal secretary.

At Florence, Maphaeus Vegius was included in the illustrious society of Medicean scholars. Flavio Blondo, Leonardo Bruni, Carlo Marsuppini, and Ambrogio Traversari were his literary confreres.

Blondus (1388–1463) praises Vegius as poet and essayist in *Italia illustrata*, one of his four monumental volumes on the antiquarian lore of Rome and Italy. To Bruni, Maphaeus dedicated two books of epigrams.[71] Among them are three in honor of Virgil:

In Virgilium et Ovidum

Nasonem Sulmo tibi dat si quaeris amores,
  Proelia si quaeris Mantua Virgilium,
Proelia si pariter, pariter si quaeris amores,
  Sufficietque unus haec tibi Virgilius.

In Virgilium

Diruta quae flammis olim Maro Pergama dixit,
  In flammas moriens iussit et inde dari.
Non tulit Augustus, rapuitque ex ignibus ignes,
  Et tristi e busto tot sacra busta ducum.
Quae vestra, o Teucri, Vulcanum iniuria laesit?
  Neptunus certe dignior ultor erat.

Qui, Maro, Castalias tantum gustaveris undas
  Mirum Lethaeas quam bene scribis aquas?
Sed qui scribit aquas Lethaeas tam bene, numquam
  Tangere, Lethaeae, debueratis, aquae.
Quid, queror? at totiens quas etsi spiritus, at non
  Saltem Lethaeas nomen adivit aquas?

The rest are on subjects varied and strange, some trivial, some coarse. They are part of the profuse expression of lavish wantonness that

[71] Luigi Raffaele, *Maffeo Vegio*, Bologna, 1909. He quotes the two books entire, pages 158 ff.

belonged to the Renaissance. The grave and ſtately chancellor of Florence bade the author employ his muse upon higher themes. Four books on the queſt of the Golden Fleece resulted from this advice.

Two books of diſtichs were inscribed to another chancellor of Florence, the no less illuſtrious Carlo Marsuppini (1399–1453), whose aſtonishing feats of memory were the admiration of his age. Immediately following the dedication of this token and pledge of love from Vegius to his new patron, are four epitaphs on Virgil:

I

Paſtor oves et arator agros: et proelia miles
Inſtruxi aeterno clarus honore Maro.

II

Ecce Maro, cuius divino carmine musa
Per silvas et agros ad fera bella venit.

III

Silvas, rura, acies cecini: mihi Mantua mater:
Nomen Virgilius: Parthenope tumulus.

IV

Pascua rusque canens peragraram, bella sequebar,
Nondum finieram: Virgilius perii.

Marsuppini acknowledged Vegius' tribute by a sequence of enthusiaſtic couplets culminating in the lines:

Diſticha tu neɕis, frondes tibi neɕat Apollo,
Impediatque tuas bina corona comas.

Leonardo Bruni and Carlo Marsuppini lie buried opposite each other in the right and left aisles of the church of Santa Croce, the Weſtminſter Abbey of Florence. Bruni's sepulchral inscription was composed by Marsuppini with the ancient epitaph of Plautus ſtill echoing in his ears:

Poſtquam Leonardus e vita migravit, Hiſtoria luget, Eloquentia muta eſt, ferturque Musas tum Graecas tum Latinas lacrimas tenere non potuisse.

The exquisite refinement of the two effigies, each a maſterpiece, that of Bruni by Bernardino Rosinello and that of Marsuppini by Disiderio

[22]

da Settignano, contributes more, perhaps, than all their Latin poems to convey to modern men the significance and charm of Italian humanism.

In Ambrogio Traversari (1380–1493), general of the Order of the Camaldulites, Maphaeus Vegius found a friend who settled the conflicting claims of Christian and pagan literature entirely in favor of the Church. Traversari was an indefatigable translator. His Latin versions of the Greek lives of the Fathers, of the *Theophrastus* of Aeneas of Gaza, and of the tracts and homilies of Saint Chrysostom were new and needed.

The Florentine biographer, Vespasiano da Bisticci, pays tribute to Traversari's learning and at the same time pictures a characteristic scene among Medicean literati in recounting the following incident:

One day, when Niccolo [de' Niccoli] and Cosimo [de' Medici] were with Brother Ambrogio he was translating Saint John Chrysostom on The Epistles of Saint Paul. He translated, and Niccolo, who was an exceedingly rapid scribe, took it down in cursive script; but he could not equal the speed with which Brother Ambrogio translated, in an elaborate style without further need of correction. After a time Niccolo said to Brother Ambrogio: "Go slowly [*andate adagio*]! I can't keep up." This version in Niccolo's handwriting is still in San Marco. You can see that the corrections are exceedingly few.[72]

Vegius also alludes to Traversari's unprecedented speed of composition in the lines:

> Clarus in eloquio Graio; clarusque Latino,
> Et pollens studiis clarus et ipse sacris.
> Si scripta attendas, fuit haud velocius ulli;
> Si vitam haud ulli mitius ingenium.[73]

Though Traversari was acknowledged to be the most rapid translator of his generation, he begrudged the time spent at the explicit command of Cosimo on his Latin rendering of Diogenes Laertius' *Lives of the Philosophers*. One might have supposed that Brother Ambrogio, who was the discoverer of Nepos' lives of Atticus and Cato, would have found his study of ancient Greek biographies a congenial

[72] Vespasiano da Bisticci, *Vite*, Florence, 1859.

[73] *Carmina poetarum italorum*, X, 313.

counterpart to the lives of the Christian Fathers; but his scruples admitted no luxurious enjoyment of pagan literature. In his whole voluminous correspondence only once does he permit himself to quote from a classic poet. This unique quotation is from Virgil's *Eclogues.*[74] Though he had been trained in Greek, Roman, and Hebrew, his true life work was not linguistic; it was not even literary, it was theological. But it can be said with truth that his study of the Church Fathers was made vivid by the new spirit of inquiry at the root of all productive scholarship of the early quattrocento.

"THE THIRTEENTH BOOK OF THE 'AENEID'": THE ALLEGORIZERS

The humanists looked at ancient literature through a prism of allegory. Donatus' (*ca.* 333) and Fulgentius' (*ca.* 520) elaborate interpretations of the *Aeneid,* which had influenced Dante and Petrarch, still conditioned the approach to Virgil of such men as Leon Battista Alberti (1404–1472), Christoforo Landini (1424–1504), and Maphaeus Vegius. In their eyes, the *Aeneid* was the symbolic journey of a hero soul to his heaven-set goal; it was, in a sense, the "Pilgrim's Progress" of antiquity. The Aeneas of Augustan Rome, the Aeneas of the allegorizers, and Bunyan's Pilgrim are typical representatives of three epochs in Western thought. The Augustan Aeneas was a hero, a Trojan aristocrat, founding, through mighty deeds, an earthly empire; the allegorical Aeneas who succeeded him in the Middle Ages and the Renaissance was a saint and spiritual guide, founding, by miracles and pious acts, a kingdom in the heavens where he was to become a kind of heavenly patron. The "Pilgrim" of the Reformation was a plain man "of a low and unconsiderable generation," "clothed in rags." When he should escape from the burdens of the world and its sin, he would become only a humble citizen of the heavenly city. Thus did paganism, medievalism, and Puritanism, each express its own peculiar aspiration for the final goal. The first emphasized a this-world end, the founding of immortal Rome. The second aspired to an other-

[74] Ambrogio Traversari, *Epistulae,* III, 99; J. E. Sandys, *A History of Classical Scholarship,* II, 44.

world end in which the social adjuſtments of feudalism were carried over into the heavenly hierarchy of the New Jerusalem. The third, likewise Chriſtian, also sought an other-world end, but this goal was an ideal congenial to the spirit which gave rise to modern democracy. According to the Puritan conception, each man counted equally before God.

Virgil's voyager was a hero, goddess-born. He set out with a divine commission. True, he was not always equally assured of the feasibility of his queſt, nor of its vaſt implications, but whenever he faltered, the holy call rang out again. After the beguiling months in Carthage, where Aeneas, who, it muſt be remembered, was the son of a mortal father, ventured to tarry for a woman's love, not only a challenge from heaven but even a descent into hell was required to sublimate the numbing memory of human happiness. Not only was renewed intercourse with his aged sire required to re-impress his obligation; he muſt actually behold the long line of his descendants, the Roman heroes to whom he owed fulfilment of his heaven-appointed task. Aeneas comes forth from Acheron by the gate of dreams, rededicated to his mission, which was the founding of Imperial Rome.

But the Middle Ages, under the combined influence of Platonic philosophy, which saw the things of sense as imperfeċt copies of ideal beauty, and of Chriſtianity with its apocalyptic hope, had vaſter ideals than those of earthly imperial ambition. Men's eyes were fixed on a better world beyond the clouds, a Celeſtial City, "not made with hands," rather than on the marble splendor set upon seven material hills. Not only were images of sense thought of as outer husks of diviner Reality, but great literature likewise, including both the Bible and the *Aeneid*, was valued as the symbolic expression of hidden truth. Many interpreters said of Moses what Maſter Phaer said of Virgil in the conclusion of his explanation of the *Aeneid*: "For you know there be many miſticall secretes in this writer." Comparetti's criticism of allegory as "a species of dialeċtical hallucination, which owes its origin to those earneſt conviċtions which are natural to a vigorous and impulsive temperament,"[75] falls far short of the truth. In the Middle

[75] D. Comparetti, *Virgil in the Middle Ages*, translated by E. F. M. Benecke (London, 1895), page 106.

Ages, allegory results from a philosophy which admitted two methods of procedure: the method of Reason to approach the half-truths of this world; and the method of Faith to attain the myſtic truths of the next. The allegorizers could by faith pierce

Wndir the cluddes of dirk poetry

to where

Hid lyis thair mony a notable hiſtory[76]

in the same way that the Chriſtian could reach through the sacraments of the Church to the inner saving grace.

The turning of men's higheſt aspirations from the things of sense to another world, and the tendency to see all things with a twofold vision, by the eye of reason and the eye of faith, resulted in a symbolic interpretation of the *Aeneid*. As a parable, however, the poem was ethically incomplete. Not only was there a this-world ending, but the saint's reward was not described. The "Thirteenth Book" found favor because it supplied these two moral demands. Its subſtance was already implicit in Virgil's prophecies in Book I; but the *Carmen Vegii* made them explicit in the completion of the narrative. Poetic technique required that an epic should never "begin at the beginning" nor "end at the end," and that it should "keep the goal in mind, but not on paper."[77] Moraliſts required that wherever hagiography began, it should at leaſt end at the end, and that the goal should be heavenly beatitude. Either Latium muſt be symbolically interpreted as the heavenly goal, or Aeneas muſt be finally translated to the ſtars. Renaissance religion, which had for its ideal not only a kingdom of heaven but also the canonization of saints, had room for both. The apotheosis of Aeneas became the symbol of heavenly assurance that the divine kingdom had been won. Thus Chriſtian exegesis, centered as it was on the supernatural and replacing the this-world ideals of the ancients with other-world aims of the Church, opened the way for a supplement to the *Aeneid* in order to bring Aeneas to heaven.

[76] Gavin Douglas, *The XIII Bukes of Eneados* (London, 1553), Prologue to Book I.

[77] R. S. Conway, *The Architecture of the Epic*, Bulletin of the John Rylands Library, Volume IX, No. 2, July, 1925.

[26]

Two passages from Maphaeus Vegius' own writings are apt illustrations of his method of allegorical interpretation. One occurs in the essay *On Education* (II, 28), the other in the tract *On Perseverance in Religion* (I, 5). Vegius recommends the two supreme epic poets, Homer and Virgil, as the basis of literary training and moral instruction for youth:

If we were not hurrying on to treat of other matters, perhaps we might touch upon the point that the whole *Aeneid* holds concealed beneath the ornament of poetic imagery the highest mystery of philosophy. But we really ought not to omit that part of the discussion which bears upon the matter which we are considering. For Virgil means to show, under the guise of Aeneas, man endowed with every virtue as he appears now in misfortune and again in happiness. By similar token, in Dido he strives to teach women, too, by what rational counsels they ought to order their lives in eager longing for praise, in fear of dishonor and pitiful ruin. For what woman is not moved by Dido's example and set on fire with zeal for goodness, as she hears how earnestly the queen devoted herself to her task, established walls for her great city, regulated institutions and laws for the people in a spirit of justice, and, even though her husband was dead, won high renown and reverence for herself and inspired fear in her neighbors by keeping her faith and promise? And yet is the heart not shaken, terrified, and affrighted by the knowledge that she fell madly in love with her guest, a mere stranger, gave up the rule of her people, spent her time in such pursuits as merrymaking and feasting, and in the end, forsaken by her lover, in grief and affliction, bereft of all hope, resolved to compass her own death? Will not a woman choose to devote herself to virtue, though it be austere, when its fruits are shown to be so sweet rather than to succumb to seductive passion, when its fruits are described as so bitter?

Vegius thinks it well to remark that the whole narrative contains not a word or phrase which could conduce to baseness.

The second passage is even more explicit in its identifications. Here Aeneas is the type of perseverance. His exhortation is quoted in full:

> "O socii (neque enim ignari sumus ante malorum),
> o passi graviora, dabit deus his quoque finem.
> vos et Scyllaeam rabiem penitusque sonantis
> accestis scopulos, vos et Cyclopia saxa
> experti; revocate animos maestumque timorem
> mittite; forsan et haec olim meminisse iuvabit

> per varios casus, per tot discrimina rerum
> tendimus in Latium, sedes ubi fata quietas
> oſtendunt; illic fas regna resurgere Troiae,
> durate, et vosmet rebus servate secundis."

It is followed by the comment:

I do not see how the thought could be expressed by any Chriſtian author in holier words or in phrases better fitted to accord with our faith than these. We are here taught to remember the paſt with joy, to bear the present bravely, to hope for a better future, and, finally, to cultivate perseverance at all times with a hero's might, and buckle it to our souls with closer bands. For if we interpret Scylla's rage and the other perils of the deep as the vexations and revilings of the world and the devils, if we subſtitute the word *heaven* for Latium and *life* for Troy, why might the passage not have come from the pen of the Apoſtle Paul?

Later in the same chapter we read:

Aeneas (whom the poet depiĉts as goodness watching and ſtriving for the benefit of others) sails this great and wide sea of earthly life. When his helms-man, Palinurus, is thrown overboard because he has fallen asleep, snared by self-indulgence, Aeneas divines that the ship of human life is swerving from its course. On his own initiative, he seizes the rudder of duty, and, through a long night of error, sweats at the helmsman's task. He does not scorn the labor, though such toil ill befits a mighty hero, because he assumes responsibility for the safety of many. Aeneas then passes in review the punishments of Avernus (that is, the miseries of the world) and observes what ills beset infancy, youth, and every other age. He visits Elysium too, where his father Anchises is seen with others, but only such as are good and upright men, at leisure for God and literature, while they abide in this life and enjoy tranquillity. Then, before he attains to promised reſt in Latium, he meets his enemy, Turnus, that is, the devil. The Latins, which is to say worldliness, wage war. Strife is had over Lavinia, who is to be interpreted as the soul. But Turnus is worſted, the Latins are put down, Lavinia is won. Aeneas rules at peace in Italy and finally is made a god. This is the reward, this the goal, for the persevering hero.

With such a view of the *Aeneid* as an allegory requiring moral completeness, it is no wonder that an ardent youth, in an age when, for sheer love of the epic, children learned it by heart, should have super-imposed upon the artiſtic completeness of Virgil's poem his own en-

thusiastic version of the heavenly reward. The surprising fact is not
that a Thirteenth Book of the *Aeneid* was composed, but that it should
have had so long a history.

Publication.—The earliest manuscript of Vegius' canto, perhaps an
autograph, is entitled *"Libri XII Aeneidos Supplementum (Papiae VI
idus Octobris 1428)."*[78] A whole generation intervened between this
date and the introduction of printing into Italy. Vegius could never
have imagined the wide popularity that was in store for the Virgilian
tribute of his gay secular youth in Pavia. He died a cleric, Canon of
Saint Peter's, in 1458, six years before the German presses of Sweyn-
heym and Pannartz were housed in the venerable religious house at
Subiaco among the Sabine hills. Just six years after those first memo-
rable experiments and only two years later than the production of the
editio princeps of Virgil (1469), the *"Supplementum"* was linked with
the *Aeneid* in the edition of 1471 printed from the types of Adam de
Ambergau at Venice. From this time on, it was broadcast over Europe.
It appeared in more than twenty Venetian editions, as well as in *Virgils*
printed at Rome, Milan, Florence, Modena, Brescia, Turin, and Pavia.
More than half a dozen Paris publications contain it, and more than a
dozen printed in London. It was three times reprinted at Basle, and at
least once each at Antwerp, Cologne, Nuremburg, Strassburg, and
Zurich.[79]

As early as 1500, however, its prestige in learned circles showed
symptoms of decline. Among cultivated judges the taste for allegory
had yielded to modern literary appreciation. In 1505 Aldus Manutius
published an edition of Virgil from which he would gladly have
omitted the *"Supplementum,"* but he included it in deference to popu-
lar demand, with the apology that he "still had to make this conces-
sion."[80] Nine years later, in a dedicatory letter to Cardinal Bembo
which precedes his beautiful edition of 1514, he proudly writes, "In
this edition you will find nothing which can detract from the majesty
of the divine poet," and Vegius' "Supplement" is here omitted.

[78] L. Raffaele, *Maffeo Vegio* (Bologna, 1909), page 83.

[79] W. A. Copinger, *Incunabula Virgiliana, Transactions of the Bibliographical
Society*, 1894, Volume II, Part 2.

[80] A. Firmin Didot, *Alde Manuce et L'Hellénisme à Venise* (Paris, 1875, page 283.

Yet it is to this same generation that Brant's captivating woodcuts (1502) belong, and a decade later Bishop Gavin Douglas was composing his vivid version of "The Threttene Buik" in the Scottish tongue. There was still amazing vitality in the reputation of a work which could call forth such echoes of genius from distant lands.

The explanation of the double phenomenon, loss of favor with the learned and unimpaired popularity with the public, is not far to seek. European printing-presses had unlocked the inheritance of literature to "men onletteryt," as Bishop Douglas terms them. The appetite for allegory was as yet unassuaged. As so often happens, a change of attitude on the part of intellectuals preceded, by a century or more, a corresponding alteration of popular taste. "The Thirteenth Book" was illustrated, as it was translated, in response to a popular craving. It continued to accompany the *Aeneid* in most of the editions published in Europe and Britain until 1650.

Criticism.—Contemporary and subsequent criticism bears additional testimony to the sustained popularity shown by frequent reprinting. Valla considered Vegius the best contemporary poet, and Filelfo spoke of him as *"alter Maro."*[81] Many literary critics and biographers are effusive in their praise. Vespasiano da Bisticci writes in his artless fashion: "So skilled was Maffeo Veggio in verse that he added with the greatest ease a thirteenth book to Virgil's *Aeneid*, which was greatly praised by all the learned men of the time."[82] Paulus Cortesius[83] is slightly skeptical. He says Vegius "was then accounted a poet, and he does show talent, but his style is sometimes exaggerated, and it is not refined enough, though this particular fault is characteristic of the age." Lilius Gyraldus[84] lists him with such prominent poets as Panormitanus and Aurispa. Paulus Jovius[85] finds him a truly Homeric bard and sets him above all other Latin writers in the preceding two hun-

---

[81] L. Raffaele, *Maffeo Vegio* (Bologna, 1909), page 46.

[82] Vespasiano da Bisticci, *Vite* (Florence, 1859), *Vita di Maffeo Veggio.*

[83] P. Cortesius, *De hominibus doctis* (Florence, 1734), page 16.

[84] L. G. Gyraldus, *De poetis nostrorum temporum*, published in *Lateinische Litteratur Denkmaler des XV und XVI Jahrhunderts*, Berlin, 1895.

[85] P. Jovius, *Elogia* (Basle, 1577), number 196.

AENEAS TRIUMPHANT

dred years, not excepting Petrarch, "though he was crowned with laurel on the capitol." Julius Caesar Scaliger[86] (1484–1558) says, "*grandis profecto poeta est.*" He devotes a whole section of his *Hyper-criticus* (Book VI of the "Poetics") to Mapheus Vegius, "so conspicuously does he stand out in that century in which scarcely any good literature flourished." "Although he is despised," continues Scaliger, "by my best and most learned instructors, I shall quote a few distinguished verses from the Supplement which he added to Virgil's divine poem . . . ." With that he quotes the opening lines of the "Thirteenth Book" and adds "here you find traces of Virgil's brilliance. With the exception of the word *revomentes,* all the rest is worthy of a consummate poet." He remarks upon two similes which he ranks as "not inferior to those of Lucan and Statius, perhaps even better." In all, seven passages are quoted and commented upon with obvious relish.

A hundred years later Vegius' praise is sung in Northern Europe as well. Gerardus Johannes Vossius[87] (1577–1649), the celebrated Dutch "*polyhistor*" and professor of eloquence at Leyden, evaluates him as the best poet between Petrarch and the graceful bard and Lucretian critic, Jovianus Pontanus (1426–1503).

Olaus Borrichius (1626–1690), whose homelier Danish name was Olaf von Borch, renowned physician of Queen Christina's court, finds him worthy of notice, though far removed from Virgil.[88]

Laelius Brisciola links Vegius' name with that of Quintus of Smyrna as author of a work which is "injudicious and inartistic."[89] Juan Luigi de la Cerda (*ca.* 1560–1645), a learned Jesuit of Madrid, in his monumental Virgil (1608–1617) writes with old-fashioned sympathy: "Maphei Vegi in supplemento Vergiliano opus laude est dignum, si versus spectes, quia multi ad umbram Maronis et modulum"; but he goes on to criticize the imputation that the *Aeneid* lacks completeness. Charles de la Rue, also of the Society of Jesus, more often called

[86] J. C. Scaliger, *Poetices libri septem* (Heidelberg, 1581, second edition), page 785.

[87] G. J. Vossius, *De veterum poetarum temporibus,* Amsterdam, 1697.

[88] Olaus Borrichius, *Dissertationes academicae de poetis* (Frankfurt, 1683), page 107.

[89] Udeno Nisiely da Vernio, *Proginnasmi poetici* (Florence, 1620), III, 102.

Ruaeus (1643–1725), expresses the same opinion in an essay *De natura Aeneidos disquisitio*.[90] Tarquinius Gallutius (1514–1549), rector of the college of Greeks in Rome, compares Vegius[91] to a wheelwright who looks at a coach, complete in every part, and thinks its four strong wheels are not enough, so he sets about adding a wretched fifth of his own make.

Abbé Claude-Pierre Gouget (1697–1767) writes pleasantly in a mood less stern: "What Vegius did for his own amusement has pleased many others. Though his little poem is far from its model, it has charms that give it value."[92] Henry Hallam (1777–1859) says in his *Literature of Europe during the Fifteenth, Sixteenth, and Seventeenth Centuries* that Maphaeus Vegius' "Thirteenth Book of the *Aeneid*" is "probably the best versification before Politian."[93]

The day of Virgilian allegory had, by this time, definitely passed. The intellectual climate of Europe had changed. For a few years scholars were vociferous in their denunciation and ridicule of the allegorical interpretation; then that phase of Virgil's influence, and with it Mapheus Vegius' "Thirteenth Book of the *Aeneid*," passed to the realm of historical interest.

Badius Ascensius' commentary.—In 1500, Erasmus' friend, the erudite French printer and editor, Iodocus Badius Ascensius, produced an elaborate and long-lived commentary for the "Thirteenth Book of the *Aeneid*"[94] so that it need no longer stand unilluminated after the richly annotated pages of the *Aeneid*.

Virgil's text had, in the space of thirty years since the *editio princeps* (1469), become literally embedded in scholia. It was a fashion of early printers to combine a number of commentaries without assuming the function of editor to fuse them into a unit. In 1500 five commentators, Servius (born *ca.* 355), Donatus (fl. *ca.* 333), Landinus

---

[90] C. Ruaeus, *Virgilii Opera*, III, 755.

[91] T. Gallutius, *Orationes tres de Vergilii allegoria*, page 246.

[92] Claude-Pierre Gouget, *Bibliothèque française* (Paris, 1742), V, 195. Quoted by N. E. Lemaire, *Virgilii Opera*, Paris, 1820.

[93] Part 2, chapter iii.

[94] T. Kerver, *Virgilii Opera*, Paris, 1500.

(1424–1504), Mancinellus (1452–1506), and Calderinus (1447–1478) were the five accepted worthies who usually expounded Virgil's text. By 1600 the li&st had been more than doubled by the addition of Pomponius Laetus (1425–1475), Beroaldus (1453–1505), Barlandus (1488–1542), Vives (1492–1540), Fabricius (1516–1571), and others.

Badius is not deceived regarding the intrinsic merit of his author, of whom he says: "Granted that he does imitate the poet and that he follows at a great di&stance and is cold in comparison, &still we cannot all do everything, and it is easier to notice defe&cts than to write without them." In a later comment he writes in more appreciative vein: "non e&st tamen usquequaque contemnenda poeta, si seorsum solusque inspiciatur, quamvis nihil ad Maronem." Badius heads his notes with the mode&st catchword, "*Ascensiani Adnotatiunculi.*" His observations exhibit no remarkable penetration. They consi&st largely of summaries or paraphrases, citations of sources, and indications of a few glaring faults and discrepancies.

Translation and parody in Great Britain.—After 1500 the enormously increased circulation of books produced a reading public so extensive and so little correlated with the citizens of the old Republic of Letters, in which Latin was the universal language, that translations of great and &standard works were required in all the languages of Europe.

The earlie&st and mo&st pi&cturesque version of "The Thirteenth Book of the *Aeneid*" was composed by Ma&ster Gavin Douglas (*ca.* 1474–1522), Bishop of Dunkel, who completed his Virgil in the Scottish tongue, the mo&st famous of his writings, and today the greate&st monument of old Scottish poetry, in 1513. This was the fir&st metrical translation of any classical author by a British scholar.[95]

Sir Walter Scott describes the learned bishop in the sixth canto (ll. 327–335) of *Marmion:*

> A bishop by the altar &stood,
> A noble lord of Douglas blood,

---

[95] H. Palmer, "Handli&st of English Editions and Translations of Greek and Latin Classics before 1641," *Bibliographical Society Publications*, Volume XII, 1911.

> With mitre sheen and rochet white
> Yet showed his meek and thoughtful eye
> But little pride of prelacy:
> More pleased that in a barbarous age
> He gave rude Scotland Virgil's page
> Than that beneath his rule he held
> The bishopric of fair Dunkeld.

Sir David Lindsay of the Mount (*ca.* 1531– *ca.* 1613), in his *Complaynt of Papingo* (ll. 33–36) alludes to Douglas' *Virgil* as composed in "our Inglis"; he continues:

> And specialy the trew translatioun
> Of Virgill, quhilk bin consolatioun
> To cunning men, to knaw his great ingyne,
> Als weill in natural science as diuyne.

As to the accuracy of the translation, the learned Francis Junius, or François du Jon (1589–1677), an exacting philologist, complains in his *Glossarium Gothicum*:

> In my perusing of this Prelate his book . . . . I stumbled on manie passages wherein this wittie Gawin doth grossly mistake Virgil, and is much led out of the way by the infection of a monkish ignorance then prevailing in church and commonwealth.

There are, to be sure, instances of misinterpretation due to meager academic equipment, and there is diffuseness due to the prevalent literary fashion. Occasional anachronisms provoke a smile. One of these occurs in the spirited lines in Book VI in which the Sibyl, who is represented as a "nwn," exhorts Aeneas to tell his beads:

> Blyn nocht, blyn nocht: thou gret Troiane Enee
> Of thi bedis nor of thi prayeris, quod sche.

Blyn is from the verb *blinnan*, "to cease."

On the whole, however, John Lesley (1527–1596), Bishop of Ross, is justified in praising Bishop Gavin for his "fragrant wit and singular erudition." His Virgil gave delight to young and old.

The reverend "Father in God," Gavin Douglas, was well aware that the right of "The Thirteenth Book" to cap the climax of the

Aeneid had been challenged; and he, like Aldus Manutius in Venice, contemplated omitting it from his *magnum opus*. He feelingly describes the welcome sense of emancipation which he experienced when, after months of toil, he completed his arduous task of translation, "every book having its particular prologue." His preface to "The Thirteenth Book" recounts in picturesque Scottish verse the manner in which he was persuaded to add this apocrypha to the accepted canon of Virgil. In summer heat, during the joyous "month time of June," when supper was done, he walked forth into the fields. Cattle and birds and busy bees were all astir to proceed to their night's rest. Down sank the sun all burning red, and Hesper rose, "forerider of the night." The beauty of the fruitful earth was shadowed o'er with darkness. Now every other thing both great and small was still, when Philomel, "the merry nightingale," began her song, and, longing to hear the "mirthful notes," the bishop sat him down beneath a laurel tree "now musing upon this and now on that" and gazing at the stars he fell asleep. Soon he heard a voice that said: "What dost thou here, under my tree, and willest me no good." Up looked the Bishop from beneath his cowl and he beheld an aged man, stern as a physician, in a strange and threadbare habit reaching to the ground. Upon his head he wore a laurel crown like to a poet of the olden time. The Bishop spoke to him with reverence:

"Father, if I have done you any offense I shall make amends so far as in me lies. And yet, as I have never seen you heretofore, I would fain know when, how or where I have trespassed against you?" " 'Tis well thou cryest for mercy," quoth the other. "Knowest thou not Mapheus Vegius, the poet that added unto Virgillis lusty bukis swete the threttene buke? I am the same, and I bear thee no good will in that thou hast rendered into thine own language the other twelve so that they may be read and sung all over Albion's isle, but of mine, thou hast taken no heed."

The Bishop answered him:

"I hear your words and seek your pardon, not that I have done you wrong, but I have overspent my time on Virgil's volume. If I longer laid aside my pressing tasks, what would folk think? Believe me, Father, there be those who hold that your book adds no more than doth a fifth wheel to a cart, and, since you be a Christian man, I pray you, let it suffice that Virgil now is at an end. A scruple irks me that I have dwelt so long upon a gentile's book."

"Ha, son!" quoth he, "wouldst thou escape me thus, why shrinkest thou from my short Christian work, and, since we speak of poetry, both mine and Virgil's are of moral tone. Lend me a fortnight, or, by my father's soul, thou shalt regret that ever thou didst Virgil know." With that he drew me from my seat and laid about him with his club, belaboring me with twenty blows while I cried "Deo! Deo! Mercy on me," and, with my right hand high upstretched, swore to translate his book, in honor of God and his apostles twelve "in the number odd." Glad at my words, he took me by the hand, then went away, and I awoke in fear. Lo! then upsprang the brilliant dawn of day that to behold was pleasant and half marvel.

> "Belyve on weyng the bissy lark vpsprang,
> To salus the blyth morrow with hir sang."

Then thought I thus, "I shall my promise keep, made thus to the poet master Maphaeus, and complete the book that I may then attend to my grave matters. For, though his style be not like that of Virgil, full well I know many shall like my text. My tongue and pen shall be the same, and this suffices common folk. Let wise men know the poets different."

The second important British version of the whole *Aeneid* and Maphaeus Vegius' "Thirteenth Book" was mainly the work of Thomas Phaer, M.D. (1510–1560). Shortly before his death he completed the first nine books and a third of the tenth in the old ballad meter called "fourteeners." He signed them with the pathetic legend *"Thomas Phaer olim tuus, nunc Dei."* His epitaph by Barnabe Googe (1540–1594), best known as the translator of Marcellus Palingenius' "Zodyake of Lyfe," was published in a collection entitled *Eglogs, Epytaphes, and Sonnettes*, 1563. This singular composition supplies the curious reader with a detailed survey of the status of Virgilian translation in England about the year 1560.

AN EPYTAPHE OF MAISTER THOMAS PHAYRE

The hawtie verse that Maro wrote, made Rome to wonder muche,
And mervayle none; for why? the style and waightynes was suche,
That all men judged Parnassus mount had clefte her selfe in twayne,
And brought forth one that seemd to drop from out Minervae's brayne.

But wonder more may Bryttayne great, when Phayre dyd florysh late,
And barreyne tong with swete accord reduced to such eſtate,
That Virgil's verse had greater grace, in forrayne foote obtaynde,
Than in his own, who, whilſt he lyved, eche other poet ſtaynde.
The noble H. Hawarde once,[96] that raught eternall fame,
With mighty ſtyle did bryng a pece of Virgil's worke in frame.
And Grimoald gave the lyke attempt,[97] and Douglas wan the ball,[98]
For famous wyt in Scottysh ryme, had made an ende of all.
But all these same did Phayre excell, I dare presume to wryte,
As much as doth Apolloe's beames the dymmeſt ſtarre in lyght.
The envious fates (O pytie great!) had great disdayne to see,
That us amongſt there shuld remayne so fine a wyt as he;
And, in the mydſt of all his toyle, dyd force, hym hence to wende,
And leave a Worke imperfyt so, that never man shall ende.

Thomas Twyne, M.D., (1543–1613) took up the translation in
the tenth book, and published in 1583 and 1584

The XIII Bookes of Aeneidos. The firſt twelve beeinge the woorke of the
divine Poet Virgil Maro, and the thirteenth, the Supplement of Maphaeus Ve-
gius. Translated into English verse to the fyrſt third part of the tenth Booke,
by Thomas Phaer, Esquire, and the residue finished, and set forth for the delite
of such as are ſtudious in Poetrie: By Thomas Twyne, Doctor of Physicke.
Imprinted at London by William How, for Abraham Veale, dwelling in Paules
Church yeard, at the sign of the Lambe.

Phaer's ſtyle has more spirit and zeſt than that of Twyne, but an
old-time quaintness of phrase and spelling prevents Thomas Twyne's
conclusion of the work from being dull reading.

In the whole sixteenth century, hardly more than ten Latin authors
were translated into English, and these were, in the main, represented
by very small portions of their work. For this reason the two complete

[96] Henry Howard, Earl of Surrey (1517[?]–1547). His translation was pub-
lished in London, 1557, with the title *Certain bokes of Virgiles Aenaeis turned into
English meter by the right noble lorde, Henry Earle of Surrey.*

[97] Nicholas Grimoald (1519–1562) made a Latin prose paraphrase of Virgil's
Georgics entitled *Maronis quattuor libros Georgicorum in soluta paraphrasis elegantis-
sima,* Oxonii in Aede Chriſti. Eduardi sexti secundo confecta, London, 1591.

[98] Translation completed 1513, published 1553.

Aeneids, that of Douglas (1513), and Phaer and Twyne (1583), have a unique importance.[99] Toward the end of the century North's famous *Plutarch* and Marlowe's *Ovid* vie with them in prominence. It was, however, almost a century before the main body of Greek and Latin literature became available to the English public.

An extraordinary cento was published by Alexander Rose or Ross (1590–1654), schoolmaster of Southampton, later chaplain of King Charles I, at London in 1638. It bears the title, *Vergilii Evangelisantis Christiados libri XIII. In quibus omnia quae de Domino nostro Iesu Christo in utroque Testamento, vel dicta vel praedicta sunt, Altisona Divina Maronis tuba suavissime dicuntur.* Alexander Ross's name occurs in a couplet in Butler's *Hudibras*, Part I, Canto II.

> There was an ancient sage philosopher
> That had read Alexander Ross over.

Some direct influence of this Virgilian cento is said to appear in the poems of John Milton.[100] The number of its books is of course due to the commonly accepted number of the books of the *Aeneid*, including the thirteenth. The "Thirteen" recalls the odd phrase of Bishop Gavin Douglas about the full tale of books in his version of the *Aeneid*, which he completed "in honor of God and his apostles twelve in the number odd."

The French translation of Virgil's poems by L. des Masures (Masurius), a work planned by Cardinal du Bellay, was reprinted in Paris in 1577 with *Le treizième livre de l'Eneide traduit de Latin en Français*, by Pierre de Mouchauld. The style is antiquated and crabbed.

When allegory had run its course, burlesque came in vogue to pique men's jaded appetites. The seventeenth century saw the publication of an anonymous Hudibrastic satire in the form of a parody upon Maphaeus Vegius' "Thirteenth Book." It came from the pen of a certain John Ellis (1698–1791), the last representative of the profession called "scriveners." The parody bears an interesting metrical title.

---

[99] H. Palmer, "List of English Editions and Translations of Greek and Latin Classics before 1641," *Bibliographical Society Publications*, Volume XII, 1911.

[100] G. A. Aitken, "Alexander Ross," *Dictionary of National Biography* (London, 1897), Volume XLIX.

The canto added by Maphaeus
To Virgil's twelve books of Aeneis
From the original bombaſtic
Done into English Hudibraſtic
With notes beneath and Latin text
To every other page annexed.

James Boswell[101] throws a pleasant light upon the author of this odd produƈtion, who also translated Ovid's epiſtles in "a very pretty way." He says (alluding to Dr. Samuel Johnson):

I remember he once observed to me, "It is wonderful, Sir, what is to be found in London. The moſt literary conversation that I ever enjoyed was at the table of Jack Ellis, a money scrivener behind the Royal Exchange, with whom I at one period used to dine—generally once a week."

The next version of Vegius' "Thirteenth Book" comes from Ireland from the pen of Mary Leadbeater (1758–1826), Dublin, 1808. Her brother's son, Richard Shackleton, had made an English prose version, which she turned into heroic couplets. This poem inclines to dullness, though some of Mrs. Leadbeater's verses are lively and melodious. Her poetic gift was well thought of by Edmund Burke, who was her father's pupil. In 1864, Cavaliere Giorgio Tornielli translated the *Aeneid* into Italian verse. In 1874, he added the "Thirteenth Book" under the title, "Canto di Maffeo Vegio da Lodi a supplemento dell' *Eneide*."

T. Seymour Burt, ſtruck with a statement in Lampriére's *Classical Diƈtionary* about "the unfinished ſtate of the *Aeneid* which exercised the talents of Maphaeus Vegius in the fifteenth century," tried to find a copy of the "Thirteenth Book" and happened upon Mary Leadbeater's metrical version, which is printed on alternate pages with the original Latin text. The "Thirteenth Book" by Vegius did not seem to him to have supplied the deficiency noted by Lampriére and commented upon by Davidson in a note on the laſt line of his English translation of Virgil's Book XII; so Burt looked up material in the firſt book of Livy's *Hiſtory* for a possible "Fourteenth Book." This

---

[101] Boswell, *Johnson*, edited by J. B. Hill, III, 24.

he found in chapters III to XVI. He rendered the prose narrative into English blank verse and offered it as a sequel, so that, to quote his own words,

if any scholar, who may feel himself equal to the task, should be willing to tax his powers by making Latin hexameters in continuation of the "Prince of Poets" work, he need only to take up Livy's Latin text . . . . to transpose it . . . . for it is almoſt poetry already, the firſt two lines forming nearly complete hexameters—and a perfeĉt narrative will be arrived at in that measure down to the death of Romulus, whom I conceive to have been the laſt descendant of the Aeneadae.

The book appeared in 1883 with the title, "*The Aeneid, Georgics, and Eclogues of Virgil* rendered into English blank verse; together with others of his poems, not hitherto translated; to which are appended Maphaeus Vegius' Book XIII, a supplement to the *Aeneid,* as well as material proposed for a Book XIV to the same by T. Seymour Burt, F.R.S., M.R.A.A., etc."

VIRGIL'S GREATEST ILLUSTRATOR AND "THE
THIRTEENTH BOOK"

Virgil's greateſt illuſtrator was the humoriſt and humaniſt, Sebastian Brant, who flourished in the old Rhine cities of Basle and Strassburg at the close of the fifteenth century. He was one of the moſt-talked-of men in Europe, largely because he never forgot that all the world loves a piĉture book. He found time, in the intervals of a successful career as juriſt, teacher, poet, ſtudent, adminiſtrator, and friend of princes, to lay before the shining eyes of his younger and older contemporaries no less than six consummate piĉture books. His famous *Virgil* of 1502 has been appropriately called "one of the moſt wonderful iﬂuſtrated books ever produced."[102]

After 1450, when the art of printing made possible the multiplication of volumes less expensive than the gorgeous codices illuminated

[102] G. R. Redgrave, "Illuſtrated Books by Sebaſtian Brant," *Bibliographica* (London, 1896), Volume II.

II   THE FUNERAL OF TURNUS

by monastic scribes, printers and readers still hankered after books that were beautiful and pictorial. Under the stimulus of popular demand, the rude planks of pear or cherry wood that had served as stamps for printing playing cards evolved within a single generation into the matchless wood blocks of Albrecht Dürer. Monochrome decoration stressed composition and design, and from the first the old prints had rare decorative quality. The fifteenth-century public was fastidious. To its nicety we owe the fact that the earliest printed books are not infrequently the handsomest. The best was none too good for connoisseurs whose taste was formed by quattrocento manuscripts. Bright boys still thought of penmanship as a possible profession, and the printer must produce a product which could hold its own in comparison with exquisite handiwork.

Sebastian Brant's first important picture book was the notorious *Narrenschiff* or "*Ship of Fools,*" that tweaked old Europe by the nose with coarse and caustic jest in 1494. The volume was a quarto, alive with woodcuts, and diversified by handsome borders designed in the Italian style. It is quite impossible to say who drew the first sketches for these prints. How much Brant had to do with them is a riddle that cannot be answered until, in a fortunate moment, some old letter or memorandum comes to light with intimate details. Many hints from the Basle woodcuts were later elaborated in Brant's Strassburg books, and it seems not at all unlikely that his hand as well as his heart was involved in their design.

The same year, 1494, or possibly the later months of 1493, witnessed the publication of a booklet, now extremely rare, which was edited by Sebastian Brant and prefaced by him with a foreword in Latin couplets. This tiny pamphlet contains a play on the capture of Granada and an illustrated text of Columbus' letter to the Crown Treasurer of Aragon announcing his great discovery. Its eight woodcuts were revamped from an earlier Basle edition of the letter. The story of the "Admiral of the Ocean Fleet" captivated the imagination of Europe. The "grave and pious" Columbus became the typical Renaissance discoverer, as Aeneas had been the voyager *par excellence* of all antiquity. It is not surprising to find that when Brant edited his famous *Virgil* at Strassburg he used Columbus' caravels as patterns for

Aeneas' ships. To Brant, as to his readers, Aeneas' weſtern voyage was fraught with all the intense significance of Columbus' journey, the greateſt event in that age of geographic discovery.[103]

Brant next concoĉted a scheme for bringing his favorite Roman poets to the notice of the prosperous citizens of Basle, who were rather prosy people, more intereſted in trade and household comfort than they were in books. He selecĉted ſtriking quotations and captivating epigrams, which he decorated in black and white with quaint intriguing designs. These broadsides he diſtributed to the men of his acquaintance. One can fancy a ſtout, velvet-coated burgher, seated before his subſtantial breakfaſt, scanning a *bon mot* from Ovid as he sipped his mug of beer.

With similar ardor Brant's pupil, Jacob Locher of Ingolſtadt, and a "prudent and honeſt" printer, Johann Grüninger by name, were engaged at Strassburg on a series of illuſtrated classics. A *Terence* appeared in 1496, a *Horace* in 1498. Block prints, variously combined from a limited selecĉtion of male and female figures, trees, and houses, decorate these editions. Each contains, in addition to the composite prints, a single magnificent symbolic design, which serves the purpose of a modern title-page. The convenient convention of the title-page did not become fixed in European printing till twenty years later.

In 1500 Brant moved to Strassburg under appointment of his admired patron, the Emperor Maximilian I, as syndic and imperial chancellor of his native city. His controlling influence firſt appears in the third volume of the Strassburg series, the *Boethius* of 1501. Here, inſtead of combined piĉtures, such as had graced the *Terence* and the *Horace*, the elaborate illuſtrations are cut on single blocks. In some inſtances, successive ſtages of narrative are indicated by a series of compartments. These are arranged like a triptich, with the main episode in the center, or in a sequence like the modern comic ſtrip.

The next year saw the publication of the crowning volume of the series, the *Virgil* of 1502, a handsome folio, crowded with vivacious woodcuts, large and small, in which "the capriceful fancy of the

---

[103] A. C. Brinton, "The Ships of Columbus in Brant's Virgil," *Art and Archaeology*, September, 1928.

    EMBASSY TO AENEAS

artist"[104] links Roman mythology arm in arm with medieval Christian symbolism. In his prefatory epigram Brant explains that this book is intended for the general rather than the scholarly reader.

> Virgilium exponant alii sermone deserto,
>   Et calamo pueris; tradere et ore iuvet,
> Pictura agresti voluit Brant; atque tabellis;
>   Edere cum indoctis; rusticolisque viris,
> Nec tamen abiectis labor hic; nec prorsus inanis,
>   Nam memori servat mente figura librum.

Dr. Henry states the whole case for these woodcuts in his own quaint language, when he says, "There is no one of them, let it only be rightly read, that is not in accord with some unseen vibrating fibril of the human heart."[105] Earlier editors had imbedded Virgil's text in an unwieldy mass of notes; Brant preserved this time-honored apparatus, while he lighted up the pages with a picture commentary designed to stimulate, not the pedantic instincts, but the imagination of his readers. On the title-page he says of his pictures

> Has tibi nemo ante hac tam plane ostenderat usquam:
>   Nemo tibi voluit pingere Virgilium.
> Nunc memorare potes monochromata cuncta Maronis
>   Quam leviter: pictis lector amice locis.

Three aspects of the *Aeneid* made irresistible appeal to the sympathetic illustrator. First and foremost, he delighted to portray the lust of battle, stormed cities, heads impaled on pikes, single combat, and funeral pyres. To the eye of gentle Virgil every one of these designs would have borne the imprint of horrid barbarity. Next he reveled in the grace and mystery of ships, as he wove the pattern of Columbus' galleons into vigorous nautical designs of storm and fair weather. Finally, here on the threshold of the northern Renaissance, that was never really a Renaissance at all in the Italian sense of the word, but rather a Reformation, medieval *courtoisie* softens the bloody chronicle of conflict into a romance of chivalry.

[104] J. Noel Humphreys, *A History of the Art of Printing* (London, 1868), page 175.

[105] James Henry, *Aeneidea* (Dublin, 1878), Volume I, Introduction, page lx.

The designer of these prints is possessed by a veritable *horror vacui*. There must be no blank spots on his paper, and no episode in his author's narrative can be ignored by the conscientious commentator. This explains the presence of little supplementary scenes in many of the cuts, portraying events earlier or later than the main subject, tucked away in sky or landscape spaces like the determinatives in Egyptian hieroglyphics. In this unique way the artist has added to his three dimensions of space a fourth dimension of time.

Six elaborate woodcuts, worthy of the most minute and attentive observation, illustrate "The Thirteenth Book of the *Aeneid*." There is no let-down in style from the Virgil pictures; Brant, Locher, and Grüninger were inspired by Vegius' narrative to design their picture commentary on the same attractive and sumptuous scale as their illustrations to Virgil's twelve books.

DESCRIPTION OF BRANT'S WOODCUTS

Plate I.—Brant's first illustration of the Thirteenth Book of the *Aeneid* quaintly synthesizes the incidents of the initial sixty lines of the poem. Lists for single combat, Turnus slain, enemy lances struck into the ground in token of surrender, these are the horizontal and vertical lines that rivet our attention. A nimble squire has removed the jeweled baldric of young prince Pallas, Evander's son, from the fallen foe. Aeneas, in kingly armor of the pattern worn in 1500 with a crown that belongs to the same period of European headdress, lifts his right hand in the ancient gesture which for Roman orator and feudal lord bespoke attention. The unarmed Latins also raise their hands with the third and fourth finger folded to the palm. This is analogous to the medieval "manulevatio," the sign of a solemn pledge. Behind on the left are the defeated Rutili still armed, but bringing their weapons to add to the breastplates, helmets, and battle axes surrendered by the Latins. Near by is a suggestion of the burial of the dead.

Troia, which is Aeneas' camp, and the city of Laurentum fill the background. There are round, weather-vaned towers like those on the old wall of Strassburg and steep, concave roofs like those of the city

[44]

IV   THE MARRIAGE OF AENEAS

within, as they are depicted in an almost contemporary print from *Scheidels Chronik*, 1493. Above the wall of Troia is a small design which might appear obscure were it not that the same object is more distinctly drawn in Plate III. A slab of marble supported by four short pillars forms an altar of sacrifice. Flames are rising to heaven from a burnt offering in token of gratitude to the gods for Aeneas' victory.

Plate II.—The center of thought and feeling in the second picture is the unadorned, but impressive coffin, on which is inscribed the one word "Turnus." Everything else, and the woodcut abounds in detail, is subordinated to the one idea, "Turnus is dead." Latinus, garbed as befitted an aged king in the great days of Brant's ideal monarch, the Emperor Maximilian I, stands at his palace gate with kerchief in hand to check his rising tears. The edifice is a noble pile dominated by two massive towers, one square, the other round, that bear a distinct resemblance to the square and round towers of the Church of Saint Thomas, one of the oldest buildings in Strassburg, as it appeared about the year 1500.

The cavalier Metiscus in handsome armor, with slashed sleeves, riding on a richly caparisoned horse, commands a guard of honor represented by three young knights with down-turned lances, weapons which in happier days would have borne the bannerets of Turnus fluttering at their points. In such mournful pomp the procession takes its way from Laurentum toward Ardea, which is first represented by towers and battlements in the upper left-hand corner and later by a fire-swept hill in the center background. Trouble is heaped on trouble for Daunus the aged king. A terrific fire demolishes his once-prosperous city. Its fortifications and homes are reduced to ashes, either because the gods have so willed or because prophetic fates give this grim foreboding of Turnus' death. As the city writhes in final agony, its spirit, transformed into the bird Ardea, rises on beating pinions from the embers. King Daunus has scarcely made his way outside the burning walls when Rumor accosts him, in the form of a messenger, with tidings that a funeral train is drawing near, bearing his dead son Turnus.

Plate III.—The embassy of a thousand heroes sent by King Latinus to Aeneas, the conqueror, to bespeak favor and offer the hand of princess Lavinia in marriage is gracefully suggeſted by five armored horsemen gaily wreathed with ivy. Even their horses' tails carry out the feſtive impression by decorative curves. Aeneas in a new corselet, wearing on his head a massive combination of turban and coronet, which can be closely paralleled among the Innsbruck ſtatues, with a huge sword in his right hand, ſtrides forth from Troia's gate to welcome the cavalcade, whose leader is Drances, famed for his much speaking. The illuſtrator does not allow us to forget, however, that this cheerful scene follows after carnage. In the lower left-hand corner two corpses are burning on a funeral pyre, and in the upper right a ſtately prieſt (perhaps Aeneas himself in changed robes) offers thanks to heaven for victory.

Plate IV.—The fourth illuſtration is a play in two acts, the arrival of the bridegroom and the wedding. In the foreground Aeneas, Ascanius, and two young squires, who have crossed the bridge from their ſtronghold on the upper left, are ſtanding before the palace gate of Laurentum. King Latinus with two royal attendants welcomes them in courteous wise. For our further edification the engraver has conſtructed an open pavilion on a higher level of the palace on the right. Here is depicted the marriage of Aeneas and Lavinia. Oddly enough Aeneas ſtands at the prieſt's left side and Lavinia at his right, an arrangement unparalleled except in Raphael's famous picture of the marriage of the Virgin Mary. Probably the engraver neglected to notice that his design would be reversed in the printing. Lavinia's ſtriped headdress in this and the following plate is almoſt exactly duplicated in Hans Holbein's portrait of the wife of the Burgomaſter Jacob Meyer in the museum at Basle.

Plate V.—The fifth woodcut in Brant's series (reproduced as the frontispiece of this volume) is perhaps the moſt attractive of the series from artiſtic and dramatic points of view. In a handsome setting of Gothic arches and tall, slender windows, with one pane of bull's-eyes characteriſtically open to admit a modicum of air, noble Aeneas and his bride Lavinia, who reſts her left hand affectionately upon her husband's arm, old Latinus, and the precocious, attractive boy Ascanius are seated at a table richly spread. A peacock, with feathers successfully reset after baking, crowns the feaſt. The handsome medieval saltcellar represents the "crater" which King Priam gave to Father Anchises and which Achates was sent to fetch as a bridal gift. To the music of pipe and drum a dapper youth and a fashionable lady lead the dance, *"variantque pedes, raptimque feruntur."*

In the background, among idyllic rocks where Aeneas is founding his new city, the heavenly sanction of the earthly wedlock is symbolically portrayed. A flame shoots up from Lavinia's head, and Aeneas stretches out his hands and prays in a loud voice to Jupiter to confirm the omen of the halo of light. As he speaks, his goddess mother stands, beside him with a prophecy of present joy and future peace, of a progeny that shall fill the world with honor, and, finally, of Aeneas' own ascension into heaven.

Plate VI.—The last of this series of woodcuts is the most bizarre of them all, with its pagan stars for Christian fig leaves and the quaint contrast between the heavy German costumes of the year of grace 1500 in which the mortals are arrayed and the complete absence of all raiment for the Roman deities. It bears witness to the incongruous ingredients of northern humanism.

A masterly description of this picture has been bequeathed us by the most singular of Virgil's critics, the Irish physician, James Henry, who retired from his medical practice to devote his life to the study of his favorite author. Dr. Henry appears not to have seen Brant's original woodcut, but an inferior copy in the Juntine edition, Venice, 1537, had come to his attention. He says:

Turn back as far as the woodcut on the verso of the last folio but one of Maphaeus Vegius's "Thirteenth Book"—ingeniously platted queue of Virgilian centos, which in this, as in some other old editions, has been pinned to, and hangs dangling from, the *Aeneis*—and observe above, on your left hand, Lavinia, Ascanius, a third person (perhaps Achates), and the city of Lavinium: in the right-hand corner, sceptred Jupiter throned on clouds, as firm to all appearance as rocks, and Venus embracing his knees and reminding him of his promise that Aeneas should be translated to heaven: below, in the right-hand corner, Latinus stretched dead on an elevated bier: the crowned head supported on a cushion, the hands crossed, the upper half of the person naked. The lower half covered with a pall carefully folded back at the upper border, and descending, at the foot and on both sides, to the very ground: still lower down, the river Numicus, with a luxuriant typha in the midst, occupying the foreground: in the left-hand corner,—corner alike of picture and river—Venus and Aeneas: Aeneas in the extreme corner on the water's edge, stretched on his back, dead, with his hands crossed, and only a swathe around his loins: Venus above her knees in the water just touching with both hands Aeneas's left shoulder, as if about to push or pull him, or as if, having pushed or pulled him so far out of the water, she does not know what step to take next. No, I beg pardon: the goddess is in no such difficulty; carry Aeneas to heaven, indeed! she, who so well knows how much trouble it cost Aeneas himself, who was more than twice as strong, to carry his father, who was less than half the weight, a few perch, here on the solid earth. She has no notion of it; she is only going to wash him—however supererogatory a work that may seem to be—before she commits him finally to the river: "*Tunc corpus nati abluere et deferre sub undas. Quicquid erat mortale iubet.*" And now prepare for a surprise. The most curious thing in the whole picture is to come yet. Put on your spectacles and tell me if you see anything on Aeneas's chin besides the beard. "Do you mean the little Lilliputian standing on it with his feet buried in the beard, and his hands lifted up and joined together as in the act of prayer?" "Exactly. Do you know who that is?" "How should I, not being the dean of St. Patrick's?" "Guess." "Perhaps queen Mab's husband; not queen Mab herself, 'for masculine he is beyond all question'." "Out; guess again." "Some tiny great-grandchild of Aeneas, playing hide-and-seek in great-grandfather's beard." "Out, again. I'll tell you, for you'll not guess till doom's day. That's Aeneas himself." "What! standing on his own chin!" "Yes; spewed out of his own mouth with his last breath, for the very purpose of being carried up to heaven with the least possible trouble to all parties." "Well, how stupid I am! Often and often as I heard there were two Aeneases, one inside and the other outside, I never before understood how it was; but I see it now with my own eyes. That's a clever artist." "You have it perfectly: two Aeneases; one inside, light and little, to be carried up into heaven; the other outside, big and heavy, to remain down here, drowned in the Numicus." "Nothing can be plainer."

PROLOGUES AND COLOPHON

It was customary in manuscripts and early printed volumes for a brief metrical summary called a *periocha* or *argumentum* to precede each individual book of a classical author. Sulpicius Apollinaris supplied a famous series of epitomes for the plays of Terence and for

   THE DEATH OF AENEAS

the twelve books of the *Aeneid*. Other *argumenta* for Virgil were pre-
pared by later hands. Maphaeus Vegius' "Thirteenth Book" was not
left long without its own metrical introduction. Two manuscripts in
the British Museum (Arundel Manuscripts 82 and 193) are prefaced
by an eleven-line hexameter summary different from the twelve-line
argumentum that appears in the Venice *Virgil* of 1471 and in all the
subsequent editions which contain the "Thirteenth Book." Maphaeus
himself may have prepared one of these *periochai* for his poem.

The eleven-line argument follows. The longer preface precedes
the printed text on page 52, below.

> Victor ut Aeneas belli fuit, illico subdunt
> Imperio sese Rutuli, datur inde per ipsum
> Hostia lausque diis, pariter congaudet Iulo
> Ac sociis pro pace suis; Turnique Latinus
> Morte dolet; patriae miseranda incendia Daunus
> Eversae et cari deflet pia funera nati.
> Conubium instaurat natae, lectosque hymenaeos
> Rex socer Aeneae genero; gens utraque pacto
> Foedere pacis ovat; tunc nomine coniugis urbem
> Instruit, et tandem placida sub pace regentem
> Transtulit Aeneas Venus astra in summa beatum.

The same Arundel manuscripts mentioned above contain an epigram
complimentary to Maphaeus Vegius and conceived in the spirit of some
of the Carmina Virgiliana quoted by Bährens in his *Poetae Latini Mi-
nores.*[106] It was a type of composition that found favor in the late
Roman period and in the Humanistic Age. Vegius himself indulged
in it freely. The lines run thus:

> Musae omnes gaudete, novus surrexit ab urbe
> Laude Maro, Vegius sua nomina data Mafeus.
> Ter decimum librum quem morte nequit adire
> Virgilius vates canit iste profarier ausus
> Alter Parthenias, dicunt, mirabile pubes
> Talia gesta refert credisque videre Maronem.

---

[106] Luigi Raffaele quotes two other poems of similar purport in his *Maffeo Vegio*
(Bologna, 1909), pages 100 f.

Adam de Ambergau's colophon, which concludes the *Virgil* of
1471, is an amusing composition that bespeaks comment. Its ligatures
and abbreviations are as elaborate as those of the medieval scribes. The
ten lines are replete with riddles almoſt amounting to charades. Poly-
syndeton is absurdly prominent. The use of *sesqui* in the fourth line
as an intensive adverb is odd and unclassical. The phrase appears to
mean "in one and the self-same identical spot." "*Parvo numerosa
iuventus*" suggeſts an extremely small edition. Only four copies have
been identified by Copinger among the Incunabula Virgiliana. Adam
addresses his reader with the words:

> Mincidae quicumque cupit cognoscere vatis
> Carmina: seu quisquis Vegi simul optat habere,
> Me legat, aut fratres, parvo numerosa iuventus,
> Uno eodemque sumus pressi sesquique locoque
> Non Solomon, neque Hiram, non Daedalus atque Sibylla,
> Graecia non omnis sapientibus inclyta quamquam,
> Non armis Romana potens aequandaque divis
> Gloria iaſtavit tali sese arte decoram.
> Nos igitur peterit patrem qui nomine primum
> Rettulit alter Adam, formis quos pressit aenis.

The .xiii. Bookes

OF ÆNEIDOS.

The first twelue beeinge the
woorke of the diuine Poet
Virgil Maro, **and the thirtenth**
the supplement of Maphæus Vegius.

Translated into English verse to
the fyrst thirdpart of the tenth Booke,
by Thomas Phaer Esquire: and the residue
finished, and now the second time newly
setforth for the delite of such as are stu-
dious in Poetrie: By Thomas Twyne,
Doctor in Physicke.

¶ Imprinted at London by
William How, for Abraham
Veale, dwelling in Paules Church
yeard, at the signe of the Lambe.
1584.

[Facsimile of the title-page of the Twyne and Phaer *Virgil* of 1584]

TEXT OF THE "EDITIO PRINCEPS"

MAFEI VEGII LAUDENSIS
LIBRI XII AENEIDOS SUPPLEMENTUM
PAPIAE VI IDUS OCTOBRIS
1428

WITH THE ENGLISH TRANSLATION
BY THOMAS TWYNE, M.D.

THE THIRTENTH BOOKE OF AENEIDOS
SUPPLIED BY
MAPHAEUS VEGIUS LAUDENSIS

TRANSLATED BY THOMAS TWYNE, M.D.
LONDON, OCTOBER 26, 1583

ARGUMENTUM

    Turnus ut extremo vitam sub Marte profudit
Subdunt se Rutuli Aeneae, Troiana sequentes
Agmina; dehinc superis meriti redduntur honores.
Congaudet nato ac sociis, memor ante malorum
5   Actorum pater Aeneas. Turni inde Latinus
Morte dolet. Patriae miseranda incendia Daunus
Eversae, et cari deflet pia funera nati.
Connubium inſtaurat natae laetosque hymenaeos
Rex socer Aeneae genero; gens utraque pacto
10   Foedere pacis ovat; tum nomine coniugis urbem
Inſtruit, et tandem placida sub pace regentem
Tranſtulit Aeneam Venus aſtra in summa beatum.

THE ARGUMENT

So soone as Aeneas had slayne Turnus, the Rutilians submitting themselves are received into the mercy of the Conquerour, not without deserved reproches for resiſting the providence of the Gods, concerning his arrivall and setling in Italy. Then Aeneas taketh Pallas belt from about Turnus, which was partlye the cause that he slue him, determining to send it for a token to king Evander. After this, honour being duly perfourmed to such as wer slain in fight, Aeneas congratulateth to his sunne Iulus and mates, their happie victories, and quiet peace purchased at laſt, after so many tempeſtes and troubles. But king Latinus bewayling the death of Turnus, with confutation of the fond enticements of Ambition, and uncerteinty of honour and kingly eſtate, sendeth the dead body unto Daunus his father, who moſt pitifully lamenteth the rashnesse and haplesse successe of his sunne, as also the deſtruction of his citie Ardea, which being consumed with fire, is transformed into a byrd of that name. Immediately Latinus sendeth Oratours unto Aeneas, Drances being cheefe, who after discommendation of Turnus whom he hated, and the excuse of king Latinus touching the breache of covenants, desireth him into the citie and pallace, where with great solemnitie Latinus coupleth unto him in marriage Lavinia his daughter, and only childe, both Troyans and Italians muche reioycing at this legue of amitie. Shortly after, Aeneas buildeth a citie, whiche by the advise of his mother Venus, hee calleth after his wives name: and king Latinus dying, hee succeedeth him in the crowne and government. And when he had raigned full three yeares, his mother Venus clensing him from contagion of mortalitie in the river Numicius neare Laurentum, she carieth him up into heaven, and translateth him into the number of the ſtarres.

Turnus ut extremo devictus Marte profudit
Effugientem animam, medioque sub agmine victor
Magnanimus stetit Aeneas, Mavortius heros,
Obstupuere omnes, gemitumque dedere Latini,
5   Et durum ex alto revomentes corde dolorem,
Concussis cecidere animis; ceu frondibus ingens
Silva dolet lapsis boreali impulsa tumultu.
Tum tela infigunt terrae, et mucronibus haerent:
Scutaque deponunt humeris, et proelia damnant,
10 Insanumque horrent optati Martis amorem:
Nec frenum, nec colla pati captiva recusant,
Et veniam orare et requiem finemque malorum.
Sicut acerba duo quando in certamina tauri
Concurrunt, largo miscentes sanguine pugnam,
15 Cuique suum pecus inclinat: sin cesserit uni
Palma duci, mox quae victo pecora ante favebant
Nunc sese imperio subdunt victoris, et ultro
Quanquam animum dolor altus habet, parere fatentur:
Non aliter Rutuli, licet ingens maeror adhausit
20 Pectora pulsa metu caesi ducis, incluta malunt
Arma sequi et Phrygium Aenean, foedusque precari
Pacis, et aeternam rebus belloque quietem.

Tunc Turnum super adsistens placido ore profatur
Aeneas: "Quae tanta animo dementia crevit,
25 Ut Teucros superum monitis, summique tonantis
Imperio huc vectos, patereris, Daunia proles,
Italia et pactis nequicquam expellere tectis?
Disce Iovem revereri et iussa facessere divum.
Magnum etiam capit ira Iovem, memoresque malorum
30 Sollicitat vindicta deos; en ultima tanti
Meta furoris adest, quo contra iura fidemque
Iliacam rupto turbasti foedere gentem.
Ecce suprema dies, aliis exempla sub aevum
Venturum missura; Iovem ne temnere frustra
35 Fas sit, et indignos bellorum accendere motus.

When Turnus in this finall fight downethrowne, his flittring ghost
Had yeelded up unto the aire, in middest of all the host
Aeneas valient victour stands, god Mavors champion bold.
The Latines stoynisht standing, from their hartes great groanes unfold,
And deepely from their inward thoughts revolving cause of care,
Their daunted minds they do let fall; Like as thick woods that are
Of bignesse huge, lament their losse when first their leaves do fall
Through furious force of northren blastes, of greene that spoiles them all.
Their weapons then on ground they pight, and on their swords do rest,
And from their shoulders lay their shieldes, and battle do detest.
The frantike love of warre, erewhile well liked, now they hate.
No pleasure of the victour they refuse, nor captive state.
But pardon crave, and rest require, all mischiefes to abate.
Like as when two couragious Bulles togither run in fight,
With stoare of blood redoubling stripes, the heards there prest in sight
As they pertayne, enclyne ech to their bull, but if one quayle,
They earst which lov'de their foyled guide, to him that did prevayle
Submit themselves, and though great greefe their harts no doubt possesse,
Do willingly yeeld up themselves as subiects naithelesse:
The Rutils so, though sorrowes great their harts did then molest,
Through feare of thus their captayne slayne, in mind did then protest.
The victour armes for to pursue, and Troyan Duke obey,
And leagues to crave, and peace eterne from warres for to enioy.
    On Turnus corps Aeneas sitting then, thus mildly spake.
What furie great from modestie thy minde so madly brake,
That Troyans by the heastes of Gods, and doome of Iove on hie
Ariving here, thou wouldst not let to dwell in Italie,
O Turnus, but in vayne from promisd houses wouldst expell?
Learne Iove to feare, and what the Gods do will, to like that well.
For mightie Iove in wrath will burne, and what thing worthye blame
Is done, the Gods will not forget for to revenge the same.
Loe here the end of all thy rage, whereby gaynst faith and right
Disturbing leagues, the Troyan bands thou didst provoke to fight.
Loe here the finall day, which unto such as shall be borne
In time hereafter may a mirrour be, not Iove to skorne
That they presume in vayne, and hateful broyles of warres to breede.

The rep-
resenta-
tion of
men dis-
comfitted
in battell

The
punish-
mente
of periurie

Nunc armis laetare tuis, heu, nobile corpus,
Turne iaces: at non tibi erit Lavinia parvo,
Nec dextra tamen Aeneae cecidisse pudebit!
Nunc, Rutuli, hinc auferte ducem veſtrum, arma virumque
40 Largior, atque omnem deflendae mortis honorem.
Sed quae Pallantis fuerant ingentia baltei
Pondera, transmittam Evandro, ut solacia caeso
Haud levia hoſte ferat, Turnoque exsultet adempto.
Vos memores tamen, Ausonii, melioribus uti
45 Discite bellorum auspiciis: ego sidera iuro,
Nunquam acies, nunquam arma libens in proelia movi:
Sed veſtris aĉtus furiis defendere toto
Optavi et licuit Troianas robore partes."

    Nec fatus plura Aeneas; se laetus ad altos
50 Vertebat muros, et Troia teĉta petebat.
·Una ipsum Teucrorum omnis conversa iuventus
Exsultans sequitur, volucresque per arva pedum vi
Quadrupedes citat, incusans acri ore Latinos,
Ignavosque vocans: strepit altus plausibus aether.
55 Et quamvis inhumata rogis dare corpora surgat
Ingens cura animo, sociosque imponere flammis,
Maius opus tamen Aeneas sub peĉtore volvens,
Primum aris meritos superum mandabat honores.
Tum pingues patrio iugulant ex more iuvencos,
60 Immittuntque sues, niveasque in templa bidentes,
Purpuream effuso pulsantes sanguine terram.
Viscera diripiunt, et caesim in fruſta trucidant,
Denudantque gregem, et flammis verubusque remittunt.
Tum vina effundunt pateris, et dona Lyaei
65 Accumulant; plenis venerantur lancibus aras;
Tura ignes adolent; onerata altaria fumant.

    Tum plausus per teĉta movent, magumque tonantem
Extollunt, Veneremque, et te, Saturnia Iuno,
Iam placidam, et meliorem ingenti laude fatentur,

But in thine armour now reioyce: A noble corps indeede
Here Turnus dead thou lieſt, but yet Lavinia coſt thee deare.
No shame that with Aeneas hand yslayne thou lieſt heare.
Now Rutils hence convay your Lord, his armour, and the man
I franckly yeelde, do honours to the dead the beſt ye can.
As for the weightie belt, which unto Pallas did belong,
To king Evander will I send, that comfort great among
For death of foes he may conceive, and ioy for Turnus slayne,
And you Ausonians these thinges repose in mindfull brayne,
Henceforth to learne some iuſter cause of battaile to ensue.
By ſtarres I sweare, that never feild nor armes I did pursue
In willing minde, but forced foorth through this your frantick moode,
With Troyan ſtrength your headlong force at wish and wil withſtoode.
    Aeneas sayd no more, but to the loftie walles with cheare
His ſteppes did turne, and to the Troyan houses drew him neare.
Him after all the troupe of Phrigian youth reioycing trace,
And wightfull ſteedes with force of nimble foote prick forth apace:
Reproving sore the Latines all by daſtardes loathsome name,
With shouts and noyses great, that ayre and skies resound the same.
And though the bodies yet untombde to burne with great desire
Within his mind doth rise, and his dead mates to waſte with fire:
Aeneas yet revolving greater matters in his breſt,
To yeeld the Gods their honours firſt right due he deemde it beſt.
Then Heickfers fat, as countries guise hath taught, forthwith they kil,
And hogges they caſt on heapes, and sheepe they drive the temples til,
And trampled earth with ſtreames of blood shead forth they purple ſtaine,
And intrailes forth they pluck, and from the flock their felles they ſtraine,
And corpses forth they cut, and broches lay to roſt at fire.
Then wine in boules they forth do fill, as cuſtome doth require.
And gifts to Bacchus up do heape, and with full cuppes adore
His sacred alters fuming fat with cense and flesh good ſtore.
Then in the houses shoutings loude they make, and Iove betweene
They do extoll, and Venus thee, and thee O Iuno Queene
More friendly and more loving now with great prayse they confesse.
And Mars himselfe, and all the troupe of Gods both more and lesse
Are there recited, and with laud extolled to the skie.

Thanks to
God to be
yielded
before
dutie to
men

[57]

70 Mavortemque ipsum: tum cetera turba deorum
In medium effertur, summis cum vocibus altos
Perlata ad caelos: ante omnes gratior unus
Aeneas duplices mittebat ad aethera palmas,
Et puerum pauca ore dabat complexus Iulum:
75 "Nate, in quo spes una patris, per tanta laborum
Quem variis actus fatis discrimina duxi,
Ecce inventa quies; ecce illa extrema malorum,
Aerumnis factura modum acceptissima semper,
Atque optata dies, quam dura in bella vocatus,
80 Saepe tibi dis auspicibus meminisse futuram
Iam memini: nunc te, cum primum Aurora rubebit
Craſtina, sublimen Rutulorum ad moenia mittam."
Dehinc sese ad gentem Iliacam volvebat, et alto
Pectore verba trahens, blando sic ore locutus:

85   "O socii, per dura ac densa pericula vecti,
Per tantos bellorum aeſtus, duplicesque furores
Armorum, per totque hiemes, per quicquid acerbum
Horrendum, grave, triſte, ingens, per quicquid iniquum
Infauſtum, et crudele foret, convertite mentem
90 In melius: iam finis adeſt: hic meta malorum
Stabit, et optatam Latia cum gente quietem
Iungemus: dabit inde mihi Lavinia coniux
Bello acri defensa, Italo cum sanguine mixtam
Troianam transferre aeterna in saecula gentem.
95 Unum oro, socii, Ausonios communiter aequo
Ferte animo, et vosmet socero observate Latino.
Sceptrum idem sublime geret: sententia mentem
Haec habet: at bello vos, et praeſtantibus armis
Discite me et pietate sequi: quae gloria nobis
100 Cesserit, in promptu eſt; sed caelum, et sidera teſtor,
Qui vos tantorum eripui de clade malorum,
Idem ego sub maiora potens vos praemia ducam."

   Talibus orabat, variosque in pectore casus

But Lord Aeneas peere of price to all the ſtanders bie,
His doubled handes in humblewise did ſtretche into the aire,
And clasping faſt his childe hee spake thus to Iülus faire.
O sunne, thy fathers only hope, whom through diſtresses ſtrange
My selfe have led, with deſtnies diverse drawne enforſt to range.
Loe, reſt at length is found, loe now that day the laſt of payne
And troubles great that bringes an ende, moſt pleasant now we gaine.
Which day moſt wished ſtill, when me to warres hard happe did call,
By Gods good will, I know, to thee I oft did tell, would fall.
And now when firſt the morning bright shall shine with purple weede,
Unto the Rutil walles I thee will send advancde indeede.
Then to the Troyan nation next he turned and deepe from out
His breſt these words he drew, and mildly spake to all the rout. [broyls
O Mates, that through sharp dangers thick and oft have paſt, through
Of warres so great, through winters many, fierce and bitter toyles,
Through what was fearefull, greevous, wofull, huge, and what uniuſt,
Unfortunate and cruell too, pluck up to better luſt
Your minds as now, the ende is come, heere shall that end be fixt
Of mischiefes all, and wished peace be setled us betwixt
And these the men of Latium. Then shall Lavinia deere
My wife, whom I in battaile fierce have woon, to Troyans cheare
Advaunce our ſtock with Itayle blood commixt to bide for aye.
This one thing Mates, the Ausonians, with equall minds, I pray,
To beare and use, and eke my sire in law Latinus King
For to obay, for he the scepter shall enioy, this thing
I have determined in minde: but you in warres and fight
Learne godlinesse of me, and trace therein my ſteppes aright.
What glory great is gaynd thereby to us, you playnly see.
But by the heaven and glittring ſtarres I sweare, eterne that bee:
I that preserved have your lives before from dangers hard,
Will after this requite your toyles with greater far reward.
    Such talke he treated then, and sundry chances in his breſt
Forepassed did revolve, not smally reckoning of his reſt
Through travaile late obtaynde, and tender love in breſt he bare
Unto his Troyans, whome to have escapte from dangers rare
He did reioyce. And like the Hen her broode that clucking guides,

Praeteritos volvens, partamque labore quietem
105 Haud parvo: nimium ardenti exundabat amore
In Teucros, gravibus tandem evasisse periclis
Exsultans: velut exiguis cum ex aethere gyrans
Incubuit pullis, et magno turbine milvus
Insiliens avido ore furit, ſtragemque minatur;
110 Tum criſtata ales perculso peɛtore mater
Consurgit, misero natorum exterrita casu,
Roſtrum acuit, totisque petit conatibus hoſtem,
Et multa expulsum vi tandem cedere cogit;
Dehinc perturbatos crocitans exquirit, et omnes
115 Attonitos cogit, pro caris anxia natis,
Et tanto ereptos gaudet superesse periclo.
Non secus Anchisa genitus mulcebat amicis
Troianos diɛtis, antiquum corde timorem
Flagrantesque agitans curas, et gaudia longis
120 Tandem parta malis, et quae perferre moleſtum
Ante fuit, meminisse iuvat: verum altior idem
Ingenti et clara Aeneas supereminet omnes
Virtute excellens, et pro tot numina donis
Exorat, summisque Iovem cum laudibus effert.

125   Interea Rutuli magnum et miserabile funus,
Exanimumque ducem tulerant sub teɛta frequentes,
Correpti maerore animos, largumque pluentes
Imbrem oculis, et iam lato clamore Latinum
Defessum, et varios agitantem peɛtore casus
130 Complerant; qui poſtquam altos crebrescere queſtus,
Et Turnum ingenti confossum vulnere vidit,
Haud tenuit lacrimas; dehinc maeſtum leniter agmen
Corripuit, manibus verbisque silentia ponens.
Ceu spumantis apri quando per viscera dentes
135 Fulmineos canis excepit praeſtantior omni
Ex numero, tunc infauſto perterrita casu
Cetera turba fugit latrantum, atque ore magiſtrum
Circumſtans querulo pavitat, magnoque ululatu

When in the ayre a kyte that soaring round in compasse glides
She doth espie, which ſtouping swift to ground with greedy bill
With furie seekes to pray, and threatneth all the birds to kill.
The combed Dame then touchte at heart, doth ſtreit her self advaunce,
Affrighted with the sodayne feare, and chickens heavie chaunce.
She whets her bill, and with her greateſt force withſtands her foe,
Until with ſturdie ſtrength she make him voyd away to goe.
Then cackling thence, she halts to seeke them earſt diſturbde with feare,
And flockes them much amazde, such love she to her younge doth beare.
None otherwise Anchisus sunne with words, and geſture milde
The Troyans did appease, while former feares and dangers wilde
Outworne he doth revolve in minde, and ioyes by troubles long,
Obteyned yet at length, which though in bearing bread him wrong
In former times, the memorie thereof yet bringes delight.
But Lord Aeneas farre excelling all in vertue bright,
Due thanks unto the Gods for gifts received earſt he payes,
And Iupiter almightie God extolles with worthie prayse.
 Therwhiles the great and wofull corps, the Rutils thick in throng,
Duke Turnus bodie dead have brought to towne in pompe along
With heavie harts perplext, and sheading ſtreams of trickling teares.
The clamour great with greefe had filled soone Latinus eares
All tired now, and caſting sundry chances in his breſt.
Who after that he heard the mone encrease with mournefull queſt,
And Turnus with a mightie wound yslayne did there behold,
His teares he could not ſtay, but meekely al the troupe controld.
And with his handes and speeches sad deepe silence did commaund.
And like as when the foming boare with tuskes fierce forth that ſtand,
Some noble hound the cheefe of all the kennell, through hath ſtuck,
The barking crue doth back retire dismayed with dreadfull luck,
And thronging thick about their maiſter round do make their mone,
And houlings great send forth with dread and greefe commixt at one.
But then the maiſter holding up his hands and bidding hush,
Their noyse they ſtraight reſtrayne, and silent sit at present push.
The Rutils so, in voices whuſt did inward sorrow presse.
Then king Latinus shedding teares, his words thus to adresse
From heart deepe drawn began. What troubles great, what often change

Infremit; at commota manu, dominique iubentis
140   Ore silet, gemitumque premit, seseque coercet.
Haud aliter Rutuli suppressa voce quierunt.

Tunc sic illacrimans rex alto corde Latinus
Verba dabat: "Quantos humana negotia motus,
Alternasque vices miscent! Quo turbine fertur
145   Vita hominum! O fragilis damnosa superbia sceptri!
O furor, O nimium dominandi innata cupido,
Mortales quo caeca vehis? Quo gloria tantis
Inflatos transfers animos quaesita periclis?
Quot tecum insidias, quot mortes, quanta malorum
150   Magnorum tormenta geris, quot tela, quot enses
Ante oculos, si cernis, habes! Heu dulce venenum,
Et mundi letalis honos! Heu tristia regni
Munera, quae haud parvo constent, et grandia rerum
Pondera, quae nunquam placidam permittere pacem,
155   Nec requiem conferre queant! Heu sortis acerbae
Et miserae regale decus, magnoque timori
Suppositos regum casus, pacisque negatos!
Quid, Turne, ingenti Ausoniam movisse tumultu,
Et dura Aeneadas turbasse in bella coactos,
160   Quid iuvat, et violasse sacrae promissa quietis
Pignora, quae tibi tanta animo impatientia venit?
Ut Martem cum gente deum iussuque tonantis
Huc vecta gereres, et nostris pellere tectis
Ultro instans velles, nataeque abrumpere foedus
165   Pollicitae genero Aeneae, et me bella negante
Dura movere manu? Quae tanta insania mentem
Implicuit? Quoties te in saevi Martis euntem
Agmina, sublimemque in equo et radiantibus armis
Tentavi revocare, et iter suspendere coeptum?
170   Corripui et pavitans cedentem in limine frustra?
Inde ego quanta tuli, testantur moenia tectis
Semirutis, magnique albentes ossibus agri,
Et Latium toto vacuatum robore, et ingens

Do mens affaires assay, and tosse their minds with whirlewind ſtrange?
O foolish fancie fayne to rule, and scepters brittle pride.
O frantike madnesse graft in men desirous realmes to guide.
To what diſtresse dooſt thou enforce mens blinded harts to run,
And glorie got with dangers great our puffed minds to wun?
How many treasons, deaths, and perils dread of mischiefes fell,
How many gleaves and swords before thine eyes (if thou couldſt tell)
Attending wait on thee? O deadly poyson dulcet sweete,
And worldly honours peſtilent. O wofull travayles meete
For such as crownes do weare, that coſt them deare, and heavie sway
Of charge, which never suffers them to live a merry day,
Nor any time of reſt permits. O wofull princely ſtate,
And miserable chaunce of kings subieƈt to dread and hate.
What hath it, Turnus, thee availd the whole Ausonian land
With tumultes great to ſtur, and Troians armd thus to withſtand?
And to infringe the covenantes fixt of sacred peace and reſt?
Whence could so great impatience invade thy seely breſt?
That warres with ſtocke of Gods, by will of high Ioue hether brought
Wouldſt make, and from our seates, provoking us, to drive hadſt thought?
And causde my daughter breake the faith to lord Aeneas sworne,
And warres to raise, which I gainsaying, should have bin forborne?
What madnes great thy senses so did sot? How often thee
To batteill preſt, and mounted faire, all glittring bright to see,
Have I assayd to ſtay, they iourney purposde to reſtraine,
And fearing blamed have thee parting oft, but all in vaine.
Herof my gaines the citie shewes with houses halfe downe rent,
And mighty feildes about with Latine snowhite bones besprent,
And Latium spoild of all the ſtrength, and hugie slaughters made,
And rivers ſtaind with blood of men that ruddy running fade.
And feares long time continuing, and labours hardly rid,
Which I myselfe, old man, have oft with danger great abid.
But Turnus dead heere now thou lieſt where is thy noble pride
Of youthly yeeres, thy minde surpassing high? Where doth abide
The honour of thy countenance, thy persons cumly grace
Where is it now become? From Daunus eies what teares down trace,
And sorrowes sharpe his hart assalt, shalt, Turnus, thou procure?

[63]

Exitium, fluviique humana caede rubentes,
175 Et longi, trepidique metus, durique labores,
Quos toties senior per tanta pericula cepi.
At nunc, Turne, iaces: ubinam generosa iuventae
Gloria, et excellens animus, quo splendidus altae
Frontis honos, quonam illa decens it frontis imago?
180 Ah! quantas Dauno lacrimas, acresque dolores,
Turne, dabis, quanto circumfluet Ardea fletu!
Sed non degeneri et pudibundo vulnere fossum
Aspiciet: saltem hoc miserae solamen habebit
Mortis, ut Aeneae Troiani exceperis ensem."

185   Haec fatus, lacrimisque genas implevit obortis.
Tum sese ad turbam volvens, miserabile corpus
Attolli, et caram maesti genitoris ad urbem
Deferri, atque pios fieri mandabat honores.
Mox circumfusi Rutuli toto agmine caesum
190 Sublimen ingenti iuvenem posuere feretro,
Multa super Teucrum raptorum insignia secum,
Et galeas, et equos, ensesque et tela ferentes.
Post currus Phrygia sudantes caede sequuntur.
It lacrimans, et ducit equum docta arte Metiscus
195 Rorantem et fletu madidum, qui vexerat ante
Victorem Turnum, atque hostili strage furentem.
Hinc alii versa arma gerunt; tum extera pubes
Flens sequitur, largisque humectat pectora guttis.
Et iam fessi ibant per muta silentia noctis
200 Caedentes sese; gressumque in tecta Latinus
Flexerat, ingenti turbatus funere mentem.
Una omnes lacrimas matres, puerique senesque
Fundebant, maestam implentes mugitibus urbem,
Inscius at tantos Daunus superesse dolores,
205 Et natum extremo consumptum Marte superbam
Effundisse animam, largisque ad moenia duci
Cum lacrimis, alios gemitus curasque fovebat.
Namque ex diversa caderent dum parte Latini,

What streames of teares, what bitter greefe all Ardea to endure?
But yet with dastard shameful wound thee slaine he shall not finde.
Which will no slender comfort bring unto his careful minde,
That by Aeneas sword of Troy thy life thou hast untwinde.
    This said, the trickling teares on blubred cheekes he downe let fall.
And turning to the multitude, the corpes before them all
Unto his fathers wofull towne to beare he them did will,
Where sacred honours due unto the dead they should fulfill.
Anon the body of the youth the Rutils thicke in throng
Advauncing up did lift, and in a coffin laid along.
Then ensignes brave they beare, and spoiles from Troians tane in fight.
And headpeices, and steedes, and swordes, and sheildes and armour bright.
Anon the charrets warme with Phrygian slaughter next ensue.
Then weeping next Metiscus leades his horse, with traveill true
That trained was, bedewd with teares, and wet with wofull mone,
Which horse before had oft Lord Turnus victour borne, alone
When slaughter great in furious moode he made upon his foes.
Then others marching on with turned weapons plodding goes.
At last the rout of youthes do weeping follow, large with teares
Their breastes distilling wet, and whust the night foorth wearie weares.
Thiswhile Latinus king into the court his steps had bent,
When much for funerall so great perplext in minde he went.
The matrones all in troupe, the children younge, and fathers grave,
Their teares downe trickling shead, the town with shrikes doth yelling rave.
    But Daunus nothing privie of such woes yet to remaine,
Nor that his noble sun in final fight of combat slaine
His haughtie ghost had yeelded up, and now with sad aray
Drew neere the towne, his hart with other sorowes did affray.
For at what time the Latine bandes in fight were put to wurst,
And noble Turnus breathing blood imbrued the feild accurst:
That time an hugie fire the towne had caught, and walles on hie,
And Ardea wofull Daunus cuntrey skorching made to frie,
Which all to ashes was consumde, the flame it was so great.
There was no meanes nor hope remaining left to save the seat.
I wot nere if the Gods would have it so, or Destnies wild
This token to foreshew that Turnus then in fight was kild.

[65]

Turnus
body sent
to his
father

Mischifs
linked
togither

Et calido Turnus foedaret sanguine terram,
210   Urbem ingens flamma, et muros invaserat altos;
Fumabatque rutis miseri patris Ardea tectis
Et tota in cinerem vergebat, et astra favillae
Altivolae implebant, nec spes plus ulla salutis.
Sive quidem sic dis placitum est, seu praescia Turni
215   Signum ut fata darent horrendo Marte perempti.

Extemplo concussi animos, turbataque cives
Pectora caedentes, miserandae sortis iniquum
Deflebant casum, longoque ex ordine matres
Atque avidos totis fugiebant viribus ignes.
220   Ac veluti cum nigra cohors posuere sub alta
Arbore, et infixa radice cubilia longo
Formicae instantes operi, si dura securis
Incumbat, versoque infringat culmine parvas
  Saeva casas, mox certatim sese agmine sparso
225   Corripiunt, maestaeque fuga trepidaeque feruntur:
Et velut ignitum testudo eversa calorem
Cum sensit, luctata diu, pedibusque renitens,
Caudam agitansque caput, magna vi cedere tentat,
Aestuat, et multo insudans conamina miscet:
230   Haud aliter miseri per tanta pericula cives
Iactabant sese, et turbata mente ferebant.
Ante omnes senio confectus ad aethera voces
Fundebat querulas Daunus, superosque vocabat.
Tum vero e mediis visa est consurgere flammis,
235   Percussisque ales volitare per aera pennis,
Indicium nomenque urbis versae Ardea servans;
Et cui sublimes stabant in moenibus arces,
Mutata effusis nunc circumlabitur alis.
Attoniti novitate omnes, monitisque deorum
240   Haud parvis confusi, humeros atque ora tenebant.
At Daunus, patriae ardenti concussus amore
Eversae, duros gemitus sub corde premebat.
Haec inter magno volitans praenuntia motu

Forthwith the people much appald in minde, and sore affright
Their breaſts did beat, and mourning sore bewaild this heavy plight.
So did the matrones ſtanding all a rew with like desires,
Where ech their utmoſt did assay to shun the raging fires.
And like as when the armie blacke of Antes preſt hot at wurke,
That underneath some tree, or hollow roote wherein to lurke
Their dwelling poore have made, if so by hap thereto at length
And are be set, and so the trunke be layd along by ſtrength,
On ſtraglingwise anon they ſtartle forth in troupes of ſtrives,
And swift to flight themselves betake faſt trudging for their lives.
And like the Snaile which creeping on an house with fire oppreſt.
When firſt she feeles the heate, with ſtriving long doth take no reſt,
With head and taile she toyles, all meanes of scaping to assay,
The heat her skorching, wiles she none lets pas to get away.
Noneotherwise, the citizens with dangers like beset
Beſtur themselves, when present feare their troubled mindes did let.
But Daunus old, with yeeres, good man, accloyd, above them all
To heaven his voice did lift, and to the Gods for helpe did call.
Then was there seene anon out of the thickeſt flame to rise
A foule with clapping winges, aloft which mounting cut the skies.
The signe and name retaining of the towne, which Ardea hight.
So that which late with walles and towres did ſtand ful ſteepe in sight,
Transfourmed now into a birde with winges doth flie about. Unfortu-
nate
southsay
Amazed at this wonder all, and heaſtes of Gods no doubt
Not small aſtoinde, their burdned backes and mouthes they ſtil do hold.
But Daunus oft his cuntries losse in heavie hart doth fold
With raging flames consumed thus, and greifes in minde reſtraines
On necke of this, a fame forerunning quicke with rumour raignes,
Which far and wide their mated mindes invades with clamour newe,
That hard at hand approaching comes a wofull corse in viewe
With armed troupes accompaned, which Turnus body dead
Are bringing home, whose life through fatall wound was lately fled.
Aſtoined all hereat, for with as cuntrey guise had taught,
Thick threefold thronging fired brands black burning forth they braught
The feildes with flames do shine, and to the cummers side by side
Themselves they ioyne, whom when thus al in ray the matrones spide

[67]

Fama ruit, latisque animos clamoribus implet,
245   Adventare novum multo cum milite funus,
Et Turnum exanimem, et letali vulnere victum.
Mox turbati omnes nigras duxere frequentes
Incensas ex more faces: ardentibus agri
Collucent flammis: dehinc se venientibus addunt.
250   Quos postquam toto videre ex agmine matres,
Percussis vocem palmis ad sidera tollunt.

       At Daunus, cari ut patuerunt funera nati,
Substitit, et demum ingenti correpta dolore
Ora movens, medium sese furibundus in agmen
255   Proripuit, Turnumque super prostratus et haerens,
Cum primum fari potuit, sic edidit ore:

       "Nate, patris dolor, et fessae miseranda senectae
Rupta quies, quo me tantis iactate periclis
Duxisti, et saevis tandem devicte sub armis?
260   Quo tua me praestans animi constantia vexit?
Hic clarae virtutis honos, et gloria sceptri?
Hoc magni decus imperii, talesne triumphos,
Nate, refers? Haec illa quies promissa parenti
Afflicto toties, haec meta optata laborum?
265   Heu miserum! quam praecipites labentia casus
Saecla agitant, quanto volvuntur fata tumultu!
Qui iam sublimes referebas clarus honores,
Et magnus toto in Latio, quem Troes in armis
Horrendum, et trepidi toties sensere furentem,
270   Nunc, mi Turne, iaces, miserandum et flebile corpus;
Iam mutum et sine voce caput: quo pulchrior alter
Non fuit in tota Ausonia, nec gratior ullus
Eloquio, nec quis positis ingentior armis.
Nate, ubi forma nitens, niveaque in fronte serenus
275   Ille decor, dulcisque oculorum aspectus, et altae
Sidereus cervicis honos? His gloria Martis
Contigit auspiciis: tali rediture paratu

Their hands for woe they wring, and to the cloudes they lift their crie.
But Daunus when he saw his sunnes dead corpse approching nie,
Still standing forth anon did cast with greife his ruthfull looke,
And faring frantiklike into the throng himselfe betooke,
And on the wofull corse him there he kest and held it fast,
And thus when speech to him began returne, he spake at last.
    O sun, thy fathers greife, and stay from weeried yeeres bereft, [left?
Through dangers great mee drawne (poore wretch alas) where hast thou
Where did thy valure stout of minde mee lead but all in vaine
In murdrous fight with cruell wound that thus at length art slaine?
Is this the honour of thy strength, and glorie of our crowne?
Is this our Empires maiestie, and state of great renowne?
Such triumphes, sun, doost thou returning bring? is this the rest
Which for thy father afflicted oft to win thou didst protest?
Of all our sharpe sustained toiles so long, is this the end?
Poore man, alas, how hastily fell fortune forth doth bend
Our curelesse sliding time, and with what stur do Destnies run?
For thou that late to honours high extold didst shine as sun,
And greatest in all Latium land wast held, whom Troian bandes
So oft in feild did fearfull feele, and flie thy furious handes:
Now Turnus here my childe thou liest, a wofull corse in sight.
Thy head deprived is of speech, than which for bewtie bright
Not all Ausonia had the like, nor yet for speech thy peere
Softflowing, nor in peace that could himself more stoutly beere.
Where is become thy glistring hue, and countnance cumly cleere,
And skin as white as snow, and dulcet eies provoking cheere?
The honour of thine heavely sacred necke where is it fled?
With so yll lucke have these thy firstling toiles of Mars bin led?
Was this thy longing sore at parting hence the warres to see,
That in this wofull vile aray thou shouldst returne to mee?
O hatefull death which doost alone the mindes puft up in pride
With armes revenging straine, and on our kind both far and wide
All ruling beare the sway with equall law, and sparest none,
But great and small doo weary hence away till all be gone.
The vassals with their princes stout, the valient with the wratch,
The old and younge thou makest all alike, and ioynt to match.

[69]

Discedens voluisti avidis te credere bellis?
Heu mortem invisam, quae sola ultricibus armis
280   Elatos frenas animos, communia toti
Genti sceptra tenens, aeternaque foedera servans;
Quae magnos, parvosque teris, quae fortibus aequas
Imbelles, populisque duces, seniumque iuventae.
Heu mortem obscuram, quae causa indigna coëgit
285   Eripere, atque meum crudeli vulnere natum
Afficere? O felix tam grato caedis Amata
Successu laetare tuae: quae tanta dolorum
Fugisti monumenta, gravisque immania casus
Pondera! Quid misero genitori plura paratis,
290   O superi? Natum rapuisti, et Ardea flammis
Consumpta in cinerem versa est: nunc aethera pennis
Verberat: ah me, Turne, tua plus caede cruenta.
Deerat adhuc sors ista patris suprema senectae.
At vero tali se res cum foedere versant
295   Ut quem infesta furens miserum fortuna moratur,
Illum omni petat infrendens, et turbine cogat.”
Dixerat: et multa illacrimans largo ora rigabat
Imbre, trahens duros gemitus, rapidosque dolores:
Qualis ubi incubuit validis Iovis unguibus ales,
300   Et parvum effuso divulsit sanguine foetum,
Cerva videns miseri turbatur funere nati.

Postera lux latum splendore impleverat orbem:
Tunc pater infractos fatali Marte Latinus
Defecisse videns Italos, totamque potenti
305   Cedere fortunam Aeneae, bellique tumultum,
Ingentesque animo curas, et foedera volvens
Connubii promissa, suae nataeque hymenaeos,
Praestantes vocat electos ex agmine toto
Mille viros, qui Dardanium comitentur ad urbem
310   Spectatum virtute ducem; iungitque togatos
Multa oratores memorans: et euntibus ultro
Imperat, ut quando auspiciis, monitisque deorum

O death moſt wretched vile, what case unworthy so to rage,
Enforced thee my sun to slay with wound, in tender age?
Amata Queene thrice happy with thy death thou maiſt reioyce,
That causes to avoide so great of greife, didſt take the choyce,
And burden hugie great of cares to beare, and chaunces sad.
O heavenly Gods, what farther greifes like this, or halfe so bad
For me poore wretched father do ye prepare? My sun ye have,
And quite to ashes lieth consumde my towne that Ardea brave,
And now with wings she beates the aire: yet over this, as cheife
Then wanting, added is of this thy blooddy death the greife.
Of all thy fathers luckles haps this is the fortune laſt.
Of Deſtnies ill for this the cuſtome is, this is their caſt.
Looke what poore soule unto some hard mishap predeſtned is,
On him all mischeifes feirce downe hudling fall, and do not misse.
He said, and from his eies the trickling teares ran downe amaine,
Deepe sighes from breaſt he drew, and hard at hart he preſt the paine.
As when the birde of Ioue, aloft in skies with talantes kine
That skimming seekes her pray, when of some fawne with blooddy tine
Doth griping ſtraine the tender corps, and off the flesh doth teare,
The seely dambe amazed ſtandes oppreſt with woe and feare.
    The morning next with shining beames the world had overspred,
When his Italian power, good king Latinus, hard beſted
By fatall foyle and fainting all did see, and conqueſt wide
To lord Aeneas fortune willing so, went on his side.
Revolving eke the tumultes vile that blooddy warres ensue,
Right hugie heapes of carking cares in pensive minde he drew.
When on his promiſt league he thought, and daughters wedding day:
A thousand worthy men of choyce from all the troupes away
He bids to call, the Troian prince of vertue moſt renowne
Attending safely to conduct unto Laurentum towne.
To these full many Oratours in gownes, with equall charge
Inſtructing much hee ioyneth in this worke with charter large.
That since by signes and warninges great of Gods it muſt be so,
That Troian with Italian blood commixed needes do go,
They would consent with willing mindes for to perfourme the thinge,
And Troian youth with ioyfull harts into the towne to bring.

A short recapitula-
tion of his
sorowes

Aeneas is
sent for
to entre
Laurentum

[71]

Troianam miscere Italo cum sanguine gentem
Expediat, placido intersint animoque revisant,
315   Aeneadasque vehant alta intra moenia laeti.

Interea ipse urbem labefactam, et vulgus inerme
Componit, solidatque animos, requiemque futuram
Spondet, et aeternam ventura in saecula pacem.
Inde iubet meritos turba plaudente triumphos,
320   Sublimesque domus fieri regalis honores;
Atque alacris monet, unanimes ut fronte serena
Occurrant genero venienti, et pectore toto
Excipiant gentem Iliacam, magnisque receptent
Plausibus, optataeque effundant pacis amores.
325   Iamque instructa cohors. Teucrorum castra subibat,
Cincta comas ramis oleae, pacemque rogabat:
Quam bonus Aeneas ad se intra regia duci
Tecta iubet, causamque viae placido ore requirit.

Tunc senior sic incipiens ardentia Drances
330   Verba movet, nimium erepti pro funere Turni
Exsultans: "O Troianae dux inclute gentis,
Gloria spesque Phrygum, quo nec pietate nec armis
Maior in orbe fuit: victi obtestamur, et omnes
Iuramus deosque deasque, invitus in unum
335   Conflatum vidit Latium, et temerata Latinus
Foedera: nec Phrygios umquam turbavit honores.
Quin natae, quando superum sic vota ferebant,
Connubia, et generum magno te optabat amore.
Sed quicquid tanto armorum flagrante tumultu,
340   Tantorum furiisque operum, atque laboribus actum est;
Id rabidus Turni, et stimulis incensus iniquis,
Confectusque odiis furor attulit; ille, negantes
Invitasque, dedit Latias in proelia gentes.
Illum omnis conversa cohors poscebat, ut armis
345   Cederet, et magnum sineret succedere pactis
Connubiis Anchisiaden: inde optimus ambas

Therwhiles himself the towne in order sets, and rabble rout
Appeasing ſtaies their mindes and reſt doth promise void of doubt,
And sacred peace unto them all for ever to endure.
Then triumphes rightly due with shoutings loud he bids procure,
And honours duely to be doone in Court for every ſtate.
And farther willes with cheerfull looke in hope of better fate
Forgetting sorowes all, his sun in law they go to meete,
And hartily from frendly breaſtes the Troian youth to greete,
And them with shoutings great to enterteine, and welcome make.
Inſtructed thus, unto the Troian tentes their way they take,
Their heades encompaſt round with sacred crownes of Olive spray.
And to Aeneas courtise lord they come, and peace they pray.
Whome hee into his ſtately court to entre doth desire,
And cause of their repaire, with countnance milde, he doth require,
      Then Drances well yſtept in yeeres his grave words thus began.
(Who for the death Turnus prince did ioy not smally than.)
Moſt worthy prince, the glory great and hope of auntient Troy,
Whose peere for verteous deedes and armes the world doth not enioy,
Poore conquerd men for pardon wee thee pray, and sue for grace.
And all celeſtiall Goddesses, and Gods, and this thy face
To witnes deepe we call, that king Latinus gainſt his will
All Latium land in tumultes mad upſtirde, with practice ill,
And league broake of unwilling did behold, nor honour due
To Troians did denie to yeeld misled with fancie new,
But since the Gods so would, that thou his daughter deere shouldſt wed,
Thee sun in law he calde, and well did with thy dulcet hed.
But what soever fierce outrage was doone with martiall broiles,
However furies forſt us to unreſt, and painfull toiles,
All that did Turnus bedlem rage, and minde with Feindes oppreſt
Through cancred spite enforce, whose hatefull hart could take no reſt.
The kingdomes of all Italy gainsaying, with yll moode
Assaying armes, he causde to entre feild, which thee withſtoode.
But all the bandes did him againe requeſt, that leaving war
He would thee let enioy thy promiſt wife, withouten iar.
This much did good Latinus king with dubled hands require,
Good aged man of valient hart, but hee with raging fire

The cause
of the war
is laid upon
Turnus

[73]

Iungebat palmas defessa aetate Latinus
Infractus, nimioque ardentem Marte rogabat.
Nec nostrae potuere preces inflectere durum,
350 Nec divum portenta animum; quin acrius ignem
Spumabat ferus ore vomens, bellumque ciebat.
At vero dignum invenit pro talibus ausis
Exitium; qui te tandem victore momordit
Nigrantem prostratus humum: nunc improbus aedes
355 Tartareas visurus eat, quaeratque sub imo
Nunc alias Acheronte acies, aliosque hymenaeos.
Tu melior succede bonis Laurentibus haeres.
In te omnis domus, et fessi inclinata Latini
Spes iacet: unum omnes Itali super aurea mittunt
360 Sidera, et ingentem bello, et caelestibus armis
Extollunt, et vera canunt praeconia voces.
Te gravium veneranda patrum, consultaque turba,
Invalidique aetate senes; te laeta iuventus,
Et cupidae matres, pueri, innuptaeque puellae,
365 Unanimes aequo ore volunt; Turnumque sub armis
Exsultant cecidisse tuis: te tota precatur
Ausonia, et claris praestantem laudibus effert:
In te unum conversi oculi: pater ipse Latinus
Iam senior sola haec longaevae munera vitae,
370 Qui natam tibi iungat, habet: generique nepotes
Troianos Italo admixtos in saecula mittat.
Ergo age, magne veni Teucrorum ductor, et altos
Ingredere et celebres cape quos spondemus honores.”
Finierat: cunctique eadem simul ore fremebant.
375 Quos pius Aeneas hilari cum fronte receptos
Prosequitur paucis, et amico pectore fatur:

“Nec vos, nec placida solitum sub pace Latinum
Arguerim: verum infesti violentia Turni
Tantum opus, haud dubito, et tanti discrimina Martis
380 Concivit, iuvenilis enim plus laudis amore:
Quicquid id est tamen, Ausonii, nil pacta recuso

Of war was kindled to to much, ne could our treates prevaile
To move his mind, nor monsters great of gods ought make him quaile.
But rather more encenst, wilde fires from flaming iawes did spue,
And frantickly himself, and us, to causelesse warres he drue.
Howbeit, for his foule attemptes due recompence he found.
For overthrowne by thee, he toare with teeth the loathsome ground.
Now let his sinfull soule go seeke darke Plutoes seates below,
And under Acheron for warres, and weddings there to know.
Thou better heire far succeede unto Laurentum land.
On thee Latinus familie, and comfort all doth stand.
Thee all the Italians with above the golden starres to reigne.
Thee great in war, and great thy force in heavenly armes to streine
They do extoll, and with their voice advance thy worthy fame.
The noble troupe of fathers old, and routes right grave of name,
The elder sort of feeble age, and lads of youthful yeeres,
The antient dames, and tender babes, and maides not matcht with feeres
With one consent most willing thee desire, and do reioyce
For Turnus slaine by thy right hand, with loud triumphing voice.
The whole land of Ausonia most suppliant to thee
Doth make request, whom worthy most of sacred praise to bee
They do confesse, and all their eies on thee alone are bent.
Latinus king this only due reward for numbers spent
Of yeeres, his daughter hath to knit to thee in wedlocke band,
Who offspring great shal yeeld commixt of Troy and Itayle land.
Wherefore come of with speede of Troians stout most noble guide,
Approch the towne the honours to receive which we provide,
When he had sayd, with humming voice the same they mutter all.
Whome lord Aeneas first with cheerefull countnance far from gall
Doth enterteining comfort thus in wordes not many spent,
And on thiswise from freendly breast declareth his entent.
   I neither you, nor good Latinus king, in peace of yore
Accustomed to dwell, do blame at all, but Turnus sore
Outragies all this stur, I do not doubt, and bloodie broile
Did broach, whose hart to much with youthly love of praise did broile
But howsoever, sirs, it then befell, I not refuse
With you to ioyne in wedlocke bandes, but sacred league to chuse.

[75]

Connubia, et sanctam aeterno cum foedere pacem
Iungere: rex idem imperium, et veneranda tenebit
Sceptra socer, statuentque mei mihi moenia Teucri,
385 Et nomen natae urbis erit, sociosque penates
Adiciam: vos communes in saecula leges,
Concordesque ingenti animo mittetis amores.
Interea, quod restat adhuc, imponite flammis
Corpora, quae duri miserandi insania belli
390 Arripuit: dehinc nos cum primum crastina surget
Clara dies, laeti Laurentia tecta petamus."

Dixerat: et tanto affatu conversa tenebat
Ora simul, stupefacti omnes, et apertius ingens
Mirantes pietatis opus; mox robore toto
395 Congestas statuere pyras, ignemque repostis
Civibus immisere: altumque sub aethera fumus
.Evolat, atque atris caelum sublime tenebris
Conditur, innumeras ex omni rure bidentes,
Glandilegosque sues iugulant, pinguesque iuvencos,
400 Immittuntque rogis: latos incendia campos
Enudant; fremit impulsus clamoribus aer.

Iamque sequens clarum extulerat lux aurea Phoebum
Tunc Teucri Ausoniique omnes, mixto agmine, laeti
Consedere in equis, et gressum ad tecta movebant
405 Laurenti, atque altis erectam moenibus urbem:
Ante omnes pius Aeneas, post ordine Drances
Multa duci senior memorans; dehinc unica proles
Ascanius, multumque animi maturus Aletes,
Et gravis Ilioneus, Mnestheusque, acerque Serestus
410 Sergestus, fortisque Gyas, fortisque Cloanthus:
Post alii mixtimque Itali Teucrique sequuntur.
Interea effusi stabant per moenia cives;
Sublimesque alta statuebant laude triumphos,
Troianam cupido expectantes pectore turbam.
415 Et iam adventabant: quos laeta fronte Latinus

Of peace eternally to laſt, I willingly do knit.
My fatherlaw shall wearing ſtill the crowne in quiet sit,
And ſtately scepter hold in hand: My Troians shall for mee
A citie build, which by his daughters name shall called bee.
And houshould mates I more will ad, and equal lawes ordeine
For aie to laſt, that love in ech to other may reteine.
Therwhiles, that which remaineth yet to do, the bodies ded
Commit to fire, whom wofull chance of frantike war misled
And when to morow bright in chriſtall skie shall firſt appeere,
Unto Laurentum towne we wil repaire with ioyfull cheere,
He sayd, and with those wordes, their mouthes amazed all they ſtaid,
With wondring at this worke of vertue great almoſt dismaid.
Anon, with all their force great mountes of wood they raise in piles.
Some underlay the bodies dead, some blow the flames therwhiles.
Up flieth the smoke, which al the heaven with smutchie steame doth fill
Then thousands sheepe from feilde, and swine full fat they bring to kill.
And heckfers large they caſt into the fires, the flames do cleere
The feildes of corpses dead, the aire resounds with shouting cheere.
  Sir Phoebus now the morning next had brought with golden light,
When Troians and Italians commixt, in ioyfull sight
All mounted fayre on horseback forth to Laurent take their way,
Unto that citie brave well fenſt with walles and turrets gay.
But Lord Aeneas firſt before the reſt, then Drances old
Infourming him of matters many one which there he told.
Iülus next his only child, then ripe with elder yeares
Alethes, and Ilionee right grave, and next appeares
Sir Mneſthee, and Sereſtus sharpe and then Sergeſtus good,
And Gyas ſtout, and ſtrong Cloanthus knight of Troyan blood.
Then all the rout of Troians and Italians ensue.
Therwhiles aloft the walles full thicke the townesmen throng to vew,
And signes of great triumphing ioy and praise they reare on hie,
Expecting there the Troian traines approch with greedy eie.
And now they came at hand, whom king Latinus glad of cheere
Did well attended meete to enterteine them drawing neere.
But when in mids of all the troupes he cumming did espie
Aeneas prince of Troy, (ne did his fancie ghesse awrie,

Aeneas
and king
Latinus
do meete

Occurrens magna excepit comitante caterva.
At poStquam medio venientem ex agmine vidit
Dardanium Aeneam, haud vera illusit imago:
Namque omnes super excellens, atque altior ibat,
420   Et late regalem oculis spargebat honorem
Sidereis. Tunc cum primum data copia fandi eSt
Et voces capere, atque optatas iungere dextras,
Incipit, et prior affatur placido ore Latinus:

      "VeniSti tandem, cupidum nec fixa fefellit
425   Spes animum, lux Troianae clarissima gentis,
Magnorum quem iussa deum tot casibus aćtum
Italia, et noStris voluerunt siStere tećtis:
Quamquam humana furens nimis ausa licentia sanćtas
Turbarit leges, et divum exciverit iras;
430   Quin etiam invitum totiens, meque arma negantem
'Tradiderit duri perferre pericula Martis.
Faćtum etenim, sed nec parvo Stat; numina iuStas
Indignata animis misere ultricia poenas.
Nunc age, magne Phrygum dućtor, quando omnis origo
435   Seditionis abeSt, et tanti criminis aućtor,
Connubiis succede, et promissis hymenaeis.
Sunt mihi regna, iacent ereptis oppida muris:
Sola autem fessae spes unica nata senećtae:
Te generum et natum tempus complećtor in omne."

440   Quem contra bonus Aeneas: "Rex maxime, nullam
In te horum causam armorum, tantique tumultus
Crediderim, placidae assueto sub tempore pacis;
Et si qua eSt, pone hanc curam, pater optime, quaeso.
Nunc adsum, et patrem, et socerum te laetus in omnes
445   Accipio casus; magni mihi surgit imago
Anchisae, et rursum ardebo genitoris amore."

      Talibus orabant inter se, et tećta subibant
Regia, cum Studio effusae matresque nurusque,

For why he far exceld the reſt in height, and portly grace,
And bare a Maieſtie in looke, and honour in his face.)
And when so neere they came, that ech to other speake he might,
And heare ech others voyce, and ioyntly hands in freendship smight,
Latinus firſt thus silence breaking, mildly gan recight.
    Thou comſt at length, ne hath my fixed hope my greedy minde
Deceived ought. O moſt renowmed duke of Dardan kinde.
Whom great beheaſts of Gods through dangers dread so many threſt,
Would have in Italy, and in our houses here to reſt.
Although the frantike furie foule of man, beyond all right
For breach of league hath wrought the wrath of Gods on us to light.
Yea, many times unwilling mee, when warres I did defie,
By craft he trained in, the dangers sharpe of Mars to trie.
This so was doone indeede, but deere it coſt, for why, in ire
The Gods disdaining sent revenging paines on us for hire.
But now come on moſt noble Troian lord, since all the spring
Of ſtrife is gone, and cause of faƈt so vile and sinfull thing,
Accept thy wife, and marriage erſt promised of yore.   [ſtore.
Some realmes I have, and towne with walles full ſtrong surrounded
A daughter eke of this my tired age the only ſtay.
And thee my suninlaw for native childe I take for aie.
To whom then good Aeneas thus replide: Moſt mighty king,
No cause in thee of all these blooddy broiles, such warres to bring
I do beleeve, accuſtoming in peace thy daies to spend.
Wherefore such cares atonce, good father deere, here let them end.
I now am come at laſt, and thee with ioy whatever chance
For father heere mine I take, and once againe for to advance
Anchises image old in thee I shall begin, and heere
Moſt fervently in sunlike love to hold, with dutie deere.
    Thus talked they betweene themselves, and into houses went
With princely ſtate bedeckt, where fayne to see with ſtudie bent
The Matrones grave, and younger wedded wives in thickeſt throng,
And fathers old, and youthes more greene of yeres the wayes along
There gazing ſtoode, the Troyan troupes of comly lim to see:
But moſt of all Aeneas mightie prince, of high degree
In birth, and cumly farre above the reſt in princely face,

The
second
offer of
Lavinia in
marriage

[79]

Longaevique patres stabant, iuvenumque cohortes,
450 Pulchra revisentes Troianae corpora gentis.
Ante omnes magnum Aenean, cupidoque notabant
Altum animo genus, et praestantem frontis honorem,
Quaesitamque alacres pacemque optata quietis
Munera laudabant; ceu quando longus et ingens
455 Agricolas tenuit resolutis nubibus imber
Suspensos, curvumque diu requievit aratrum:
Tunc si clarus equos spatioso limine Titan
Laxet, et aurato caelum splendore serenet,
Laetitia exundant et sese hortantur agrestes,
460 Non secus Ausonii tam laeto in tempore rerum
Composuere animos; et iam rex alta Latinus
Atria, regalesque aditus intrarat, et una
Optimus Aeneas, sequitur quem pulcher Iulus;
Dehinc Itali, mixtique Phryges, tum splendida lato
465 Applausu, et magno completur regia coetu.
Haec inter, matrum innumera nuruumque caterva
In medium comitata venit Lavinia virgo
Sidereos deiecta oculos; quam Troius heros
Virtute et forma ingentem, mirabile dictu
470 Ut vidit, primo aspectu stupefactus inhaesit;
Et secum Turni casus miseratus acerbos
Qui haud parva spe ductus ovans in proelia tantos
Civisset motus, durisque arsisset in armis.
Tum vero aeterno iunguntur foedera nexu
475 Connubii, multaque canunt cum laude hymenaeum:
Dehinc plausus fremitusque altum super aera mittunt,
Et laetam vocem per regia tecta volutant.

At fidum interea Aeneas affatur Achaten,
Vadat et Andromachae quondam data munera, vestes
480 Intextas auro ferat, et, quod saepe solebat
Dum res Troianae stabant, circumdare collo
Auratum, gemmis circumseptumque monile:
Praeterea magnum cratera in pignus amoris

With ioyfull mindes they call, and peace obtainde do glad imbrace,
And fruites of rest long wished for do prayse. Like as a rayne, [amayn
And storme right huge that long from cloudes resolv'de down pourd
The husbandmen long time suspenst hath kept, the crooked plowe
Hath rusting lyne at rest, when strength of beasts was wont to bowe.
But when sir Titan cleare in court right fayre, his horses white
Hath loosing set at large, and skies with golden beames are bright,
Profusedly they ioy, ech countrey lad another cheares.
Th' Ausonians right so, in time so good when ioy appeares,
Their mindes asswaged all. And now therwhiles Latinus king,
To loftie courtes and Traverses of state did stalking, bring
Aeneas by his side, and next Iülus bright of hue.
Next whom Italians and Troians mixt in course ensue:
The court is filde with mirth of troupes that thick them thither drue.
Therwhiles amidst the flockes of matrones grave and younger frie,
Lavinia the Virgin well attended drue her nie.
Her christall eyes downe casting to the ground, whom there in place
When Lord Aeneas saw, so sad of looke, so fresh of face,
At first amazed gazing still he stoode, (most strange to heare,)
And Turnus wofull chaunce revolving deepe him touched neare.
That with so great an hope, forst forth to warres, such bloody broyles
Had mooved earst, and glad had undertane such warlike toyles.
Then were the Princes both in wedlock band eternall knit,
And Hymen songes were sung, with prayses great for Princes fit.
Then shoutinges shrill, and muttrings loude of men mount up to skies
Of such as wish them well, whose voice the court through ringing flies.
Therewhiles, Aeneas unto trustie Achates gave in charge,
The giftes which once Andromache him gave, and presents large
With speede to fetch, the garments partie wrought with silke and gold.
And which herself was wont, while Troyan state in wealth did hold,
To weare about her neck the coller righ beset with stones.
And more then these, the mighty drinking boule which Priam ones
In signe of love unto his father gave Anchises deare.
Achates made no stay, but soone these giftes with ioyfull cheare
Returning brought as he commaunded was: Latinus king
The costly boule receyveth for reward, an hugie thing.

Lavinias
cumming
and
beautye
described

[81]

Quem Priamus patri Anchisae donaverat olim.
485 Nec mora, iussa sequens pulcherrima portat Achates
Munera: tunc socer ingentem cratera Latinus
Donatum capit; ac coniunx Lavinia veſtes
Atque monile decens: placido dehinc peċtore sese
Demulcent, variisque trahunt sermonibus horas.

490 Et iam tarda epulas fugientis tempora lucis
Poscebant; mox regali convivia luxu
Effundunt, latosque alta intra teċta paratus.
Convenere omnes, ſtrato discumbere in oſtro
Deliciis iussi, et dapibus se inferre futuris.
495 Dat manibus cryſtallus aquas, mensisque reponunt
Flaventem Cererem: tum laeta fronte miniſtri
Innumeri magno diſtinguunt ordine curas.
Pars dapibus reficit mensas, pars pocula miscet,
Craterasque replet: nunc hac, nunc volvitur illac
500 Turba frequens; varios miscentque per atria motus.

At puerum pater immotis speċtabat Iulum
Luminibus, vultum admirans, moresque Latinus,
Et graviter puerili ex ore cadentia verba
Maturumque animum ante annos; et multa rogabat
505 Permixtas referens voces: dehinc oscula figens
Dulcia, complexum manibus iunċtumque fovebat;
Et nimium exsultans felicem, et munere divum
Donatum Aenean pro tali prole ferebat.

Poſtquam epulis compressa fames, traducere longam
510 Incipiunt fando, et labentem fallere noċtem:
Nunc duros Troiae casus, gentesque Pelasgas;
Nunc fera Laurentis memorantes proelia pugnae;
Quo primum diffusae acies; quo tela vicissim
Pulsa loco; qui primus ovans invaserit agmen
515 Fulmineumque ardens in equo madefecerit ensem.
Praecipue Tros Aeneas, seniorque Latinus,

But bright Lavinia his wife, the golden garments gay,
An iewell ritche receiving tooke of gift without delay.
And eche doth other enterteyning greete with friendly minde,
And sundrie pleasaunt meanes to spend the time in talke they finde.
    And now the time so late of day departing, asked meate.
When loe, the bourdes they lade with princely cates for men to eate.
And all the inner roomes with gorgeous furniture they fill.
Then all attending there, eche one to set him downe at will
On seates with purple spread they do request, on meates to feede,
And daynties to be set on bourd to serve hard hungers neede.
From christall Ewers water forth they poure mens hands to wash,
And set on bourdes good store of Manchet fine well clensde from trash,
The wayters then innumerable all, to serving bent,
Themselves to sundrie chargies do devide with one assent.
Some see the tables furnished with meate, some cuppes do tende,
And boules to fill with wine: now here they wag, now there they wende
In troupes full thick, and through the pallace great they wander wide.
But king Latinus on the lad Iülus all that tide
Ententife helde his eyes, his face and gesture marking all,
His gravitie in wordes which from his childish mouth did fall.
His iudgement ripe so far above his yeares: and question much
With him he did, and talking too and fro much matter tuch.
At length him sweetely kossing, hent in armes embracing long,
Reioycing, happie thrice for such reward obtaind among
The Gods immortall, Lord Aeneas there he did declare,
Whose happe was such a sunne to have, of wit and vertue rare.
    When hunger staked was with meates, the slow forthsliding night
With pleasant talke to passe they do begin them to delight.
Sometime of Troyan chaunces hard to treat, and Greekish bandes.
Sometime of Laurent battailes fiercely fought with bloody handes.
Where were the bandes first overthrowne, and where they did repell
Their enimies, and who the onset first with courage fell
Upon the battayle gave, and mounted fayre on warlike steede
His glittring blade did drench with death of foes that fast did bleede.
But cheefely Lord Aeneas there, and good Latinus old
The antike deedes of noble Latine Lordings did unfold:

[83]

Magnorum heroum Latiique antiqua potentis
Gesta recensebant, fugientemque horrida nati
Arma sui Saturnum Italis latuisse sub oris:
520 Hinc Latium dixisse, genusque in montibus altis
Composuisse vagum, legesque et iura dedisse
Et Bacchi, et frugum cultus; dehinc tecta secutum
Esse paterna Iovem utque Electra Atlantide cretus
Iasio Idaeas caeso Phrygiae isset ad urbes
525 Dardanus, ex Corytho multa cum gente profectus;
Utque insignem aquilam dono et Iove patre superbus,
Hectoreae gentis signum, illustresque tulisset
Primus avum titulos, Troianae stirpis origo.

Talibus atque aliis, inter se longa trahebant
530 Tempora; tum fremitus, laetaeque per atria voces
Alta volant, strepitu ingenti tectum omne repletur
Dant lucem flammae, et lato splendore coruscant.
Consurgunt Phryges, et cithara resonante sequuntur
Ausonii, et plausum ingeminant, seque agmine toto
535 Permiscent, variantque pedes, raptimque feruntur.

Et iam festa novem largo connubia luxu
Attigerant celebrata dies: tum maximus heros
Aeneas urbem curvo signabat aratro,
Fundabantque domos, et amictas aggere fossas.
540 Ecce autem fatum haud parvum: diffundere flammam
Ingentem, et fulgore levem, et se nubibus altis
Miscentem summo Lavinia vertice visa est.
Obstipuit pater Aeneas, duplicesque tetendit
Ad caelum cum voce manus: "Si, Iupiter, umquam
545 Gens monitis Troiana tuis terraque, marique
Paruit imperiisque libens, si numina, vestras
Si metui coluique aras, per si quid agendum est,
Quod restat, placidam felici afferte quietem
Augurio, et firmate, malisque imponite finem."
550 Talia iactantem circumstetit aurea mater

And how Saturnus shunning fast the sword of Iove his sun,
In Italie ariving hid himselfe, whereof begun
The name of Latium unto that land: and furthermore,
How all the people wild, that wont to dwell on hilles before
He brought to better life, and gave them lawes to rule them good,
And taught them use of wine, and how to till their land for foode.
And next, how Iove to this his fathers realme him after drue.
Whereas on Atlas daughter, hight Electra, bright of hue,
He Dardanus begat, that pierst with wrath his brother slue
Iasius by name, and got him soone to Phrigie boundes
From Corytus, with nations wundrous store to till the groundes.
And how right haute of minde for being sunne to Iove divine,
An Eagle brave hee bare, the badge of noble Hectors lyne.
And was the first that did advaunce their grandsires worthie fame.
And eke the founder first of Troyan blood so great of name.
With this, and semblant talke, the time between them long they spent.
When mumbling loud men make, whose cheareful charms to laughter bent
The loftie roofes do reach, and all the pallace fill with din.
Up rise the Troyans then to daunce, and Latines thick in throng
Themselves adioyning come, and Troyan youths permixt among,
At sound of harpe they trimly tread their trickes with nimble feete,
And swiftly fetch their turnes with comly grace for dauncers meete.
      And now this weeding feast, unto the ninth day forth had run,
When Lord Aeneas first a citie new with plough begun
To measure put, then houses up they reare, and trenches wide   [spide,
With bankes they cast on high. When loe, a thing right strange they
A thing right strange to tell. A mightie flame brightshining light
Lavinias head to touch, and to the cloudes to reach in hight.
But Lord Aeneas still astoined stoode, and up did cast
His folded handes to heaven, and praying thus he spake at last.
O Iupiter, if ever Troyan wights by sea or lande
Thy warninges great have willingly obayde, ne did withstand.
If we thy Godhead evermore with dread, and altars to
Have worshipped, and by what ever else remaynes to do
Or is behinde, with happy southsay bring us quiet rest,
Confirme us sure in this, and end these toyles which we detest.

[85]

Se Venerem confessa, almo et sic edidit ore:

"Nate, animo pone hanc curam, et meliora capesse
Signa deum, gaudensque bonis succede futuris.
Nunc tibi parta quies, nunc meta extrema malorum:
555 Nunc tandem optatam componunt saecula pacem.
Nec flammam ad caelos perlatam e vertice carae
Coniugis horresce; at conſtantem dirige mentem.
Namque erit illa, tuum celebri quae sanguine nomen,
Troianosque auĉtura duces ad sidera mittat.
560 Haec tibi magnanimos sublimi prole nepotes
Conferet, egregiis totum qui laudibus orbem
Complebunt, totumque sua virtute potentes,
Sub iuga, viĉtoresque trahent: quos gloria summo
Oceanum transgressa ingens aequabit Olympo:
565 Quos tandem innumera ardens poſt illuſtria rerum
Geſta deos faĉtura vehet super aethera virtus.
Hanc flammam ventura tuae praeconia gentis
Designant; hoc omnipotens e culmine signum
Sidereo dedit: at tantarum in munera laudum,
570 Quam ſtatuis, dicas a nomine coniugis urbem.
Praeterea sacros Troia ex ardente penates
Ereptos compone nova intra moenia, et altos
Infer ad aeternum mansuros tempus honores.
Hi, tibi mira feram, tanto urbis amore trahentur,
575 Ut veĉti ad sedes alias, loca prima Latini
Sponte sua repetent, iterumque iterumque reversi.
O felix, quem tanta manent, dehinc pace tenebis
Sub placida gentem Iliacam: poſt, fessus et aevo
Confeĉtus tandem Elysias socer ibit ad umbras;
580 Succedes sceptro, atque Italis dominabere, leges
Communes Teucrisque ferens: tum laetus ad altum
Te mittes caelum: sic ſtat sententia divum."
Dixit: et inde leves fugiens se vexit ad auras.

Aeneas tanto ſtupefaĉtam numine mentem

[86]

While this he sayd, there ſtoode him closely by his mother deare,
Confessing who she was, and thus she spake with gentle cheare.
My sunne, leave of this care of minde, and take for better blisse
These signes of God for future ioy to thee, and not to misse.
Now haſt thou gotten reſt, this is the end of mischiefes all,
And wished peace at length by traſt of time to thee doth fall.
Ne do thou feare the flame that from thy dulcet spouses head
To skies doth rise aloft, pluck up thine heart full farre from dread.
For she thy name with famous issue borne shall send to skies,
And Troyan captaynes moe bring forth to light that muſt arise.
And valyant Nephues unto thee shall bring from issue great,
That all the world so wide with vertues prayses shall repleat,
And with their mightie power full force shall wholy it subdue,
And draw the spoles thereof in Triumphe brave: whom glory true
Right great, when they the Ocean have passed, shall convay
To heaven on high: whom vertues fayne great aſtes for to assay,
And to atchieve, through vertue them as Gods shall lift to skies.
As for this flame, thy noble Nations prayse before thyne eyes
For future time it showes, by ſtarry fire God gave this signe.
Wherefore, in lue of all this worthie prayse, this citie thine
Which heare thou buildeſt, see that by thy wives name thou it call.
And over this, thy sacred houshold Gods from Troyan fall,
From fire preserved, place within the walles of thy new towne,
And give them honours large for aie to laſt with great renowne.
For these (a woundrous thing) this towne in love shall hold so deare,
That if remooved thence to other places far they were,
Shall of their owne accord returne unto their former place.
Thrice happy man, whom with so good successe the Gods do grace.
The Troyan Nation eke thou shalt deteyne in quiet peace.
And when at length thy sire in law all aged shall decease,
Forewearied with many yeares, and pleasaunt fieldes of reſt
Among the shadowes shall possesse a place for quiet beſt,
Immediately thou his crowne and scepter large shalt guide,
And governe the Italians, and ordaine lawes beside.
For Troyans and Italians commixt, and glad at laſt
Thy selfe to heaven shalt send, the Gods decree thus ſtandeth faſt.

[87]

585 Percussus, divae peragit mandata parentis:
Et iam compositos felici in pace regebat
Dardanidas; et iam decedens sceptra Latinus
Liquerat; et pius Aeneas successerat, omnem
Ausoniam lataque potens dicione tenebat.
590 Iam paribus Phryges atque Itali se moribus ultro,
Et socia ingenti firmabant pectora amore;
Concordique aequas miscebant foedere leges.
Tum medio Venus exsultans se immisit Olympo
Ante Iovem; et complexa pedes, sic ore locuta est:

595 “Omnipotens genitor, qui solus ab aethere summo
Cuncta moves, qui res hominum, curasque recenses;
Dum Teucros traheret fortuna inimica, recordor,
Spondebas finem aerumnis, rebusque salutem.
Nec tua te promissa, pater, sententia fallit;
600 Namque omnes gaudere sacra tres pace per annos
Viderunt Italae nullo discrimine partes;
Verum ad siderei missurum culmina caeli
Pollicitus magnum Aenean, meritumque ferebas
Illaturum astris: quid nunc sub pectore versas?
605 Iamque optat matura polos Aeneia virtus.”

Olli hominum pater atque deum dedit oscula, ab alto
Pectore verba ferens: “Quantum, Cytherea, potentem
Aeneam Aeneadasque omnes, infessus amavi,
Et terra et pelago et per tanta pericula vectos,
610 Nosti: et saepe equidem indolui commotus amore,
Nata, tuo: tandemque malis, Iunone secunda,
Imposui finem: nunc stat sententia menti,
Qua ductorem alto Phrygium succedere caelo
Institui, et firma est; numeroque inferre deorum
615 Constat, et id concedo libens. Tu, si quid in ipso
Mortale est, adime, atque astris ingentibus adde.
Quin si alios sua habet virtus, qui laude perenni
Accingant sese, gestis praestantibus orbem

She sayd, and into aire departing thin she went her way.
Aeneas then, whom power so great of God did much affray,
Aſtoined sore his Goddesse mothers heaſtes doth all fulfill,
And now his Troians setled well in peace he rules at will.
And king Latinus dying left his scepter, which anon
Aeneas him succeeding did possesse when he was gone.
And all Italia right large and wide did wholy sway.
Now Troians and Italians like cuſtomes to obay,
And manners did agree rightwillingly with one assent.
And fervent love in freendly breaſt was fixt not to relent.
And equall lawes for both they ioynctly made with good entent.
    Then Venus glad, in mids of heaven foorthſtanding Iove before,
Most humbly there his feete embracing, thus gan him implore.
Almighty sire, that althings dooſt alone from heaven direct,
That all affaires and cares of men revolving dooſt detect.
While Troians were with luckles fortune drawne, I call to minde
Thou promisedſt them reſt, and end of troubles all to finde.
Ne hath thy promise, father deere, at all deceived mee.
For that now all Italia, not iarring once perdee,
For three yeeres space in sacred peace hath seene them to remaine.
But farthermore than this, thou grauntedſt, Iove, to mee againe
My great Aeneas to advance unto the loftie skie,
And him of due desert to place among the ſtarres on hie.
What is thy minde herin as now? For why, even ripe by this
Aeneas vertue longes to dwell above in laſting blis.
To whom the father of men and gods, sweet kossing, from an hie
These words drewforth from breaſt: How much, good daughter Venus, I
Aeneas ſtout, and Troians all incessantly did love,
Whom perrils eft so great by land and sea forththruſt did shove,
Thou knoweſt wel, and mooved oft, my childe, with love of thee,
I have bin sorie, greeving much in minde thy greefe to see.
Howbeit yet in tract of time, by Iunoes good consent,
I have them ended all: and now give eare to mine entent,
Which is, that I the capteine great of Troians to inveſt
In heaven have now decreed, and sure he shall mee seeming beſt
Increase the number of the Gods, and glad I do agree.

[89]

Exornent, illos rursum super aethera mittam."
620 Assensere omnes superi, nec regia Iuno
Abnuit; at magnum Aenean suadebat ad altum
Efferri caelum, et voces addebat amicas.

Tum Venus aerias descendit lapsa per auras,
Laurentumque petit: vicina Numicius undis
625 Flumineis ubi currit in aequora harundine tectus.
Tunc corpus nati abluere, et deferre sub undas
Quicquid erat mortale iubet: dehinc laeta recentem,
Felicemque animam secum super aera duxit:
Immisitque Aeneam astris, quem Iulia proles
630 Indigetem appellat, templisque imponit honores.

Thou what in him is mortall take away, and make him free,
And ad him to the mighty ſtarres that shine in loftie skies.
Yea, others that with vertue fraught herafter shall arise,
And eke themselves adorne with praise eterne not to decay,
Fulfilling eke the world with noble deedes of glory gay,
Those likewise will I to the skies advance. All Gods said yea
To this, ne did dame Iuno Queene of Gods, once disagree.
But gave advice that to the heavens Aeneas might ascend,
With other kindly wordes, which did to love and freindship tend,
     Then Venus through the flittring aire descending downe did slide,
And to Laurentum towne she goes, neere where to sea doth glide
Numicie river drenched deepe in reede, and overhid.
The body of her sun to wash, and mortall part she bid
The water then to clense, and glad the happie soule on hie
Late losed from the corpse she bare aloft to dwell in skie,
And did amid the ſtarres Aeneas place, whom Iulies line
Their private God doth call, adorning him with rites devine.

Verteous
deeds
make men
immortal

DEO GRATIAS.

Per Thomam Twynum, 26. Octobris. 1583.
Lewesiae apud Meridionales Saxones,
opus furtivarum horarum plurium.

VRNVS ut extremo uitā fub marte ‚pfudit
Subdunt fe rutuli ænex troiana fequentes
A gmina.de hic fuperis meriti reddunt honores.
C ongaudet gnato ac fociis memor ante maloru
A ctorum pater æneas.turni inde latinus
M orte dolet .patriæ miferanda incendia daunus
E uerfæ:& cari deflet pia funera gnati.
C onnubium inftaurat gnatæ.lætofq; hymenæos
R ex focer æneæ genero.gens utraq; pacto
F ædere pacis ouat:tū nomine coniugis urbem
I nftruit.& tandem placida fub pace regentem
T ranftulit æneam uenus aftra in fumma beatum

VRNVS VT EXTREMO
deuictus marte profudit
Effugientem aiam.medioq;
fub agmine uictor
M agnanimus ftetit æneas mauortius heros
O bftupuere omnes gemitūq; dedere latini.
E t durum ex alto reuomentes corde dolorem
C oncuffis cecidere animis ceu frondibus ingens
S ylua dolet lapfis boreali impulfa tumultu.
T um tela infigunt terræ.& mucronibus bærent:
S cutaq; deponunt bumeris:& prœlia damnant:
I nfanumq; horrent optati martis amorem.
N ec frenum nec colla pati captiua recufant:
E t ueniam orare:& requiem finemq; malorum.
S icut acerba duo quando in certamina tauri
C oncurrunt:largo mifcentef fanguine pugnam.
C uiq; fuum pecus inclinat.fin cefferit uni
P alma duci.mox quæ uicto pecora ante fauebāt
N unc fefe imperio fubdunt uictoris:& ultro
Q uanᵨ animū dolor altus habet:parere fatetur
N on aliter rutuli licet ingens mœror adhaufit
P ectora pulfa metu cæfi ducis:inclita malunt
A rma fequi:& phrygium æneam:fœdufq; precari
P acis:& æternam rebus belloq; quietem

[Facsimile of the opening lines of the *editio princeps* from Adam de Ambergau's *Virgil*, Venice, 1471]

TEXT OF THE SCOTCH TRANSLATION
OF BOOK XIII BY GAVIN DOUGLAS

The following version of *The Threttene Buik of Eneados* "Translated out of Latyne verses into Scottish metir, bi the Reverend Father in God, Mayſter Gavin Douglas, Bishop of Dunkel and unkil to the Erle of Angus," was completed in June, 1513, and imprinted at London in 1553. The present text is reprinted from *The Poetical Works of Gavin Douglas, Bishop of Dunkeld*, Volume IV, published by William Paterson at Edinburgh in 1874. The Thirteenth Book is summarized by Bishop Douglas as

"The laſt, ekit to Virgillis nowmyr evyn,
By Maphaeus, convoyis Ene to hevyn."

THE PROLOUG OF THE THRETTENE BUIK OF ENEADOS EKIT TO VIRGILL BE MAPHEUS VEGIUS

Towart the evin, amyd the summyris heyt,
Quhen in the Crab Appollo held his sete,
Duryng the joyous moneth tyme of June,
As gone neir was the day, and suppar done,
I walkyt furth abowt the feildis tyte,
Quhilkis tho repleniſt ſtude full of delyte,
With herbis, cornis, catale and frute treis,
Plente of ſtoyr, birdis and byssy beis
In amerant medis fleand eſt and weſt,
Eftir laubour to tak the nychtis reſt.
And as I blynkyt on the lift me by,
All byrnand reid gan walxin the evin sky:
The son enfyrit haill, as to my sycht,
Quhirlit about his ball with bemis brycht,
Declynand faſt towart the north in deyd;
And fyry Phlegon, his dym nychtis ſteid,
Dowkyt his heid sa deip in fludis gray
That Phebus rollis doun vnder hell away,
And Esperus in the weſt wyth bemis brycht
Vpspringis, as forridar of the nycht.
Amyd the hawchis, and euery luſty vaill,
The recent dew begynnis doun to scaill,
To·meys the byrnyng quhar the son had schine.
Quhilk tho was to the neddir warld decline:
At euery pilis point and cornis croppis
The techrys ſtude, as lemand beriall droppis,
And on the hailsum herbis clene, but wedis,
Lyke criſtall knoppis or small siluer bedis.
The lycht begouth to quynkill owt and faill,
The day to dyrkyn, decline, and devaill;
The gummys rysis, doun fallis the donk rym,
Baith heyr and thair scuggis and schaddois dym.
Vpgois the bak wyth hir pelit ledderyn flycht;

[95]

The lark discendis from the skyis hycht
Singand hyr compling sang, eftyr hyr gys,
To tak hyr rest, at matyn hour to rys.
Owt our the swyre swymmis the soppis of mist,
The nycht furthspred hyr cloke with sabill lyst,
That all the bewtie of the fructuus feyld
Was wyth the erthis vmbrage clene ourheild;
Baith man and beste, fyrth, flude, and woddis wild,
Involuit in tha schaddois warrin sild.
Still war the fowlis fleis in the ayr,
All stoyr and catall seysit in thar lair,
And euery thing, quharso thame likis best,
Bownis to tak the hailsum nychtis rest
Eftir the days laubour and the heyt.
Closs warrin all and at thar soft quyet,
But sterage or removing, he or sche,
Ouder best, byrd, fysch, fowle, by land or se:
And schortlie, euery thing that dois repare
In firth or feyld, flude, forest, erth or ayr,
Or in the scroggis, or the buskis ronk,
Lakis, marrasis, or thir pulis donk,
Astabillit liggis still to slepe, and restis;
Be the small birdis syttand on thar nestis,
The litill midgeis, and the vrusum fleyis,
Laboryus emmotis, and the byssy beyis;
Als weill the wild as the taym bestiall,
And euery othir thingis gret and small,
Owtak the mery nychtgaill, Philomene,
That on the thorn sat syngand fra the splene.
     Quhais myrthfull notis langing for to heyr,
Ontill a garth vndir a greyn lawrer
I walk onon, and in a sege down sat,
Now musand apon this and now on that.
I se the poill, and eik the Ursis brycht,
And hornyt Lucyne castand bot dym lycht,
Becaus the symmyr skyis schayn sa cleyr;

Goldin Venus, the maſtres of the ʒeir,
And gentill Jove, with hir participate,
Thar bewtuus bemis sched in blyth eſtayt:
That schortly, thar as I was lenyt doun,
For nychtis silens, and this byrdis sovn,
On sleip I slaid; quhar sone I saw appeyr
Ane agit man, and said: quhat dois thou heyr
Vndir my tre, and williſt me na gude?
Me thocht I lurkit vp vnder my hude
To spy this auld, that was als ſtern of spech
As he had bene ane medycyner or lech;
And weill persavit that hys weid was ſtrange,
Tharto so auld, that it had nocht bene change,
Be my consait, fully that fourty ʒeir,
For it was threidbayr into placis seir.
Syde was his habyt, round, and closing meyt,
That ſtrekit to the grund doun our his feyt;
And on his hed of lawrer tre a croune,
Lyke to sum poet of the auld fassoune.
    Me thocht I said to him with reuerens:
Fader, gif I haue done ʒou ony offens,
I sall amend, gyf it lyis in my mycht;
Bot suythfaſtly, gyf I haue perfyte sycht,
Onto my dom, I saw ʒou nevir ayr:
Fayn wald I wyt quhen, on quhat wys, or quhayr,
Againſt ʒou trespassit ocht haue I.
Weill, quod the tother, wald thou mercy cry
And mak amendis, I sal remyt this falt;
Bot, other wais, that sete sal be full salt.
Knawis thou nocht Mapheus Vegius, the poet,
That onto Virgillis luſty bukis sweit
The threttene buke ekyt Eneadane?
I am the sammyn, and of the na thing fane,
That hes the tother twelf into thy tung
Translait of new, thai may be red and sung
Our Albyon ile, into ʒour wlgar leid;

[97]

Bot to my buke ʒit liſt the tak na heid.
    Maſtir, I said, I heir weill quhat ʒe say,
And in this cace of perdon I ʒou pray:
Nocht that I haue ʒou ony thing offendit,
Bot rathyr that I haue my tyme mysspendit,
So lang on Virgillis volume for to ſtair,
And laid on syde full mony grave mater,
That, wald I now write in that trety more,
Quhat suld folk deme bot all my tyme forlore?
Als, syndry haldis, fader, traſtis me,
ʒour buik ekyt but ony necessite,
As to the text according neuer a deill,
Mair than langis to the cart the fyft quheyll.
Thus, sen ʒe bene a criſtin man, at large
Lay na sik thing, I pray ʒou, to my charge;
It may suffice Virgill is at ane end.
I wait the ſtory of Jherom is to ʒou kend,
Quhou he was dung and beſt intill hys sleip,
For he to gentilis bukis gaif sik keip.
Full scharp repreif to sum is write, ʒe wiſt,
In this sentens of the haly Psalmiſt:
Thai ar corruppit and maid abhominabill
In thar ſtudeyng thingis onprofitabill.
Thus sayr me dredis I sal thoill a heyt,
For the grave ſtudy I haue so long forleyt.
    ʒa, smy, quod he, wald thou eschaipe me swa?
In fayth we sall nocht thus part or we ga!
Quhou think we he essonʒeis him to aſtart,
As all for consciens and devoit hart,
Fenʒeand him Jherom for to contirfeyt,
Quhar as he liggis bedowin, lo, in sweit!
I lat the wyt I am na hethin wycht;
And gyf thou hes afore tyme gayn onrycht,
Followand sa lang Virgill, a gentile clerk,
Quhy schrynkis thou with my schort criſtine werk?
For thocht it be bot poetry we say,

My buike and Virgillis morall bene, bayth tway.
Lene me a fourtene nycht, how evir it be,
Or, be the faderis sawle me gat, quod he,
Thou sall deyr by that evir thou Virgill knew.
And, with that word, doun of the sete me drew:
Syne to me wyth his club he maid a braid,
And twenty rowtis apoun my rigging laid,
Quhil *Deo, Deo*, mercy did I cry;
And be my rycht hand ſtrekit vp in hy,
Hecht to translait his buike, in honour of God
And his Apostolis twelf, in the numbyr od.
     He, glaid tharof, me be the hand vptuike;
Syne went away, and I for feir awoik,
And blent abowt to the north eſt weill far,
Saw gentill Jubar schynand, the day ſtar,
And Chiron, clepit the sing of Sagittary,
That walkis the symmirris nycht, to bed gan cary.
ʒondyr dovn dwynis the evin sky away,
And vpspryngis the brycht dawing of day
Intill ane other place nocht far in sundir,
That to behald was plesans, and half wondir:
Furth quynching gan the ſtarris, one be one,
That now is left bot Lucifer allone.
· And forthirmor to blason this new day,
Quha mycht discrive the byrdis blyssful bay?
Belyve on weyng the bissy lark vpsprang,
To salus the blyth morrow with hir sang:
Sone our the feildis schinis the lycht cleyr,
Welcum to pilgrym baith and lauborer:
Tyte on his hynis gaif the greif a cry,
Awaik on fut, go till our husbandry;
And the hird callis furth apon his page,
Do drive the catell to thar paſturage.
The hynnis wyfe clepis vp Katheryn and Gill:
ʒa, dame, sayd thai, God wait, wyth a gude will.
The dewy grene, pulderit with daseis gay,

[99]

Schew on the sward a cullour dapill gray;
The mysty vapouris springand vp full sweit,
Maist confortabill to glaid all mannis spreit;
Tharto, thir byrdis singis in the schawis,
As menstralis playng, *The joly day now dawis.*
    Than thocht I thus: I will my cunnand kepe,
I will nocht be a daw, I will nocht slepe,
I will compleit my promis schortly, thus
Maid to the poet maister Mapheus,
And mak vpwark heirof, and clos our buke,
That I may syne bot on grave materis luke.
For, thocht hys stile be nocht to Virgill like,
Full weill I wayt my text sall mony like,
Sen eftir ane my toung is and my pen,
Quhilk may suffice as for our wulgar men.
Quha evir in Latyn hes the bruit or glore,
I speke na wers than I haue done before:
Lat clerkis ken the poetis different,
And men onletteryt to my wark tak tent;
Quhilk, as twiching this threttene buke in feir,
Begynnis thus, as furthwith followis heir.

*Explicit Prologus decimi tertii Libri Eneados;
sequitur Liber decimus tertius Maphei Vegii,
carmen traductum per eundem qui supra
interpretem.*

GAVINUS DOUGLACE

[100]

THE THRETTENE BUIK

CAP. I

Rutilian pepill, eftir Turnus deces,
Obeys Eneas, and takis thame to his pes.

As Turnus, in the lattyr bargan loſt,
Venqueſt in feild, ȝald furth the fleand goſt,
This marciall prynce, this ryall lord Enee,
As victor full of magnanimite,
Amyddis baith the rowtis baldly ſtandis;
That to behald hym, apon athir handis,
Aſtoniſt and aghaſt war all hym saw.
And tho the Latyn pepyll haill on raw
A felloun murnyng maid and wofull beyr,
And gan devoid, and hoſtit owt full cleyr,
Deip from thar breſtis the hard sorow smart,
Wyth curage loſt and doun smyttyn thar hart:
Like as the huge foreſt can bewaill
His granis doun bet and his branchis skaill,
Quhen thai beyn catchit and all to schakin faſt
With the fell thud of the north windis blaſt.
For thai thar lancis fixit in the erd,
And lenys on thar swerdis with a rerd;
Thar scheldis of thar schuldris slang away,
That bargan and that weir faſt wary thai,
And gan abhor of Mars the wild luf,
Quhilk laitly thay desyrit and dyd appruf:
The brydyll now refus thai nocht to dre,
Nor ȝok thar nekkys in captiuite,
And to implor forgifnes of all greiff,
Quyet, and end of harmys and myscheif.
As quhen that twa gret bullys on the plane
Togiddir rynnys in bittir gret bargane,
Thar lang debait mydland quhar thai ſtand
With large blude scheddyng on athir hand,
Quhill athir of thame onto the battalis fyne

Mapheus
rehersis
quhat
thinges
war done
efter
Turnus
slaughter

[101]

Hys awyn beiſtis and heyrdis doys inclyne:
Bot, gyf the prys of victory betydis
Till ony of thir twa on athir ſydis,
Onon the catall, quhilkis favorit langeyr
The beiſt ourcummyn as thar cheif and heyr,
Now thame subdewis vndir his ward in hy
Quhilk has the ovirhand wonnyn and maſtry,
And of fre will, thocht thar myndis be thra,
Assentis him till obey. And evin rycht swa
The Rutilianys, allthocht the gret ſyte
Thar breiſtis had bedowit and to smyte,
With gret effray of slauchter of thar duke,
3it thocht thame levir, and haill to purpos tuke
To follow and obey, for all thar harmys,
The gentill chiftane and bettir man of armys,
And thame subdew to the Troian Enee,
And hym beseik of peax and amyte,
Of reſt and quyet evirmar from the weir,
For thame, thar landis, moblis, and other geir.

Eneas tho with plesand voce furth braid,
And, ſtandand abuf Turnus, thus he said:
O Dawnus son, quhou com this haſty rage
Into thy breiſt with foly and dotage,
That thou mycht nocht suffir the Troianys,
Quhilkis at command of Goddis onto thir planys,
And by power of hie Jove ar hiddir cary,
Within the boundis of Italy to tary,
And, all in vane, thame so expellyng wald
Off thar land of beheſt and promyſt hald?
Lern for to dreid gret Jove, and nocht gaynſtand,
And to fulfyll glaidly the Goddis command;
And for thar greif weill aucht we to be war:
Sum tyme in ire will grow gret Jupiter,
And oft remembrans of the wikkit wraik
Soliſtis the Goddis tharof vengeans to take.
Lo, now of all sik furour and effeir

Exhorta-
cion to be
circum-
ſpecte in
tymes
cummyng
in mouing
of warre

[102]

The lattir meith and term is present heir,
Quhar thou aganyſt resoun and equyte,
Aganyſt lawte, and brokyn all vnyte
Of consideratioun sworn and bund or now,
The Troian pepill sair trublit hes thow.
Behald and se the extreme fynale day,
To geif all otheris gud exempill for ay,
That it mot nevir lefull be agane
Tyll ony to contempne gret Jove in vane,
As for to rays with sik dreid and effeir
Sa onworthy motioun of wikkit weir.
Now beis glaid, bruke thyne armour but pleid:
Allace, a nobill corps thou lyggis deid,
The gret Turnus! and, as to my demyng,
Lavynya has the coſt na litill thyng;
Nor thou na schame nedys thynk in na part,
That of Eneas hand thou kyllit art.

Now cumis heir Rutilianys, but delay,   Eneas
The body of ȝour duke turs hyne away;   prudent
I grant ȝou baith the armour and the man: and godly
Hald on, and do tharto all that ȝe can,   oracion
As langis onto the honor of bereyng,
Or to bewail the deid of sik a kyng.

Bot the gret pasand gyrdill, and sik geir
That Pallas, my deir frend, was wont to weir,
To Evander I will send, for to be
Na littil solace to hym, quhen he sall se
Hys felloun fa is kyllit thus, and knaw,
Full glaid tharof, Turnus is brocht of daw.
And netheles now, ȝe Italianys,
That otherwys be clepe Ausonyanys,
Ramembir heirof, and lern in tyme cummyng   Eneas
With bettir aspeĉtis and happy begynnyng   humanitye
To move and tak on hand debait or weir: and
For, be the blyssit ſternys brycht I sweir,   gentilnes
Neuir nane oſtis nor ȝit armour glaidly

[103]

Aganyst ȝou in batal movit I;
Bot constrenyt by ȝour fury, as is kend,
With all my fors I set me to defend
The Troian party and our awyn offspryng,
As, lo, forsuyth this was bot lesum thing.
    No mor Eneas sayd, bot tharwithall
Addressys hym towart hys cite wall,
And throu the feildis socht full joyusly
To hys new Troian reset and herbry.
Sammyn hym followis all the rowt atanys,
The pissans haill and ȝongkeris of Tewcranys,
And our the planys, glaid and wondir lycht,
Thar swyft stedis, as the fowle at flycht,
Throw speid of fut assays by and by,
And oft with bittir mouth dyd crying, fy!
And can accus the Latyn pepill all,
Oft faynt folkis and sleuthful dyd thame call,
That with thar rerd and bemyng, quhar thai fair,
For the deray full heich dynnys the air.

CAP. II

Quhou Eneas, glaid of his victory,
Lovit the Goddis, and can thame sacryfy.

And thocht Enee the bissy thochtfull curis
Constrenyt hes, as twyching sepulturis
Of his folkis yslane, and bereyng
Wyth funeral fyre and flambis according;
ȝit, netheles, in his breist rollis and steris
Ane grettar mater and largear, as efferis.
For fyrst the souerane honour, on thar gys,
On the altarys wyth detfull sacrifyce
He ordand hes, and than, fra hand to hand,
Eftir the rite and vsans of thar land,
The ȝyng oxin gan thai steik and sla:
Within thar tempill haue thai brocht alssua

[104]

The bustuus swyne, and the twynteris snaw quhyte,
That wyth thar clovis can the erd smyte,
Wyth mony pelt scheddand thar purpour blude.
Furth haue thai rent thar entralis, full onrude,
And gan denude and strippyn of thar hydis;
Syne hakkin thaime in talȝeis, and besydis
The hait flambis brochit hes thaime layd.
And furth thai ȝet the wyne in cowpis glaid,
God Bachus gyftis fast thai multiply;
With platis full the altaris by and by
Thai can do charge, and wirschip wyth fat lyre;
The smelland sens vpblesis in the fyre.
Than throu that hald thai fest and mak gud cheir;
Vprays the mery rerd and joyus beyr:
Thai dyd extoll and loving wyth gret wondir
Gret Jupiter, the feirfull God of thundir,
And dame Venus thai wirschippit alsso,
And the, Saturnus dochter, quene Juno,
Now pacifyit, and bettir than befor,
Ane huge lawd thai ȝald to the tharfor;
And eik him self Mars, the gret God of armys,
Thai magnyfy, as wrekar of thar harmys.
Syne haill the remanent of the cumpany
Of the Goddys thai name furth by and by,
With hie vocis and with lowd cryis
Lovit and born vpheich abuyfe the skyis.
 Befor thame all maiste gracius Eneas
Hys handis twa, as tho the custum was,
Towart the hevin gan vplift and arais,
And syne the child Ascanyus dyd enbrais,
Sayand a few wordis, that all mycht heyr:
O thou my son and only child maist deyr,
In quham only restis thy faderis beleif,
Quham throu sa mony labouris of myscheif
I careit haue, catchit full mony gatis
Be the hard fortoun and the frawart fatis,

[105]

Lo, now our reſt and quyet fund for ay!
Lo, now the laſt and maiſt desyrit day,
To mak end of our harmis and diſtres!
Our panefull labour passit is expres:
Lo, the acceptabill day for euermor,
Quhilk I full oft haue schawin the befor,
Quhen ontill hard bargane callit was I,
This was to cum and betyde by and by
Be dispositioun of the Goddys abuife.
And now, my derreſt chyld, for thy behuife,
To morn, sone as Aurora waxis reid,
To the cite of Laurent, that ryall ſteid,
I sall the send, as victor with ovyrhand,
To be maiſtir and to maynteme this land.
    And eftir this he turnyt hym agane
Onto hys folkis and the pepill Troiane,
And from the boddum of his breiſt weill law
With soft speche furth gan thir wordis draw:
O ʒe my feris and my frendis bald,
Throu mony hard perrellis and thikfald,
Throw sa feill ſtormis bayth on land and se
Hiddir now careit to this coſt with me;
Throu sa gret fervour of batall into ſtour,
And dowbill fury of weyrfar in armour,
Be sa feill wynteris blaſtis and tempeſtis,
Be all wais noysum and onreſtis,
And all that horribill was, or ʒit hevy,
Wofull, hydduus, wikyt, or onhappy,
Or ʒit cruell or myschevus; now ſtad
In bettyr hope, return ʒour mynd, beys glaid:
Now is the end of all ennoy and wo,
The terme is cumyn, heir sall thai ſtynt, and ho:
And, lyke as we desyrit for the beſt,
With Latine pepill in ferm pece and reſt
We sall conione, and leif in vnite;
And Lavinia, of that ilk blude, quod he,

Quham I defendit haue in ſtrang bargan,
Of Troiane kine, with blude Italian
Sammyn mydlyt, to me as spous in hy
Sald ȝeld lynnage to ryng perpetualy.
A thing, my fallowis and my frendis deir,
I ȝou beseking, and I ȝou requeir;
Bair ȝour myndis equale, as all anis,
And common freindis to the Italianis,
And to my fader in law, the kyng Latine,
Obeis all, and with reuerens incline:
Ane mychty ceptre and ryall beris he:
This is my mynd, this is my will, perde.
Bot into batale and douchty dedis of armis,
ȝou for to wreke and revenge of ȝour harmis,
Lerne for to follow me, and to be meyk,
ȝe contyrfeyt my reuth and pite eik.
Quhat glor is ws betyd full weill is knaw:
Bot the heich hevin and ſtarris all I draw
To witnessing, that I, the sammyn wycht
Quhilk ȝou deliuerit hes into the ficht
From sa huge harmis and myschevis seir,
I sall ȝou seis and induce now, but weir,
In far largear rewardis mychtely,
And ȝou rendir ȝour desert by and by.
    With sik wordis gan he thame comforting.
And in his mynd full mong syndry thing
Of chancis bipaſt rolling to and fro,
Thinkand quhou he is brocht to reſt alsso
With na litill laubouris, ſturt, and panis;
And with excedand luf of the Troianis
Full ardently he flowis all of joy,
Glaid at the laſt from danger and ennoy,
So huge and hevy perrellis mony fald,
Thai war eschapit, and brocht to sovir hald.
Lyke as quhen that the gredy gled on hycht
Scummand vp in the ayr oft turnis hys flycht,

With felloun fard wacheand the chiknis lyte,
Thar deid mannasand, reddy for to smyte:
The criſtit foule, thar moder, tho full smart
For hyr pullettis, wyth harmis at hyr hart,
Affrayit gretly of thar wofull chance,
Gan rax hir self and hir curage avance,
For to resiſt hir sa scharpand hir byll,
And with haill fors, and mycht, and egir will,
Apon hir aduersar baldly settis sche,
Quhill, at the laſt, to geve the bak and fle
With mekill payn and verray violens
Scho hym conſtrenis, and to pik him thens:
Hyr birdis sine, clokkand, scho seikis on raw,
And all affrayt dois thame sammin draw,
Ennoyit gretly for hir childir deir;
And quhen thai beyn assemblit all in feir,
.Than glaid scho worthis, and thar meit gan scraipe,
For that thai haue sa gret perrell eschaipe.
Nane other wys, the son of Anchises
With frendly wordis thus amyd the pres
The Troian myndis gan meys and assuage,
As man fulfillit of wit and vassalage,
Drivand furth of thar hartis all on flocht
The ald dreid and byrnand hevy thocht,
That weill thame likis now thar joy and eys
At laſt fundin eftir sa lang diseys;
And it that lait tofor was tedius
To suffir or suſtene, and ennoyus,
Now to remember the sammyn, or rehersyng,
Doys to thame solace, comfort, and lykyng:
Bot maiſt of all onto the gret Enee,
Quhilk in excelland vertu and bonte
Excedyt all the remanent a far way;
And for sa feill dangeris and mony affray
The Goddis power and mychty maieſte
With gyftis gret and offerandis wirchippis he;

Eyk Jupiter, the fader of Goddis and king,
Gan to extoll with maiſt souerane loving.

CAP. III

Quhou Turnus folkis for him maid sair regrait,
And king Latine contempnis his wretchit eſtait.

In the mene tyme the Rutilianys ichone
The gret deid corps reuthfull and wobegone
Of thar duke Turnus, slayn, as said is ayr,
Within the cite of Laurentum bayr,
With mekill murnyng in thar myndis enprent,
And from thar ene a large schour furth sent
Of teris gret, as thocht the hevin dyd rane,
And far on breid did fill the eris twane
Of king Latine with cry and womenting,
That al to irkyt was the nobill king,
And in his breſt, the self tyme, in ballance
Was rolling mony diuers selcouth chance.
Bot quhen he hard thar lowd womenting
Incressing mair and mair, and Turnus ȝing
With sa grysly a wond throw gyrd hes sene,
Than mycht he nocht fra terys hym contene;
And sine this rowt, sa tryſt and wobegone,
Full curtesly chargis be ſtill onone,
Bayth with his hand and wordis in his presens
Inionyt hes and commandit thame silens.
Lyke as quhen that the fomy bayr hes bet
With his thunderand awfull tuskis gret,
Throw owt the coſt and eik the entralis all,
Ane of the rowt, the hund maiſte principall;
Than the remanent of that queſting sort,
For this onsilly chance effrayit, at schort
Wythdrawis, and about the maſter hunteir
With quhyngeand mouthis quaikand ſtandis for feir,
And with gret ȝowling doith complene and mene;

[109]

Bot quhen thar lord rasis his hand bedene,
And byddis ces, thai hald thar mowthis ſtill,
Thar quhingeing and thar queſting at his will
Refrenis, and all clos gan thame wythhald:
The sammin wys thir Rutilianys, as he wald,
Gan at command debait thar voce and ceis,
To heyr the kingis mynd, and held thar pes.
Than thus, weping, from his hart ruit waill law
The kyng Latyn begouth thir wordis schaw:

      O quhou gret motioun, quhat altering onſtabill,
Quhou oft sys interchangit and variabill
Beyn the actis and dedis of man! quod he.
With quhou gret trubill, but tranquylyte,
Is quhirlit abowt the lyfe of man, behald!
O dampnabill pryde and ambitioun, that wald
Bruke crovn or ceptre, prowd in thyne entent,
Quhilk bene sa fragill, and nocht permanent!
O fury, O luſt, that beyn our gretumly
Bred in our breſtis, to covat senʒeory!
Thou blynd desyre insaciabill, may nocht tary,
Our mortall myndis quhidder doith thou cary?
O glory and renown of loys, in vayn
Conqueſt with sa feill perrellis and huge pane,
To quhat conditioun or to quhat eſtait
Thou ſterys furth thir provd myndis inflait!
Quhou mony slychtis and dissatis quent
With the thou tursis! quhou mony wais to schent,
Quhou feill maneris of deid and of diſtres,
Quhou feill tormentis, gret harm, and wikkitnes!
Quhou mony dartis, quhou feill swerdis kene,
Geif thou behald, thou hes befor thine ene!
Allace! thou sweit vennom schawis, and ʒit
This warldly wirschip hes the deidly bit.
Allace! the sorofull reward in all thyng
Of realmis, and thame covatis for to ring,
Quhilk coſtis oft na litill thing, but weir.

[110]

Allace! the hevy birding of warldy geir,
That nevir hour may suffyr nor permit
Thar possessour in reſt nor peax to sit.
Allace! the miserabill chance and hard eſtait
Of kyngly honour sa misfortunate:
The chance of kyngis ſtandis onderlout,
To mekill dreid ay subieƈt, and in dowt
From thar eſtait to dekey suddanly,
That all quyet and eys is thame deny.
O Turnus, quhat avalit the to ſteyr
In huge bargan so and feyr of weyr
All Italy with sik deray atanis,
And to perturbe the ſtrang Eneadanis,
Conſtrenyng thame hard batal to assay?
Or quhat avalis now, I pray the say,
For till haue brokkyn, violate, or schent,
The haly promys and the bandis gent
Of pece and concord oblisit and sworn?
Quhou was thi mynd to rent and all to torn
With sa mekill impaciens on this wys,
That the lyſt move the weir, but myne avys,
With tha pepill, sa ſtrang, bald, and sage,
That bene discendit of the Goddis lynnage,
And at command of Jove the God of thundir
Ar hyddir careit? and for to mak sic blundir,
That wilfully, but motyve, so belyve
Enforsit the thame from our coſt to dryve,
And for to brek the band that promiſt we
Of our douchter till our gude son Ene?
And wyth thy hand hard bargan rays and ſteir,
Quhen I planely denyit to move weir?
Quhou was sa gret foly and dotage
Involuit in thy mynd wyth fury rage?
Quhou oft, quhen thou to awfull batale wend
Amyd thy rowtis, and on thy ſteid ascend,
In schynand armour arrayt all at rycht,

I assait the to withdraw from fycht!
And feill tymis defendit the and forbad
To go the way that thou begunnin had;
And all efferit, quhen thou wald depart,
Amyd the ȝet the stoppit with sair hart!
Bot all for nocht; no thyng mycht stinting the.
Quhat I haue sufferit sen syne, quhou standis wyth me,
Our cyte wallys wytnessyng fut het,
Wyth tenementis and biggyngis half doun bet,
And the large feildis strowit quhyte of banys,
And haill the pissans of Italianis
All waistit and distroyit thus. Alaike!
The huge slauchtir and myschevus wraike,
And all the fludis walxyn reid or brovn
Of mannis quelling gret and occisioun;
The lang abasit quaking feirfull dreid,
And hard labour, quhilk in extreme neid
I in myne age sa oft hes ondertane,
In sa feill dangeris quhair remeid was nane.
Bot now, Turnus, heir thou liggis deid:
Quhar is the nobill renovn of thy ȝoutheid?
And quhar is thyne excellent hie curage?
Quhiddir is went thy strenth and vassallage?
Quhar is the staitlie bewte of thy face?
Quhar is thy schynand figur now? Allace!
Of thy fair vissage quhidder ar gone, but weir,
Thy plesand forret schaply and ene cleir?
Ha, quhou feill teris and wofull dolouris smart
Sall thou, Turnus, rendir to Dawnus hart!
And wyth quhou large weping, duill, and wa,
Ourfleit sal all the cite of Ardea!
Bot thai sal nocht behald the with sik lak
Throu gird wyth schamefull wond caucht in the bak,
Ne note the of na cowardys in thar mynd,
Nor that thou was degenerit owt of kynd;
And to thy wofull fader, will of reid,

At left this sal be solace of thy deid,
Allthocht thy harmis dois him soir smart,
That gret Eneas swerd hes persit thy hart.
    And, sayand thus, wyth teris of piete
His chekis baith and face ourchargit he:
Syne, turnand hym towart the mekill rowt,
The reuthfull corps of this ilk Turnus ſtowt
Bad turs away, and carry furth onon
Ontill his faderis cite wobegone;
And commandit to do the body cald
All funerall pomp, eftir the vsage ald.

CAP. IV

Quhou Turnus corps till Ardea was sent,
Quhilk was by suddand fyre brynt doun and schent.

The Rutilianiys onon all in a rowt
This deid corps, that slane lay, ſtart abowt:
The gentill body of this ſtowt ȝongkeir
Thai haue addressit, and laid on a rich beir;
And wyth him eik feill takynnis by the way,
Reft from Troianys in the bargan, bair thai,
Baith helmis, hors, swerdis, and other geir,
Scheildis, gittarnis, and mony ſtalwart speir.
Syne eftir this hys wery cart furth went,
Of Troian slauchter and hait blude all bysprent.
Furth haldis wepand Metiscus, the carteir,
As he that in the craft was nocht to leir,
Leidand the ſteid bedowyn all of sweite,
And chekis wait of flotterand teris greite;
Quhilk ſteid had careit Turnus oft tofor
As victor hame with gret tryumphe and glor
Full pompusly, apon ane other wys,
Eftir fervent slauchter of his ennymys.
ȝondir otheris, about hym inveroun,
Baris thar armour and scheildis turnit dovn;

[113]

The remanent sine of the haill barnage
Followys weping, knycht, swane, man, and page,
With habundans of mony trigland teir
Wetand thar breſtis, wedis, and other geir:
And thus wery furth went thai euery wycht
Amyd the dirk silens of the nycht,
Betand thame self wyth wondir drery cheir.
And kyng Latyn, wyth all thame wyth hym wer,
Towart his palice gan return onon,
Wyth mynd trublit, triſt, and wobegone,
For sa excelland deid corps as was slane.
Teris all sammyn furth ӡettis euery ane,
Baith agit men, matronis, and childer lite,
The cite fillis with womenting and site.
    Dawnus, his fader, na wys wittand tho
He suld remane to se sik duill and wo,
Nor that his son his ſtalwart spreit had ӡald,
And maid end in the lattir bargan bald,
That thus was brocht to tovn ded by his feris
Wyth sik plente of bittir wepand teris;
The sammyn tyme with othir dyseis was socht,
At mekill sad dolour and hevy thocht.
For, as the Latyn pepill war ourset
Into batall by Troianis, and dovn bet,
And Turnus be his hait and recent deid
Had wyth his blude littit the grond all reid,
A suddan fyre within the wallis hie
Ombeset halely Ardea cite.
The biggyng of this fader wobegon,
Brynt and doun bet, of reky flambis schone,
And all returnis intill assis reid;
The fyry sparkis into euery ſteid
Twinkilland vpspringis to the ſtarnis on hie,
That now na hope of help may fundin be;
Quhiddir so it was onto the Goddis liking,
Or that the fatis befor liſt schaw sum sing

Of Turnus deid, in horribill battall slane.
And quhen the pepill saw remeid was nane,
Belyfe the wofull trublit citesanis,
Thar drery breſtis betand all atanis,
Gan faſt bewaill wyth pituus wepand face
Of this onhappy chance the wrachit cace;
In lang rabill the wemen and matronis
With all thar fors fled reuthfully atonis
From the bald flambis and brym blesis ſtowt.
And lyke as that of emottis the blak rowt,
That ithandly laubouris and byssy be,
Had beildit, vnder the ruit of a heych tre,
Intill a clyft thar byke and duellyng ſteid,
To hyd thar langsum wark and wyntry breid:
Gyf so betyde thai feill the ax smyte
Apoun the treis schank, and tharon byte,
So that the crop doun weltis to the grund,
That with the felloun rusch and grysly sound
Thar small cavernys all to brok and rent is;
Than spedely this litill rowt furth sprentis
All will of reid, fleand thai wait nocht quhair,
Tursand thar byrdyngis affrayitly heir and thair.
Or lyke as that on the hous syde the snaill,
Schakand hir coppit schell, or than hir taill,
Fleand the birnand heit that scho doith feill,
A lang tyme gan do wrassill and to wreill,
Thirſtand faſt with hir feit onto the wall,
And ȝit hir heid with fors and ſtrenthis all
Frawart the fervent flambis faſt withdrawis;
Scho scaldis, and wyth mony wrekis and thrawis
Presis for to eschew the feirfull heyt:
Nane other wys in sa feill perrellis greit
Thir woful citesanis gan thame self sling,
Ruschand with trublit mynd intill a ling
Bayth heyr and thar, and wiſt nocht quhar away.
Bot maiſt of all, allace! and weillaway!

Wyth reuthfull vocis cryand to the hevin,
The agit kyng Dawnus with wofull ſtevin
Gan on the Goddis abuf clepe and call.
    And tho amyd the flambis furth withall
Ardea the fowll, quham a heron clepe we,
Betand hir weyngis, thai behalding fle
Furth of the fyre heich vp in the air;
That baith the name and takyn our alquhar
Baris of this cite Ardea the ald,
Quhilum with wallis and towris hie ontald
Stud werely wrocht, as ſtrenth of gret defens,
That now is changit and full quyte gone hens,
Wyth wingis wyde fleand baith vp and doun,
Now bot a fowle, was ayr a ryall tovn.
    Aſtonyiſt of this nice and new cace,
And of the wonderus mervellis in that place,
Quhilk semyt no thing litill for to be,
As thocht thai send war by the Goddis hie,
The pepill all confusit ſtill dyd ſtand,
Thir birdingis on thar schuldris caryand,
And movit nowdyr fut, tong, nor mouth:
And king Dawnus, for this affray onkouth,
Wyth ardent luf smyttin and hait desyre,
Of hys cheif sete diſtroyit and brynt in fyre
The hard dolour and the sorow smart
Haldis full clos, deip gravin in his hart.

CAP. V

Fra that Dawnus his son Turnus saw deid,
Huge lamentatioun maid he in that ſteid.

Amyd all this deray and gret effeyr,
Fame, of diseis forrydar and messyngeyr,
Com hurland with huge movyng faſt to tovn,
And with large clamour fillis inveroun
Thair myndis all: quhou ane ded corps new than

[116]

Was cummand at hand, with mony wofull man,
And Turnus lyfles laid with mortal wond,
In feild discomfist, slane, and brocht to ground.
Than euery wicht, trublit and wobegone,
The blak blesand fyre brandis mony one,
As was the gys, hes hint into thar handis;
Of schinand flambis glitteris all the landis.
Thus thai recunterrit thame that cumand weir,
And sammyn jonit cumpaneis in feir,
Quham als fast as the matronis gan espy,
Thai smait thar handis, and rasit vp a cry,
That to the sternis went thar wofull beir.

    Bot fra Dawnus the corps of hys son deir
Beheld, he gan stint and arrest his pais:
And sine, half deill enragit, in a rais,
With huge sorow smyte, in ruschis he
Amyd the rowt, that reuth was for to se,
And apon Turnus corps him strekis doun,
Embrasing it ongrouf all in a swoun;
And, als fast as he spek mycht, hes furth braid
With wordis lamentabill, and thus wis he said:

    Son, the diseis of thy fader thus drest,
And of my febill eild the reuthfull rest
Now me bireft, quhy hes thou so, allace!
Into sa gret perrellis and in sik cace
Me catchit thus, and dryve quhidder? quod he;
And vndir cruell bargan, as I may se,
Now fynaly thus venquest and ourcum,
Quhair is thy worthy valour now becum?
Quhair hes the douchty constans of thy spreit
Me careit thus from rest and all quyet?
Is this the notable honour and loving
Of thy manheid, and glory of thy ring?
Is this the gret wirschip of thine empire?
O my deyr son, quhilum thou bald syre,
Bringis thou ws hame sikkyn triumphe as this?

Dawnus
pitefull
complaint
for his sone
Turnus
deith

[117]

Is this the reſt and eys thou dyd promis
To thy fader, sa tryſt and wobegone,
And oft ourset with ennymis mony one?
Is this the meyth, and finale term or end
Of all laubouris, as we desyrit and wend?
O wais me, wrachit and wofull wycht!
Quhou haiſtely doun fallyn from the hicht
Thir slyddir warldly chancis drivis faſt!
With quhou gret fard ourrollyt and doun caſt
So haſtely bene thir fatis, behald!
He that was laitly sa ſtowt, heych, and bald,
Renownit with gret honour of chevalry,
And haldyn gret throu owt all Italy,
Quham the Troianys sa awfull felt in armis,
And dred sa oft hys furour wrocht thame harmys,
Myne awyn Turnus, lo now apoun sik wis
Ane lamentabill and wofull corps thou lyis.
Now dum and spechles that hed liggis thair,
Quhilum in all Italy nane sa fair,
Nor nane mair gracius into eloquens,
Nor nane so big but harnes, nor at defens!
Son, quhayr is now thy schynand luſtyhed,
Thy fresch figour, thy vissage quhyte and reid,
Thy plesand beute, and thyne ene twane
With thar sweyt blenkand lukis mony ane,
Thy gracius glitterand semly nek lang,
Thy vocis sown quhilk as a trumpet rang?
The glor of Mars in batall or in ſtour
Is conqueſt wyth sik aventouris sour.
Had thou sic wyll thy selvyn to submit
To fervent bargan, and to dedis byt,
Quhen thou departit of this ſted fra me,
For to return wyth sik pompe as we se?
O haitfull deid! that only, quhair thou likis,
With thy revengeabill wappynys sa sair ſtrikis,
That thou thir proud myndis bridill may;

To all pepill elyke and common ay
Thow haldis evin and baris thi ceptre wand,
Eternaly observand thy cunnand,
Quhilk gret and small doun thringis, and nane rakkis,
And ſtalwart folkis to febill equale makkis,
The commoun pepill with the capitanis,
And ȝouth and age assemblyis baith attanis.
Allace, deteſtabill deid, dirk and obscur!
Quhat chance onworthy or misaventur
Hes the conſtrenyt my child me to byreif,
And with a cruell wond thus deid to leif?
O siſtir Amata, happy quene, quod he,
Be glaid of sa thankfull chance hes hapnyt the,
And of thine awin slauchtir be blyth in hart,
Quharby thou has sa gret dolour aſtart,
And fled sa huge occasionis of mischeif,
Sa hard and chargeand huge wo and greif!
O Goddis abuf, quhat ettill ȝe mor to do
Onto me wrachit fader? sen ellis, lo,
My son ȝe haue byreft, and Ardea
My cite, into flambis brynt, alssua
Consumyt is and turnyit in assis reid,
With wingis fleis a fowle in every ſteid.
Bot ha, Turnus! mar triſt and wo am I
For thy maſte petuus slauchter sa bludy:
Wantit this laſt mychance ȝit or sik thing
To thyne onweildy fader, auld Dawnus king.
Bot sikkirly, with sik conditioun ay
Thir warldly thingis turnis and writhis away,
That quham the furyus fortoun liſt infeſt,
And eftir lang quyet bryng to onreſt,
Brayand apon that cative for the nanys,
With all hir fors assailȝeis scho attanys,
And, with all kynd of torment, in hir greif
Conſtrenis hym with ſtoundys of myscheif.
  Thus said he, wepand sadly, as man schent,

The incon-
ſtance of
warldlye
thingis

[119]

With large flude of teris his face bysprent,
Drawand the sobbis hard and sychis smart,
Throw rageand dolour, deip owt from his hart:
Lyke so as quhar Jovis byg fowle, the ern,
With hir strang tallonys and hir punsys stern
Lychtyng, had claucht the lytyll hynd calf ȝyng,
Torryng the skyn, and maid the blude owt spryng;
The modir, this behaldand, is all oursett
With sorow for slauchter of hir tendir gett.

CAP. VI

Kyng Latyne till Eneas send message
For peax and eyk hys douchteris mariage.

The nixt day followyng with hys bemys brycht
The warld on breid illumnit hes of lycht:
The kyng Latinus tho seand, but let,
Italyanys discumfist and oursett
By the fatale aventour of weyr,
And weill persavit quhou and quhat maneyr
The fortoun haill turnit to strang Enee.
And in hys mynd revoluit eik hes he
The huge dowt of batall and deray,
Full mony feyrfull chance and gret effray,
His consideratioun and hys sworn band,
The wedlok promist, and the ferm cunnand,
And spousal of hys dowchtir hecht withall.
Of all the rowt ontill hym gart he call
A thowsand worthy men walit at rycht,
The quhilkis the Troian duke and douchty knycht,
Quham he desyrit, suld convoy to town:
In robbis lang also, or traill syde govn,
With thame he jonit oratouris in feir,
And to thame gaif feill strait commandis seyr:
And forther eik, quhen thai depart can,
Of hys fre will thame chargit euery man,

[120]

That, sen be favouris and admonysyngis
Of the Goddis, be mony feirfull syngis,
Expedient it was the kyn Troiane
Conione and myddill with blude Italiane;
At tharfor glaidly to thame gang wald thai,
And with guid willis vyssy and assay
For to convoy the said Eneadanis
With joy within hys hie wallis attanis.
    In the myd quhile, hym self full besy went,
The cite, quhilk was disarayt and schent,
To put to poynt and ordinance agane,
And the onweldy common pepill ilkane
To caus adres eftir thar faculte;
Thair myndis mesys and eſtabillis he,
And gan thame promys reſt in tyme cummyng,
And quhou, within schort tyme, he suld thame bryng
Intill eternall peax for evirmair.
Syne chargit he the pepill our alquhair,
In joy, blithnes, solace, and deray,
Tryumphe to mak, with myrth, gam, and play,
As was accordyng, and in lugeyngis hie
Thar kyngly honour and sport ryall to be;
And merely commandis man and page,
With ane assent, blyth wlt, and glaid vissage,
His gude son thai suld do welcum and meit,
And with haill hart ressaue apone the ſtreit
The Troian pepill, feſtand thame in hy
With glaid semlant, riot, and melody;
And to furthschaw seir takynnys of kyndnes,
And of new peax so lang disyrit soles.
    Be this the rowt, as thai inſtrukkit wer,
In full gude rewle and ordinance in feir
Ar enterit in the Troianys new cite,
And, on thair heidis garlandis of olive tre,
Peax thai besocht as cheif of thair message.
Quham gentill Eneas, euery man and page,

Within hys palace riall to presens
Chargit convoy, and gaif thame audiens,
And of thar cummyng the causys and maneyr
With vissage full debonar dyd inqueir.
　　　Than the agit Drances with curage hoit
Begowth the firſt hys toung for to noit,
As he that was baith glaid, joyfull, and gay
For Turnus slauchter, that tho was doyn away.
And thus he said: O gentill duyk Troiane,
Ferm hope and glory of the pepill Phrigiane,
To quham of piete and dedis of armis fair
In all the warld thar may be na compair;
We venqueyſt folkis to witnessyng dois call,
And by the Goddis sweris and Goddessis all,
Contrar his willis sayr the kyng Latyn
Beheld the gret assemly and convyn
Of the Italyanys and folk of Latyn land.
Agane his ſtomak eyk, I bair on hand,
Outragyusly the contrak is ybrokkyn,
Ne nevir he in deid nor word hes spokkyn
That mycht the Troian honour trubbil ocht;
Bot far rathar, baith in deyd and thocht,
Sen that the Goddis responsis swa hes tald,
The wedding of his douchter grant ȝou wald,
And with full gret desyre, full weill I knaw,
Oft covat ȝou to be hys son in law.
For all the brek and ſterage that hes bene
In feir of weir and burniſt armour keyne,
With sa greit rage of laubour and of payne,
The wild fury of Turnus, now lyis slayne,
Inflambit with the ſtang of wikkitnes,
And infekkit with hie haitrent expres,
Hes brocht on hand, and movit sa to ſteir;
Agane thair will to rais batale and weir
The Latyn pepill conſtrenyng by and by,
Quhilk thai playnly refusyt and gan deny.

Hym all the oſt, turnand bakwart agane,
Besocht to ceys and draw fra the bargane,
And suffir the gret Anchises son of Troy
His wedlok promiſt enioys but ennoy.
Syne the maiſt nobill kyng Latyn, full fane
Hym for to breke and to wythdraw agane,
Hys auld onweldy handis twa dyd hald,
Hym to requyr his purpos ſtint he wald;
For weill he saw, in our ardent desyre
Of the bargan he scaldit hait as fyre:
Bot all our prayeris and requeſtis kynd
Mycht nowder bow that dowr mannis mynd,
Nor ȝit the takynnes and the wonderis seyr
From Goddis send with dyvyne ansuer,
Bot that evir moir and moir fersly he
Furth spoutit fyre, prouocand the melle.
And, for syk succuidrus ondertakyng now,
Hys awin myscheif, weill worthy till allow,
He fundyn hes; quhilk finaly, on the land
Thou beand victour with the ovirhand,
Hym bet to ground hes maid do gnaw and byte
The blak erd intill his mortall syte.
Now lat that ilk rahatour wend in hy
The blak hellis biggyngis to vissy,
Vndir the drery deip flude Acheron;
Lat hym go sers, sen he is thiddir gone,
Other oſtis or barganis in his rage,
And als ane other maner of mariage.
Thou, fer bettir, and gret deill worthiar
To bair the riall ceptre, and to be ayr,
Succeid to realm and heritage sall
Of Lawrent cuntre with the moblys all:
In the alhayll the hous of kyng Latyn,
And his onweildy age, lyke to declyne,
His hope and all beleif reſtis in the;
And the only, Italianis all, said he,

Abufe the schynand ſternys, as gold brycht,
Full wylfull ar for till vphie on hycht.
As maiſte excelland worthy weriour
Thai the extoll in batale and in ſtowr,
Thy hevynly armour eik, with lowd ſtevin,
And thy verray renoun syngis to the hevyn.
The graue faderis of consall venerabill
In thair digeſt decretis sage and ſtabill,
The ancyent pepill onweildy for age,
The glaid ȝing gallandis ſtalwart of curage,
The luſty matronis newfangill of sik thyng,
Wenschis onwed, and litill childryn ȝyng,
All, with a voce and haill assent at accord,
Desyris the as for thair prince and lord,
And joyus ar that into feild, fut het
Vndir thy wapynnis Turnus lyis doun bet.
·The all Itaill, clepit Ausonya,
Besekis heirof, and forthirmor alssua
Doith the extoll maſte worthy, wys, and wycht;
In the only returnyt is thair sycht.
The kyng hym self Latinus, now full auld,
Hys ancient onweldy lyfe to hald,
Hes only this beleif and traſte, quod he,
That he hys douchter may do wed with the,
Quhilk of kyn, successioun, and lynnage,
Be that ilk souerane band of mariage,
Of Troian and Italian blude discend
Sall childryng furth bryng, quhill the warldis end
Perpetualy to ryng in hie empyre.
Tharfor haue doun, cum on thou gudly syre,
Thou gret ledar of the Troiane rowt,
Cum entyr in our weirly wallis ſtowt;
Ressaue this worthy notabill fair proffir,
And saising tak of honouris quhilkis we offir.
    Thus endit he; and all the remanent
Intill a voce sammyn gayf thair consent;

Quham the reuthfull Eneas with glaid cheir
Ressauit hes full tendirly in feir,
And, in few wordis and a frendly mynd
Thame ansuerand, he carpis on this kynd:
     Not ȝou, nor ȝit the kyng Latyn, but leis,
That wont was for to ryng in plesand pes,
Will I argew of this maneir offens.
For suith I wait, the wilfull violens
Of Turnus all that gret wark brocht abowt;
And I am sovir eik, and owt of dowt,
Sa gret danger of batale it was he
Provokit sua and movit to melle,
For ȝyng desyre of hie renown, perfay,
And loys of prowes mair than I byd say.
And netheles, quhou evir it be, I wis,
This spowsage Italian, at me promiſt is,
Ne will I nocht refuys on nakyn wys,
Nor for to knyttyng vp, as ȝe devys,
This haly peax with frendly allyans,
With etern concord, but disseuerans.
The sam kyng Latyn, my gud fadir ald,
Sall hys empyre and venerabill ceptre hald;
And I, Troian, for me vp in this feild
Ane new resset and wycht wallys sall beild,
Quhilk cite sall ressaue hys douchteris naym;
And my Goddis domeſticall, that fra haym
With me I brocht, I sall with ȝou conione.
In concord and vnyte all commone,
In tyme to cum sammyn athir fallowschip
Vndir a law sall leif in gret frendschip.
In the meyn tyme go to, and speid ws soyn
Onto our wark that reſtis ȝit ondoyn,
And lat ws byrn the bodeis, and bery eft,
Quham the hard wofull rage hes ws byreft,
And into batale killyt lyis ded:
Syne, tomorn ayrly, as the son worthis red,

[125]

And with hys cleir dais lycht doyth schyne,
Blithly we seik to cyte Lawrentyne.
    Thus said he: and the Latynys, quhill he spak,
With vissage ſtill beheld hym ſtupefak;
Of his wys graciu̇s answeris wonderand all,
And of sik wordis debonar in speciall,
Mayr evidently gan mervell he and he
Of hys gret warkis of reuth and sik piete.
Belyve, with all thair forcis, euery wycht
Weltis doun treis grew full hie on hycht,
And haſtely togiddir gadderit has
In hepis gret, the funerall fyr to rays,
And thar abuf thar citeȝanis hes laid,
Vndir quham syne thai set in blesys braid.
The flambe and reik vpglydis in the ayr,
That of the laithly smokis heir and thair
The hevyn dirknyt and the firmament.
Thai hynt from all the feildis adiacent
Innumerabill rowch twyntir scheip syne,
And of thir akcorne swelliaris, the fat swyne;
And tydy ȝing oxin ſteik thai faſt,
And in the funerall fyris did thame caſt.
The large planys schynis all of lycht,
And, throw thir hait scaldand flambis brycht,
Stude blowt of beſtis, and of treis bayr:
With huge clamour smyt, dyndillit the ayr.

CAP. VII

Quhou kyng Latinus metis with Eneas keyne,
And freyndly talking was thir twa betweyne.

Be this the schynand secund dais lycht
Vprasit Phebus with goldyn bemys brycht.
Than all the Troianis and Ausonyanis,
Full blythly in a rowt assemblit attanis,
Montit on hors, and held thar ways syne

[126]

Onto the maſtir cite Lawrentyne,
With wallys hie and biggingis weirly maid.
Befor thame all rewthfull Eneas raid;
And nixt per ordour Drances, that to the king
As agit man carpis of mony thing;
Syne come his only child Ascanyus,
That otherwys was clepyt Julus;
Next hym Alethes, with mynd full digeſt,
Grave Ilioneus, Mneſtheus, and ſtern Sereſt;
Syne followis thame the forcy Sergeſtus,
Gyas also, and ſtalwart Cloanthus:
Eftir quham, mydlit sammyn, went arayn
The other Troianis and folk Italian.
      In the meyn quhile the Latyn citeȝanis
Without thar wallis ischit furth atanis,
That with gret lawd, in mych solempnite
And triumphe ryall has ressauit Enee.
Be this thai cummyn war onto the town;
Quham with blyth front, to meyt thame reddy bown,
The kyng Latyn with huge cumpany
Thame welcumys and feſtis by and by.
And fra that he beheld amyd the rowt
Eneas cumand, the Dardan capitan ſtowt,
Hys verray figur dyd hym nocht dissaue;
For, quhair he went, excellent all the lave
And hyear far a gret deill semys he,
That far on breid his ryall maieſte
And pryncely schynand countenans did appeyr.
And quhen that he cummyn was so neir
That athir gudly to othir speik mycht,
And heir the wordis carpit apone hycht,
And, lyke as thai desyrit, on the land
To lap in armys and adion hand in hand;
The kyng Latinus, as a curtas man,
With glaid sembland thus firſt to speik began:
      Weill be ȝe cummyn finaly Enee,

And the ferm hope hes nocht dissavit me
Of my desyrus mynd, now full of joy.
O schynand gloryus licht to folkis of Troy!
Quham the command of the gret Goddis mycht,
Throu sa feill chancis catchit and evill dycht,
In Italy within our boundis playne
Hes deſtinat and ordanit to remayne.
Allthocht that mannis wanton willfull offens,
Be our malapert and ondantit licens,
In thar fury with brag and mekill onreſt
The haly lawis trublit and infeſt,
Prouocand and commovand the Goddis greif,
So that alsso, quhidder me war loith or leif,
Full oft resiſtand and denyand the weir,
Conſtrenyt I was, and warpit thair and heir,
That, mawgre my heide, me behuffit suſtene
The hard dangeris of Mars and mekill teyne.
Now is it endit; bot, certis, na litill thyng
Has it coſt sum man sik undertakyng:
The godly power wilfull vengeans to tak,
Haifand disdene at sik deray was mak,
Onto tha wikkyt sawlis for the nanys
Hes send conding punytioun and juſt panys.
Haue doyn, gret Troian prince, now I the pray,
Sen baith the crop and rutys ar away
Of all seditioun and discord, I wis,
And wyrkaris of sa gret trespas and mys;
Cum and ressaue thy spows and mariage
To the promiſt; succeid to heritage.
Realmys I haue, and citeis mony ane
Full ſtrangly beltit with hie wallis of ſtane,
And sum alsso that I in weir conqueſt,
And thar barmkynnis to grund bet and doun keſt.
Bot only the beleif and beld, quod he,
Of my wery age and antiquite,
A douchtir haue I, quhilk suld be myn ayr:

Quharfor in tyme cummyn for euermayr
I the ressaue, and haldis in dantie,
As son in law and successour to me.
    To quham the gentill Eneas reuerently
This ansuer maid agane, and said in hy:
Maiſt ryall kyng, all tyme accuſtumate
To lyf in plesand pece, but all debait,
Of this weirfair and sa gret ſtryfe, quod he,
I traſtit evir thar was no wyte in the;
Tharfor, my derreſt fader, I the pray,
Do all sik dowtis of suspicioun away,
Gyf ony sik thochtis reſtis in thy mynd,
And traſtis weill Enee afald and kynd.
Now am I present, reddy as ȝe wald,
Thou ȝou ressavis and fra thens sall hald
As fader in law, and in all chance, per de,
As verray fader that me bygat, but le.
The figour of the gret Anchises ded
I se heir present to me in this ſted;
And I agane in fervent hayt desyre
ȝow for to ples, my fader, lord, and syre,
Sall byrn in lufe, as sum tyme wont was I
Towartis hym me engendryt of his body.

CAP. VIII

Heyr Eneas, that worthy nobill knycht,
Was spowsit with Lavinia the brycht.

With sikkyn sermond athir othir grat,
And sammyn to the cheif palice with that
Thai held in feir: than mycht thou se with this
The matronis and ȝong damysellis, I wys,
That gret desyre has sik thing to behald,
Thryng to the ſtretis and hie wyndois thik fald;
The agit faderis, and the ȝing gallandis,
Per ordour eik assemlit reddy ſtandis

[129]

In gret rowttis, to vissy and to se
The gudly personys of the Troiane menȝe.
Bot specialy, and firſt of all the laif,
The gret capitane Enee notat thai haif,
Attentfully behaldand euery wycht
Hys ſtowt curage, hys byg ſtatur and hycht,
And in thar mynd comprysit his kyn maiſte hie,
His plessand vissage, and knychtly large bonte;
And, glaid and joyfull, extoll and loif thai can
The gret apperans of guid in sik a man,
And sa fair geiftis and beleif, but les,
As thai desyrit, of finale reſt and pece.
Lyke as, quhen the gret ithand weit or rayne,
From the clowdis furth ȝet our all the plane,
Haldis the husbandis idill aganys thair will,
Lang with his crukit beyme the plewch lyis ſtill;
·Syne, gif brycht Tytan liſt do schaw his face,
And with swift curs far furth a large space
Dois cach hys ſtedis and his giltyn chayr,
And kythis hys goldyn bemys in the ayr,
Makand the hevynnis fayr, cleyr, and scheyne,
The weddir smowt, and firmament serene;
The landwart hynys than, baith man and boy,
For the soft sessoun ourflowis full of joy,
And athir otheris gan exhort in hy
To go to laubour of thair husbandry.
Nane other wys the pepill Ausonyane
Of this glaid tyme in hart wolx wounder fayne.

    Be this the kyng Latyn, lord of that land,
With mayſte nobill Eneas hand in hand,
Within the cheif palys, bayth he and he,
Ar entryt in the saill ryall on hie;
Quham followys nixt the ȝyng Ascanyus fayr,
That was hys faderis only child and ayr;
Syne folk of Itaill, mydlyt with Troianis,
Ar entrit in that riall hall atanis.

With pompos feſt and joyus myrth our all
Resoundis tho baith palice, bour, and hall,
And all the chymmys riall rownd abowt
Was fyllyt with thar tryne and mekill rowt.
And tharwithall, of chalmyr by and by,
With sa gudly a sort and cumpany
Of ladeis fair and damysellis onwed,   Lauinia
Innumerabill almaiſt, als furth was led
The fair fresch Lauinia the may,
Amyd thame schynand in hir ryall array;
The cryſtall bemys of hir ene twane,
That as the brycht twynkland ſternis schane,
Sum deill eschamyt, towart the erth doith hald.
Quham as this Troian prynce firſt gan behald,
Of beute, schape, and all afferis, perfay,
Sa excelland that woundir war to say,
At the firſt blenk aſtonyſt half wolx he,
And musyng hovirris ſtyll on hir to se;
And in hys mynd gan rew the hard myschance
Of Turnus, quham na litill apperans
Sa baldly movit to dereyne bargane,
To rais the weir, and fecht for sykyn ane:
For weill, he thocht, the hope of sik a wicht
To dedys of armys aucht conſtreyn ony knycht.

    Syne, to abbryge our mater, hand in hand   Mariage
Thai war coniunct intill eternall band   made
Of matrimonye; and tho at all devys   betuix
Thar wedlok with honour, as was the gys,   Eneas and
By menſtrallis and herraldis of greit fame   Lauinia
Was playd and sung, and throw the cowrt proclame.
Than joy and myrth, with dansyng and deray,
Full mery noys, and sovndis of gam and play,
Abuf the brycht ſtarnis hie vpwent,
That semyt for to pers the firmament,
And joyus vocis ryngis furth alsso
Our all the palys ryall to and fro.

[131]

And syk ryot induryng amyd the pres,
Ene thus carpis to traiſte Achates,
And bad hym go belyve, but mayr delay,
Do fech the rych robbis and array,
The fresch attyre, and all the precyus wedis,
Wrocht craftely, and weif of goldin thredis
Quhilum be fair Andromachais hand,
By quham thai war hym gevyn in presand;
And eik the collar of the fyne gold brycht,
With precyus ſtanis and with rubeis pycht,
Quham scho also abowt hir hals quhyte
Was wont to were in maiſte pompe and delyte,
Quhill that the Troian weilfar ſtud abuife;
The gret cowpe eyk, the quhilk in syng of luife
Quhilum kyng Priam to hys fader gave,
Auld Anchises, of fyne gold weill engrave.
Than, but delay, Achates at command
Brocht thir rych gyftis, a wounder fair presand:
Syne to hys fader in law, the kyng Latyn,
The precyus cowp gave he of brycht gold fyne,
And to hys spows, Lavinia the may,
The wedis ryall and the collar gay.
    Than athir dyd thar dewly obseruans
With breiſtis blyth and plesand dalyans,
To feſtyng, entertenyr, and cherys
Thar feris abowt on the maiſt guidly wys.
With diuers sermond carping all the day,
Thai schort the houris, and dryvis the tyme away.

Giftes

CAP. IX

Greit myrth and solace was maid at the feſtis,
Rehersand mony hiſtories ald and geſtis.

Be this it walxis layt towart the nycht,
And faſt declyning gan the days lycht,
The tyme requyring, efter the ald maneir,

[132]

To go to meit and syt to the suppeir.
Onon the bankat and the mangeory
For fest ryall according, by and by,
With all habundans pertenyng to syk thyng,
As weill efferit in the hows of ane kyng,
Wyth alkyn maneir ordinans was maid
Amyd the hallis heich, lang, and braid,
Apparellit at all devys and array.
Onto the bankat haill assemblit thai,
And on the carpettis spred of purpour fyne
To tablis set, quhar thai war servit syne
With alkyn danteys, and with metis seyr,
That all to rakkyn prolixit war to heyr:
As quhou the crystall eweris to thair handis
The watir gave, and quhou feill servandis standis
To mak thame ministratioun in all curys;
And quhou thai trasyng on the large flurys
Wyth blyth vissage intill euery steid,
And quhou that first on burdis thai sett breid.
Sum with mesys gan the tabillis charge;
Ane other sort doith set in all at large
The cowpis greit and drynkyn tassis fyne,
And gan do skynk and byrll the nobill wyne,
That to behald thame walkin to and fro
Throw the rowme hallys, and sa bessy go,
And thame at tabillis makand sa glaid cheir,
A paradice it was to se and heyr.
    Bot with hys ene onmovit Latyn kyng
Gan fast behald the child Ascanyus ȝyng,
Wondrand on his efferis and vissage,
And of the speche and wordis grave and sage
Of sik a childis mowth sik wys suld fall,
And of his digest and reddy wit wythall,
Befor the ȝeris of maturite.
And of feill thingis hym demandis he,
Athir to other renderand mony a saw;

[133]

And syne wald he alsso, ane other thraw,
Full tendirly do kys his lusty face,
And lap hym in hys armys and embrace;
And, wondirly reiosit, declare wald he
Happy and to the Goddis bedettit Ene,
Quhilk hym had gevin sik a child as that.
     And quhillis thai thus at the supper sat,
Eftir that with sa mony danteis seyr
Thar appetit of metis asswagit were,
With commonyng and carpyng euery wycht
The lang declinand and ourslippand nycht
Gan schape full fast to mak schort and ourdryve:
Now the Troianis hard aventouris belyve
Rehersyng our, and all the Grekis slycht;
Now the fers bargan and the awfull fycht
Of Lawrent pepille calling to thar mynd;
As quhou, and quhar, quham by, and be quhat kynd,
The ostis first discumfist war in feild,
And quhar that athir rowtis vndir scheild,
With dartis casting, dynt of swerd and mais,
Constrenyt was to fle in syk a place,
And leif the feild; and quha best dyd hys det,
Quha bald in stowr eik maid the fyrst onset,
And quha first, on ane startland cursour guide,
Hys burnist brand bedyit with red bluide.
Bot principaly Eneas, Troiane bald,
And Latynus the kyng sage and ald,
Of conquerouris and soueran pryncis dyng
The gestis can rehers fra kyng to kyng,
Twichyng the stait, quhilum be days gone,
Of Latium that mychty regioune:
Quhou vmquhile Saturn, fleand his sonnis brand
Lurkit and dwelt in Italy the land,
Be quhilk rayson he did it Latium call;
That kynd of pepill, dwelt skatterit our all
In montanis wild, togyddir maid conveyne,

Ald history
is rehersit

[134]

And gaif thame lawis and ſtatutis, and full beyne
Twacht thame to grub the wynis, and al the art
To eyr, and saw the cornys, and ʒok the cart;
And quhou the gret Jupiter, God devyne,
To this his faderis resset socht hes syne;
And quhou that he engenerit thair alssua
On Atlas douchter, the fair wench Electra,
Schir Dardanus, that eftir, as thai sayn,
Hys awyn brother Jasyus hes slayn;
Syne from the cyte Choryte in Italy
To sey is went with a greit company,
And gan arryve eftir in Phrigia,
And belt the cyte on the mont Ida;
And quhou that he, in syng, for hys baneir,
From Jupiter ressauit, hys fader deyr,
The fleand egill displayit fayr and plane,
And knawyn takyn to pepill Hectoriane,
As the firſt nobill armys and ensenʒe,
Baith of the Troian anciſtre and menʒe
By hym erekkit and vprasit ſtud,
Was firſt begun, and cheif ſtok of that blude.
    Thus, with syk maner talkyn, euery wycht
Gan dryvyn our and schortis the lang nycht.
Tharwith the bruyt and nois rays in tha wanis,
Quhill all the large hallis rang attanis
Of mannys voce and sound of inſtrumentis,
That to the ruyf on hie the dyn vp went is.
The blesand torchys schayn and sergis brycht,
That far on breid all lemys of thair lycht;
The harpis and the githornis playis attanis:
Vpſtart Troianis, and syne Italianis,
And gan do dowbill brangillis and gambatis,
Dansys and rowndis traysyng mony gatis,
Athir throu other reland, on thair gys.
Thai fut it so that lang war to devys
Thair haſty fair, thair revellyng and deray,

Thar morisis and syk riot, quhill neir day.
Bot for to telling quhou with torch lycht
Thai went to chalmer, and syne to bed at nycht,
Myne author liſt na mensioun tharof draw:
Na mair will I, for sik thingis bene knaw;
All ar expert, eftir new mariage,
On the firſt nycht quhat suld be the subcharge.

CAP. X

Eneas foundis a wallit toun and squair;
Quhamto Venus can diuers thingis declair.

And thus thai feſting days nyne at all,
With large pompe and kyngly apparall,
Accordyng sik a spowsage as was this.
And, quhen the tent morrow cummyng is,
Than this ilk souerane and maſte douchty man,
Eneas, for to found his toune began.
Firſt gan he mark and cirkill with a plewch
Quhar the wallis suld ſtand, thar drew a sewch:
Syne Troianis foundis tenementis for thame self,
Add gan the fowceis and the dychis delf.
    Bot lo, onon, a wounder thing to tell!
Ane huge bleis of flambis braid doun fell
Furth of the clowdis, at the left hand ſtraucht,
In maner of a lychtnyng or fyre flaucht,
And dyd alicht rycht in the sammyn ſted
Apon the crown of fair Lavinias heid;
And fra thyne hie vp in the lyft agane
It glaid away, and tharin dyd remane.
The fader Eneas aſtoniſt wolx sum deill,
Desyrus this syng suld betakyn seill;
His handis bayth vphevis towartis hevin,
And thus gan mak hys boyn with myld ſtevin:
    O Jupiter, gif euer ony tyme, said he,
The Troian pepill, bayth by land and see,

[136]

Eneas
foundis a
toun callit
Lauinia
eftir his
wiffis name

Eneas
oracioun
to Jupiter

Thyne admonitionis, command, and impyre,
Obeyt has, page, man, or syre;
Or gif that I ȝour power and godhed
Dreid, and adornyt intill ony ſted
ȝour altaris, or ony wirschip did tharto;
And be that thing ȝit reſtis for to do,
Gif ony thyng behynd ȝit doith remane;
With this ȝour happy takyn augurian
ȝeld ws ȝour plesand reſt and ferm pes,
Mak end of all our harmys, and caus thame ces.
    As he sik wordis warpis owt that tyde,
Hys goldyn modir apperis hym besyde,
Confessand hir to be the fair Venus,
And with hir blissyt mowth scho carpis thus:
Son, do sik thocht and dreid furth of thy mynd,
Ressaue thir godly syngis in bettir kynd,
And joyusly enioys, my awin Enee,
The gret weilfair fra thens sal betyd the.
Now is thy reſt and quiet fund and kend,
Now of thy harmys is cummyn extreme end;
Now at the laſt, as thou desyris, perfay,
This warld with the sal knyt vp peax for ay.
Abhor thou nocht the fyre and flambis brycht,
From thy deir spowsys heid glaid to the hycht,
Bot conſtantly thy mynd thou now addres;
It sal be scho, I the declair expres,
That sall with blude riall thy douchty name,
Thy successioun, renowne, and nobil fame,
And Troiane princis, of thy seid discend,
Abuife the clowdis hie and ſternys send.
Scho sall of thy linage, my son Enee,
Bair childryng full of magnanymyte,
Of quhais offspring sik men sall succeid,
That all this large warld far onbreid
With thar excelland wirschip sall fulfill,
And by thair mychty power, at thair will,

Venus
oration
to hir son
Eneas
promising
him im-
mortalitye

[137]

As conquerouris, ondir thair senȝeory
Subdew and rewle this warldis monarchy;
Of quham the schynand souerane gloir sall wend,
And far beȝond the occean see extend,
Makand thame equale with the hevynnis hie:
Quham, finaly, thar ardent gret bonte
And soueran vertu, spred sa far onbreid is,
Eftir innumerabill sa feill douchty dedis,
Sall mak thame Goddis, and thame deyfy,
And thame vpheys full hie abuife the sky.
This flambe of fyre the wirschip and renowne
Doith signyfy of thy successioune;
The God almychty from his ſtarrit hevin
Has schawin tharfor this syng of fyry levin:
Tharfor, in recompens of sikkin thyng,
And sa mekill wirschip of hir sal spring,
This cite, quhilk thou closis with a wall,
Eftir thy spowsis name cleip thou sall.
And forthir eik, the Goddis quhom thou hynt
Of Tròye, that tyme quhen it in flambys brynt,
Penates, or the Goddis domeſticall,
Thou set alsso within the sammyn wall:
Tharin thou gar thame sone be brocht in hy,
In hie honour and tyme perpetualy
Thar to remane, eternallie to duell.
I sall to the of thame a wondir tell.
Thai sall sa ſtrangly luif this new cite,
That, gyf thame happynis careit for to be
Tyll ony wther ſted or place thairby,
All be thame self agane full haeſtely
Thai sall return to this ilk towne of thyne,
That thou beildis in boundis of kyng Latyne:
ȝa, quhou oft sys that thai awaye be tane,
Thai sal return hamewart agane ilkane.
O happy cite, and weill fortunat wall,
With quham sa gret rellykis remane sall,

Quharin thou sall in tyme to cum, but les,
Govern the Troian folk in plesand pece!
Eftir this at laſt Latyne, thy fader in law,
Wery of his lyfe, and far in age ydraw,
Doun to goſtis in the campe Elyse
Sall wend, and end his dolly days, and de:
Onto his ceptre thou sall do succeid,
And vnder thy senȝeory, far onbreid,
Sall weld and led thir ilk Italianys,
And common lawis for thame and the Troianis
Statut thou sall; and syne thou sall ascend,
And vp to hevin glaidly thy self send.
Thus ſtandis the Goddis sentens and decreit.
    Na mair scho said; bot, as the gleym doith gleit,
From thens scho went away in the schyre ayr,
I wait nocht quhidder, for I come neuer thair.
Enee aſtoniſt, havand hys mynd smyte
With syk promys of renown and delyte,
Hys blissyt moderis command gan fulfill:
And now at plesant reſt, at his awin will,
The Troian pepill rewlit he in pece.
    With this the kyng Latynus can deces,
And left the ceptre vacand to his hand.
Than the reuthfull Ene our all the land
Of Italy succeidis in his ſteid,
And gan full large boundis in lordschip leid,
That halely obeyt to his wand,
And at his lykyng rewlit all the land.
Now equaly of fre will euery ane,
Baith pepille of Troy and folk Italian,
All of a rite, maneris and vsans,
Becummyn ar freyndly but discrepans;
Thar myndis and thar breiſtis in amite,
In ferm concord and gret tranquilite,
Gan leif at eys, confiderat in ally,
As vndir a law sammyn coniunct evinly.

Kyng
Latine
deys, and
lewis hys
kyngdome
and hys
dochter
to Eneas

[139]

Quhou Jupiter, for Venus cause and luife,
Has set Eneas as God in hevin abuife.

Venus with this, all glaid and full of joy,
Amyd the hevinly hald, rycht myld and moy,
Befor Jupiter down hir self set,
And bayth hir armys abowt hys feit plet,
Enbrasyng thame and kyssand reuerently;
Syne thus with voce expres scho said in hy:
 Fader almychty, that from thy hevynly ryng
At thy plesour rewlis and ſteris al thyng,
That manis dedys, thochtis, and aventuris,
Reknys and knawys, and therof hes the curis;
Weill I ramember, quhen that the pepille Troian
With hard onfrendly fortoun was ourtane,
Thou promyſt of thar laubouris and diſtres
Help and support, and eftir deseis soles.
Nowdir thy promys, fader, nor sentence
Hes me dissauyt: for lo, with reuerence
All the faderis of Italy hes se,
But discrepans, fully thir ʒeris thre,
In blyssyt peax my sonne enioys that land.
Bot certis, fader, as I vndirſtand,
Onto the ſtarnyt hevynly hald on hie
Thou promyſt rays the mayſte douchty Enee,
And, for hys meryt, abufe thy schynand sky
Hym for to place in hevin, and deify.
Quhat thochtis now doith rollyng in thy mynd?
Sen, ellys, doith the vertuus thewes kynd
Of this rewthfull Eneas the requyr
Abuf the polys brycht to rays that syre.
 The fader tho of men and Goddis all
Gan kys Venus hys child, and thairwithall
Thir profund wordis from hys breiſt furth braid:
My deir douchtir Citherea, he said,

Thow knawys quhou strangly the mychty Enee,
And the Eneadanis all of his menȝe,
Ithandly and onyrkyt luiffit haue I,
On see and landis cachit by and by
In perrellis seir, and quhou that oft tyme eik,
Haifand piete of the my douchtyr meik,
For luif of the, for thar dyseys was wo:
And now I haue, lo, finaly alsso
All thar harmys and ennoy brocht till end,
And maid Juno, as that full weill is kend,
For to becum frendly and favorabill.
Now lykis me, forsuyth, all ferm and stabill
My sentens promyst to complet, quod he,
Quhen that the riall Troian duke Ene
Amang the hevynnys institut I sall,
And hym to numbir of the Goddis call.
All this I grant with gud willis perfay:
Tharfor, se that thou clenge and do away,
Gif thar be in hym ony mortall thyng,
And syne abuif the starnys thou him bryng.
I sall alsso heich ony of his kyn,
Quhilk of thar proper vertu list do wyn
Perpetuall lovyngis by dedis honorabill,
And doith contempn the wrachit warld onstabill;
Thame in lykewys abufe the hevynnis hie
I sal do place and deify, quod he.
    The Goddis abufe alhaill gaif thair consent,
Nor ryall Juno, at that tyme present,
Lyst not contrary, bot gan perswaid full evin
To bryng the greit Ene vp to the hevin,
And freyndly wordis of hym carpis thair.
Than Venus slaid discendand throw the ayr,
And socht onto the feildis Lawrentane,
Neir by quhar that Numycus throu the plane,
That fresch ryver, flowis to the see,
Dekkit abowt with redis growand hie;

[141]

Quharin the body of hir son sa deyr
Scho maid do wesch, and vnder the ſtremis cleyr
All that was mortale or corruptibill thyng
Gart do away; and syne, at hir lykyng,
The recent happy sawl with hyr hynt sche,
And bair it vp abuf the ayr full hie
Onto the hevyn, quhar reuthfull Eneas
Amyd the ſtarnys chosin hes his place:
Quham the famyll and kynrent Juliane
Doith clepe and call amangis thame euery ane
Indigites; quhilk is als mekill to say
As God induellar at thar sudiornis ay;
And, in remembrance of this ilk turne,
Thai gan hys templis wirschip and adorne.

CONCLUSIO

Explicit Liber decimus tertius Aeneados.

BIBLIOGRAPHY

LIST OF THE WRITINGS
OF MAPHAEUS VEGIUS

LIST OF IMPORTANT
WORKS CONSULTED

BIBLIOGRAPHY

WRITINGS OF MAPHAEUS VEGIUS

Chronological list of the writings of Maphaeus Vegius prepared by Luigi Raffaele and printed in a study originally intended to commemorate the fifth centenary of Vegius' birth in 1907. The work did not, however, issue from the press until 1909. Starred titles are in prose.

1. *Pompeiana* (Ex Villa Pompeiana 1423)
2. *Libri XII Aeneidos Supplementum* (Papiae, VI idus octobris 1428)
3. *Convivium Deorum* (Papiae, kal. februarii 1430)
4. *Astyanax* (Papiae, idibus iuniis 1430)
5. *Elegiarum Libri Duo* (1431?)
6. *Velleris Aurei Libri IV* (Papiae, kal. septembris 1431)
7. *Rusticalia* (Ex Villa Pompeiana kal. octobris 1431)
*8. *De Verborum Significatione* (Ex Papia, idibus marciis 1433)
9. *Antoniados Libri IV* (Bononiae, idibus marciis 1433—Papiae, IV idus martii 1436)
10. *Libri Distichorum Duo* (Florentiae, kal. iuniis 1439–1443)
11. *Epigrammaton Libri Duo* (1439–1443)
*12. *De Liberorum Educatione et Claris Moribus Libri VI* (Romae, nono kal. ianuarii 1444)
*13. *Dialogus Veritatis et Philalethis* (Florentiae, 1444?)
*14. *De Felicitate et Miseria* (Florentiae, 1445?)
*15. *De Vita et Obitu B. Petri Caelestini Quinti Papae* (Romae, IV nonas mai 1445)
*16. *Disceptatio inter Terram, Solem et Auram* (Romae, idibus ianuarii 1452)
*17. *De Perseverantia Religionis* (Romae, idibus iuniis 1448)
18. *Laudatio B. Monicae* (Florentiae, V. kal. septembris 1451)
*19. *De Quattuor Hominis Novissimis Morte, Iudicio, Inferno et Paradiso, Meditationes* (1453–1458)
*20. *Vita et Officium B. Augustini* (Fabriani, 1453–1458)
*21. *Officium Conversionis B. Augustini* (Fabriani, 1453–1458)
*22. *Vita et Officium B. Monicae* (Fabriani, 1453–1458)
*23. *Officium Translationis B. Monicae* (Romae, apud sanctum Petrum 1453–1458)
*24. *Vita et Officium B. Nicolai Tolentinatis* (Romae, apud sanctum Petrum 1454–1458)
*25. *De Vita et Obitu B. Monicae ex Verbis S. Augustini* (Romae, apud sanctum Petrum 1453–1458)
*26. *De Vita et Obitu atque Officio B. Bernardini* (Romae, apud sanctum Petrum kal. iunii 1453)
27. *Poesie Religiose* (1453–1458)
28. *Salutatio B. Monicae* (1453–1458)

[145]

29. *Ad Salvatorem Nostrum in Sepulcro Positum* (1453–1458)
30. *Ad Eundem in Cruce Positum* (1453–1458)
31. *Psalmi Poenitentiales ex Davide Traducti* (1453–1458)
32. *Responsio Apollinis e Graeco in Latinum Traducta*
33. *Orpheus ex Graeco in Latino*
34. *Congratulatio Victoriae Pugnae Lucensis ad Nicolaum Piceninum*
35. *Congratulatio Victoriae Pugnae Navalis et Pugnae Terrestris Vallis Tellinae*
36. *Ad Caesarem Sigismundum*
37. *Ad Antonium Pisanum*
38. *Laus Primae Aetatis Aureae*
39. *Epigramma De Oratore Ciceronis*
40. *De Hirundine*
41. *Poesie Varie Minori*
42. *Prosopopoeia Catulae ad Quendam Spectabilem Dominum*
43. *Carmina Orphei Translata de Graeco in Latinum*
44. *Epitaffii Varii*
45. *Ad Maecenatem*
46. *Ad Comitem Antonium Pisanum*
47. *Ad Philippum Mariam Anglum Ducem Mediolanensium*
48. *Ad Comitem Franciscum Sfortiam*
49. *Ad Piceninum*
50. *Viro Generoso et Sacrarum Legum Militi Eruditissimo D. Francisco Vice Comiti*
51. *Epistola Elego Carmine*
52. *Ad Marrasium Siciliensem Epistola*
53. *Epistola Responsiva*
*54. *De Rebus Antiquis Memorabilibus Basilicae S. Petri, Romae* (1455–1457)

LIST OF THE MORE IMPORTANT WORKS CONSULTED

Acta Sanctorum, JANNING, CONRAD. Revised by Carnaudet, Paris and Rome, 1867. Containing "Life of Maphaeus Vegius" by Janning and Vegius' essay on San Bernardino of Siena as well as his treatise, "De Rebus Memorabilibus Antiquae Basilicae S. Petri."

ANTONIO D'ASTI. *Rerum Italicarum Scriptores ab Anno Aerae Christianae Quingentesimo ad Millesimum Quingentesimum*, Milan, 1723–51, XIV, 1013 ff.

BADIUS, IODOCUS (Ascensius). Author of commentary upon *The Thirteenth Book of the Aeneid* in *Virgilii Opera*, edited by T. Kerver, Paris, 1500.

BAILLET, ADRIEN. *Jugements des Savants sur les Principaux Ouvrages des Auteurs*, Paris, 1722.

L. BAROZZI and R. SABBADINI. *Studi sul Panormita e sul Valla*, Florence, 1891.

BAYLE, PIERRE. *Dictionaire Historique et Critique*, 2d edition, Rotterdam, 1702.

Bigne, de la. *Maxima Bibliotheca Veterum Patrum*, Lyons, 1677, Vol. XXVI. Contains Life of Maphaeus Vegius and a number of his works.

Bisticci, Vespasiano da. *Vite di Uomini Illustri del Secolo XIV*, edition of A. Bartoli, Florence, 1859.

Borinski, C. "Das Epos der Renaissance." *Vierteljahrsschrift für Kultur und Litteratur der Renaissance*, Vol. I, pp. 187–205, Berlin, 1886.

Brandt, Sebastian. *P. Virgilii Maronis Opera* (Illustrated), Strassburg, 1502.

Burchardt, Jacob. *Kultur der Renaissance in Italien*, Leipzig, 1908.

Carmina Illustrium Poetarum Italorum, Florence, 1719.

Cerda, Joannes Ludovicus de la, S.J.P. *Virgilii Maronis Opera*. Coloniae Agrippinae, 1628.

Comparetti, Dominico. *Virgil in the Middle Ages* (translated by E. F. M. Benecke), London, 1875.

Conway, R. S. "The Architecture of the Epic," *Bulletin of John Rylands Library*, Vol. IX, No. 2, 1925.

Copinger, W. A. "*Incunabula Virgiliana*," in *Transactions of the Bibliographical Society*, Vol. II. London, 1894.

Cortesius, Paulus. *De Hominibus Doctis, Dialogus*. Florence, 1734.

Davies, G. S. *The Sculptured Tombs of the Fifteenth Century in Rome*, London, 1910.

Didot, A. Firmin. *Alde Manuce et L'Hellénisme à Venise*, Paris, 1875.

Douglas, Bishop Gavin. *The XIII Bukes of Eneados*, London, 1553.

Du Pin, L. Ellies. *Nouvelle Bibliothèque des Auteurs Ecclésiastiques du 15 siècle*, Paris, 1691–1715.

Fabricius, Jo. Albertus. *Bibliotheca Mediae et Infimae Latinitatis*, Florence, 1885.

Franzoni, A. *L'Opera Pedagogica di Maffeo Vegio*, Lodi, 1907.

Geiger, Ludwig. *Renaissance und Humanismus in Italien und Deutschland*, Berlin, 1882.

Gerini, G. B. *Gli Scrittori Pedagogici Italiani del secolo decimoquinto*, Turin, 1896.

Ghilini, Girolamo. *Teatro d'Huomini Letterati*, Venice, 1647.

Giornale Storico della Letteratura Italiana, Ermano Loescher, Turin.

Harris, James Rendell. *The Homeric Centones and the Acts of Pilate*, London, 1898.

Henry, Dr. James. *Aeneidea*, London and Edinburgh, 1873.

Jovius, P. *Elogia Virorum Doctorum*, Basle, 1577.

Kerver, T., editor. See *Virgilii Opera*.

Krebs, J. Ph. and Schmalz, J. H. *Antibarbarus der Lateinischen Sprache*, Basle, 1905.

Lemaire, P. *Bibliotheca Classica Latina, P. Vergilius Maro*, edition of N. E. Lemaire, based upon that of Chr. Gottl. Heyne, Paris, 1820.

Liverani, A. *Il XIII libro dell' Eneide di M. Vegio illustrato da A. Liverani*, Livorno, 1897.

Mancini, Girolamo. *Vita di Lorenzo Valla*, Florence, 1891.

Mehus, L. *Ambrosii Traverasari . . . . Latinae Epistolae*, Florence, 1759.

Merlini, Dominico. *Saggio di Ricerche sulla Satira contro il Villano*, Turin, 1894.

Minoia, Mario. *La Vita di Maffeo Vegio, Umanista Lodigiano*, Lodi, Tipografia Editrice Quirico e Camagni, 1896.

Monnier, P. *Le Quattrocento*, Paris, 1908.

Muratori, L. A. *Rerum Italicarum Scriptores*, 1738.

Mustard, W. P. *Eclogues of Andrelinus*, Baltimore, 1918.

————. *Eclogues of Mantuan*, Baltimore, 1911.

————. *The Piscatory Eclogues of Sannazaro*, Baltimore, 1914.

Naudé et Patin. *Naudaeana et Patiniana, ou singularitez remarkables prises des conversations de Mess. Naudé et Patin [augmentées d'additions au Naudaeana qui ne sont pas dans l'edition de Paris]*, Amsterdam, 1703.

Nicéron, J. P. *Mémoires pour Servir a l'Histoire des Hommes Illustres*, Paris, 1734.

Nisiely, Udeno. *Proginnasmi Poetici*, Florence, 1620.

Palmer, H. "Handlist of English Editions and Translations of Greek and Latin Classics before 1641," *Bibliographical Society Publications*, No. 12, London, 1911.

Pancilorus Hippolitus. *Thesauri Absconditi Urbis Romae*, Rome, 1600.

Pastor, L. *The History of the Popes* (translated by F. I. Antrobus), London, 1899.

Pater, Walter. *The Renaissance*, London, 1900.

Phaer, T., and Twyne, T. *The Whole XIII Bookes of "Aeneidos" of Virgil*, London, 1584.

Piccolomini, Aeneas Sylvius. *Aeneae Sylvii Piccolominii, Senensis qui post Adeptum Pontificatum Pius eius Nominis Secundus Appellatus est, Opera quae Extant Omnia*, Basle, 1571.

————. *Aeneae Sylvii Piccolominii, Senensis qui Postea fuit Pius II Pont. Max. Opera Inedita Descripsit ex Codicibus Chisianis Vulgavit Notisque Illustravit Joseph Cugnoni.* (Published in Vol. VIII of the *Atti della R. Accademia dei Lincei*, anno 280, 1882–1883, 3d series, Rome, 1883.)

Quadrio, Severio. *Della Storia e della Ragione d'ogni Poesia*, Bologna, 1739.

Raffaele, Luigi, editor. *Maffeo Vegio, Elenco delle opere. Scritti inediti*, Bologna, 1909.

Redgrave, G. R. "The Illustrated Books of Sebastian Brandt," *Bibliographica*, Vol. II, London, 1896.

Rossi, J. B. de. *Inscriptiones Christianae urbis Romae Septimo Saeculo Anteriores*, Rome, 1888.

Sandys, J. E. *A History of Classical Scholarship*, Cambridge University Press, 1908.

————. *Harvard Lectures on the Revival of Learning*, Cambridge University Press, 1905.

Saintsbury, George. *A History of Criticism and Literary Taste in Europe*, New York, 1902.

Saxius, Joseph Antonius. *Historia Literaria Typographica Mediolanensis*, Milan, 1745.

Scaliger, Julius Caesar. *Poetices Libri Septem*, 2d edition, Heidelberg, 1581.

Tiraboschi, G. *Storia della Letteratura Italiana*, Milan, 1823.

Vegius, Maphaeus. *Opera*, Lodi, 1613.

Vierteljahrsschrift für Kultur und Litteratur der Renaissance, Berlin, 1886.

Virgilii Opera. P. Virgilii Maronis . . . . Buccolica et Georgica et Aeneis . . . . Cum Familiarissima Iodoci Badii Ascensii Elucidatione. Accessit ad hoc Mapphei Vegii Liber Addititius cum Ascensianis Adnotatiunculis, Paris, 1500.

Voigt, George. *Aeneas Silvius de' Piccolomini als Pabst Pius der Zweite, und sein Zeitalter*, Berlin, 1858.

————. *Die Wiederbelebung des classischen Alterthums, oder erste Jahrhundert des Humanismus*, Berlin, 1893.

Wadding, L. *Annales Minorum*, Rome, Ancona, Naples, 1731–1860.

COMMENTARY

NOTES TO THE LATIN TEXT
PARALLEL PASSAGES

COMMENTARY

NOTES

[The references are to the line numbers in the original Latin text.]

2. sub is used here to obviate elision. It appears in lines 33 and 102 for the same reason. In lines 377 and 578 no metrical necessity dictates its use. Compare *Aeneid* xii . 410, *duro sub Marte*. A curious parallel to Vegius' use of *sub* occurs in the motto of the state of Massachusetts written by Algernon Sidney (1622–1683), *ense petit placidam sub libertate quietam*.

5. revomentes, *revomentem* is employed in its literal significance in *Aeneid* v . 182. Its figurative use is late, and with *corde* bad. Compare Florus ii . 10, 3, *cum sanguine et spiritu male partam revomuere victoriam*. Compare also Ambrosius, *Hexaëmeron* 4, n. 15, *malitiae venena revomere*. J. C. Scaliger in *Poetices Libri Septem*, p. 785, quotes the first six lines of Vegius' *Thirteenth Book of the Aeneid* and comments: "in quibus Virgilianae lucis vestigia invenias. Tolle enim vocem illam *revomentes,* caetera omnia optimi poetae opinione digna sunt. Nec minoris aut operae aut gratiae sexdecim proximi versus qui sequuntur, in quibus duae illae comparationes longae optimae; neque eis inferiores quae in Lucani atque Statii libris positae sunt: ac fortasse etiam meliores."

11. Nec frenum, nec colla pati captiva recusant, as the line stands *colla pati* may possibly be parallel with such a phrase as *collum date,* 'to submit,' 'to acknowledge defeat,' compare Propertius ii . 10, 15, *India quin, Auguste, tuo dat colla triumpho*. In medieval Latin, however, *collum* is sometimes used in the sense of 'a burden' or 'load,' see Du Cange, *Glossarium* II, 439: "collum, fascis, onus quod ad collum portatur. *Covent. Saonae, Anno 1526,* 'Pro qualibet sarcina et unoquoque collo seu fascio omnium, denarios sex monetae Saonae'."

62. trucidant is used in classical Latin in the sense 'to slay' as, for example, *primosque trucidant immissi Danai,* in *Aeneid* ii . 494, and xii . 577, *primosque trucidant*. Horace in *Epistles* i . 12, 21 makes use of this verb: "seu piscis seu porrum et caepe trucidas." Possibly Vegius mistook Horace (who talked about "slaying" onions, etc., though he really meant 'cutting them up,') and used quite seriously an expression which is intelligible only in a playful context.

71 f. altos .... ad caelos, compare *Georgics* iv . 227, *caelo alto; Aeneid* v . 542; vii . 141; viii . 423; x . 633. *Caelum* is used only in the singular by Virgil. Vegius here uses the plural, perhaps to avoid elision, perhaps because the plural was more frequently used than the singular in his time. See H. A. J. Monro's note on Lucretius ii . 1097, "*caeli* for *caelum* was a Hebraism of Church writers." W. A. Merrill, in a note on the same verse says, "the plural, always masculine, is mainly ecclesiastical and a Hebraism." In line 544 Vegius uses *ad caelum*.

83. dehinc, a monosyllable by synizesis as always in the *Thirteenth Book*. Virgil uses *dehinc* as a monosyllable four times (*Aeneid* i . 131, 256; vi . 678; ix . 480) and as a dissyllable five times (*Georgics* iii . 167; *Aeneid* iii . 464; v . 722; viii . 337; xii . 87). Virgil never begins a line with *dehinc*. Vegius uses *dehinc* eleven times in the *Thirteenth Book* (Virgil uses it nine times in his entire works).

[153]

sese . . . . volvebat, see Du Cange, *Glossarium* VI, 877; *volvere se* for *vertere,* a Gallicism, compare *se tourner. Acta Sanctae Francescae Romanae,* Vol. 2, Martii, page 105, *Quibus dictis volvit se Regina caeli ad beatam Franciscam.* (Saint Francesca Romana was a contemporary of Maphaeus Vegius.)

88. Compare *Aeneid* iii . 658, "Monstrum horrendum, informe, ingens, cui lumen ademptum," also *Vellus Aureum,* I, 140–142: "quis deinde asprum immanemque draconem | tuto adeat, taetrum informem, cui lumina semper | insopita, trucique ardescunt, ignea visu."

91. With this verse compare line 558, which clearly implies that Vegius assumes that the Roman race is to trace its origin to Lavinia. Compare also notes on lines 312 and 370.

109. insiliens, a parallel to this use is found in *Vulgaris Interpretatio Regum* x . 10, "et insiluit super eum Spiritus Domini."

116. An interesting parallel to this simile is found in *The Four Seasons,* "Spring" by Anne Bradstreet, quoted by E. W. Martin, *The Birds of the Latin Poets,* p. 148:

> The clocking hen her chirping chickins leads,
> With wings and beak defends them from the gleads.

With the simile of a hen and her chickens, compare Matthew 23:37 and Luke 13:34.

134 ff. The dog rent in pieces by the wild boar is Turnus, the other dogs of the pack are the Latins, the huntsman is Latinus. While the simile is picturesque, its vague connection with the context makes it appear rather a patch.

143 ff. J. C. Scaliger, *Poetices Libri Septem,* p. 786: "Oratio deinde Aeneae frigida, nec multo meliora quae deinde ponit, nec plenior aut felicior oratio Latini."

185. Compare Vegius' *Astyanax,* 83, *oculos suffundit obortis* | *siderios lacrimis.*

211. Ardea (an interesting article on Ardea appears in *Archaeologia,* XLIX, 169 ff.), compare *Aeneid* vii . 409–414, especially the lines, *locus Ardea quondam* | *dictus avis, et nunc magnum manet Ardea nomen* | *sed fortuna fuit.* Vegius has in mind also the fall of Ardea as described by Ovid in *Metamorphoses* xiv . 573 ff. It is of interest that Ardea was captured by Pope Martin V and restored to the Roman Church. The Colonna family, of which the Pope was a member, kept the city under its immediate control. This probably took place at about the time of the composition of the *Thirteenth Book of the Aeneid.*

221. infixa radice, Fabricius and Lemaire read *in fissa radice.* The older editions agree in reading *infixa.* **radice,** governed by *sub,* means 'under a root that is held fast in the earth, but for part of its length protrudes above ground.' *in fissa radice* implies a forked root.

226 ff. Testudo—conamine miscet, compare Seneca, *Epistles* 121 (Book xx, Epistle 4), 8 and 9: "Animalia quaedam tergi durioris inversa tamdiu se torquent, ac pedes exserunt, et obliquant, donec ad locum reponantur. Nullum tormentum sentit supina testudo, inquieta est tamen desiderio naturalis status nec ante desinit (niti), quatere se quam in pedes constitit." Badius (quoted by Lemaire) remarks: "Ponit secundam comparationem, sumptam a testudine, animali quidem imbelli, sed pertinaciter parieti domus incensae adhaerenti; et non nisi cum summa indignatione eam relinquenti, quomodo et cives ex incendio, res suas tantisper dum possunt recipiunt: nec deserunt nisi vi summa repulsi, ingruente scilicet igne. Potest autem prior comparatio (*simile of the ants*) referri ad strenue migrantes; posterior ad tarde discedentes."

229. insudans refers to the effect of heat upon the tortoise shell and supplies the immediate reason for *conamina miscet,* which suggests the turtle's frantic efforts. The figure seems to describe the Rutili, who are so paralyzed by the disaster that they make all sorts of futile efforts before they at last succeed in escaping from the flames.

238. circumlabitur, a verb of which only the present participle is used in classical Latin (Forcellini), compare Lucan vi . 484, *prospectumque dedit circumlabentis Olympi. Circumvolo* is the usual word. Compare also Lactantius, *Fabula* 14: "Turno ab Aenea interempto Ardea urbs, regnum Turni, incendio in cinerem redacta, ex quo volucris emersa est, quae patrio eius nomine vocaretur a posteris Ardea." The bird "Ardea" is mentioned by Virgil, *Georgics* i . 364; *Lucan* v . 554; *Anthologia Latina* 772, 37; Isidorus, *Origines* XII, 7, 21 (E. W. Martin, *The Birds of the Latin Poets*).

effusis .... circumlabitur alis, 'it circles on poised wings,' an unusual and late use of *effundo,* due possibly to some such reminiscence from Virgil as *Aeneid* v . 818, *effundit habenas.*

256. Compare Vegius' *Astyanax,* lines 261 and following.

275 f. altae | sidereus cervicis honos, *id est splendor et relucentia, ac nitor cervicis altae, quia ipse altus erat,* says Badius. *Siderius* would have seemed more appropriate as a modifier for **oculorum aspectus;** compare line 468, **sidereos deiecta oculos;** also Vegius' *Astyanax,* line 264, *quae tibi sidereos rapuit mors impia vultus.* For *honos,* see line 179.

286. Badius comments: *magnus dolor sed ineptus.*

312 ff. quando auspiciis, monitisque deorum | Troianam miscere Italo cum sanguine gentem | expediat, ... intersint, compare *Aeneid* vii . 271 f., *qui sanguine nostrum | nomen in astra ferant* also *Aeneid* xii . 838, *hinc genus Ausonio mixtum quod sanguine surget.* 'He bids them be present and in calmness of mind discover when it is meet in accordance with the omens and signs of the gods to unite the Trojan race with the folk of Italy.' Compare notes on lines 91 and 370.

326. Compare Vegius' *Vellus Aureum,* lines 35–37.

346. f. ambas | iungebat palmas, i.e. in supplication, Badius amplifies the phrase thus: *coniunctis manibus orabat et rogabat.* This is a medieval touch; the Virgilian expression might have been *genua amplectens* or *complexa pedes.* Handclasping was thought dangerous by the Romans. If the palms were held, *pectinatim inter se implexis,* bad luck was considered inevitable. Such postures were "a let and hindrance to business of every sort, and at a council of war or a meeting of magistrates, at prayers and sacrifices, no man was suffered to cross his legs or clasp his hands" (Frazer, *"The Golden Bough,"* "The Taboo and the Perils of the Soul," p. 298, and note 4). See also Pliny, *Naturalis Historia* xxviii . 17; Hippocrates, *De Morbo,* Vol. I, p. 589, ed. Kuhn, Leipzig, 1825. An interesting passage on hand-clapping occurs in Vegius' *Astyanax,* lines 14 f., *tendebat utrasque | iungebatque manus.*

365. unanimes, post-classical. Claudianus, *In consulatum Olybrii et Probini,* 231 : *unanimes fratres cinctos stipante senatur.*

370. qui, Badius comments: *id est, utpote is qui et mittat nepotes: in secula, id est in perpetuam successionem, scilicet Troianos; admixtos generi, id est progenei: Italo, hoc est sanguini Italico, ex parte materna.* The order is unusual, the meaning seems to be, 'now let aged father Latinus who has but this one treasure of his old age give you his daughter in marriage and send down to future ages Trojan descendants sprung from the Italian race.' Compare lines 91 and 312.

394. pietatis opus, Forcellini explains, *opus dicitur sensu morali quaecumque actio sive bona, sive mala, quocumque modo fuerit patrata.* Compare *Vulgaris Interpretatio Jacobus* ii.25, *fides sine operibus mortua est,* and Forcellini's comment, *pietas, item clementia, mitis animus, et facile miserans et parcens.* Compare also *Acta Sanctorum Saturnini, Dativi et aliorum plurimorum martyrorum in Africa,* (7): "Subveni, rogo, Christe, habe pietatem, serva animam meam."

401. enudant, *enudo* in the sense of 'to despoil' is late, compare Cassiodorus, *Variarum Libri xii,* 10.13, *ut nec Roma suis civibus enudetur,* Forcellini.

411. mixtim, compare Lucretius iii.566, *per venas et viscera mixtim.* Merrill comments: "The word is comparatively frequent in late Latin." Du Cange, *Glossarium* IV, 451, "mixtim pro mistim. *Vetus ceremoniale MS B. M. Deauratae Tolos,* 'Et post omnes similiter tendunt ad mensam tam monachi quam seculares; sed qui sunt honorabiliores debent esse primi mixtim cum monachis'."

415. laeta fronte Latinus, Badius feelingly explains, *potius fronte, quam animo dixit: quia licet propter Amatae suspendium doleret, tamen 'premit altum corde dolorem'.*

417 f. postquam .... venientem .... vidit .... haud vera illusit imago, compare *Aeneid* x.456, *haud alia est Turni venientis imago. haud* is here used with *illusit* by analogy to its use with such verbs as *errare* and *ignorare.* Krebs and Schmalz, *Antibarbarus,* Vol. I, p. 646.

Imago, compare Vegius' *Astyanax,* lines 286 f., *simillima imago | patris erat.*
438. Compare Vegius' *Astyanax,* line 97.
448 ff. Compare *Astyanax,* line 69.
454. ceu quando .... agrestes, J. C. Scaliger, *Poetices Libri Septem,* p. 786: "Illa vero comparatio valde bona est."
470. Compare Vegius' *Vellus Aureum,* line 72.
472. qui haud, a harsh elision unusual in the thesis of the first foot.
479. Andromachae quondam data munera. See *Aeneid* iii.483.
480. intextas auro. Compare *Aeneid* i.647 f., *munera .... | ferre iubet, pallam signis auroque rigentem.*
490. tarda, 'late,' not 'slow.' *tarda .... tempora;* Du Cange, *Glossarium* VI, 508, "Serotinus *tarda hora* a Gallico *tard, ad vesperum.*"
526. Vegius credits Dardanus, the mythical founder of Troy, with the original introduction of the symbol which became the Roman eagle. For the eagle as a military standard see Ovid, *Ex Ponto* ii.8, 1.70; Ovid, *Fasti* v.586; *Silius Italicus* vi.25 ff. (E. W. Martin, *The Birds of the Latin Poets,* p. 38): Badius enlarges on the subject and concludes: "Hanc autem Romani pro insigni habebant, quia per auspicium aquilarum inditum est a Romulo urbi nomen." This seems to have been a current misconception. Contrast Livy vii.1: "Priori Remo augurium venisse fertur sex vultures, iamque nuntiato augurio cum duplex numerus Romulo sese ostendisset."

535. variantque pedes, Badius explains, *scilicet saltando, ad modulos psallen-*
tium, unde ductitantium choreas gestum exprimit, Lemaire cites *Aeneid* vi . 644:
pars pedibus plaudunt choreas, but one is tempted to think that medieval custom
has colored the description.

raptimque feruntur further suggests dancing in the modern sense.

541. In the Virgilian portent in *Aeneid* ii . 683 ff. the flame is described as a
point of light; in *Aeneid* vii . 73 ff., the phrase *totis Volcanum spargere tectis,* gives
an impression of more fire, Vegius increases it still further to **flammam | ingentem
. . . . nubibus altis | miscentem.**

levem, compare *Aeneid* ii . 682, *levis . . . . lumen apex.*

560. Lavinia's son is described in the prophecy, *Aeneid* vi . 760 ff.

563 f. quos gloria summo | Oceanum transgressa ingens aequabit Olympo;
contrast *Aeneid* i . 287, *imperium Oceano . . . . qui terminet.* Thomas Twyne,
London, 1583, remarks with confidence: "He alludeth to the Romaines conquest
of Britain."

583. Compare Vegius' *Vellus Aureum,* II, 251.

593. medio . . . . Olympo, Badius has the following curious note: "non incon-
grue autem datur illi in caelo, locus medius, quia sidus Veneris est proximum sub
sole, qui medius planetarum est."

595. omnipotens genitor, compare the beginning of Aeneas' prayer, *Aeneid*
x . 668, and Venus' prayer *Aeneid* i . 229 ff. Vegius imitates the same passages in
Astyanax, 82 ff.

602 ff. The concluding lines of the poem are based on Ovid's *Metamorphoses,*
xiv . 581–608.

612. Compare Vegius' *Astyanax,* line 79.

616. An interesting parallel to these lines occurs in Vegius' *Astyanax,* 113 ff.

> "non tamen Iliacas omnino extinguere vires
> Decretum est, tuus Aeneas servabitur, unde
> Magni opibusque, animisque duces nascentur, et armis
> Qui tandem domitas cogent parere Mycenas;
> Quorum ingens toti nomen dominabitur orbi,
> Illum ego, post multos pelagi, terraeque labores,
> Sublimen ad coelum mittam, et divum numero addam."

624. Compare Livy i . 2 (end): "Situs est, quemcumque eum dici ius fasque
est super Numicium flumen: Iovem indigetem appellant."

626. J. C. Scaliger (*Poetices Libri Septem,* p. 787), "nuptiae vero, et convivium
non sine ineptiis, neque caetera meliora ad finem usque; qui sane non est ignobilis."

1. The same rhythm occurs in *Aeneid* xii.1; **profudit** has the same position in the line as in *Aeneid* xii.154.

3. **magnanimus....Aeneas:** *Aeneid* i.260; v.17, 407; ix.204.
Mavortius: *Aeneid* vi.777; ix.685.

4. **obstupuere omnes;** line 393, **stupefacti omnes;** line 470, **stupefactus;** line 543, **obstupuit pater Aeneas:** compare *Georgics* iv.351, *omnes obstipuere.*

gemitumque dedere Latini, compare *Aeneid* xii.928, *consurgunt gemitu Rutuli.*

8. **tum tela infigunt terrae,** compare *Aeneid* ix.746, *portaeque infigitur hasta.*

10. **insanum....horrent optati Martis amorem,** compare *Eclogues* x.44 f., *nunc insanus amor duri me Martis in armis |....detinet.*

12. **veniam orare,** compare *Aeneid* xi.358, *veniamque oremus ab ipso.*

requiem....malorum, compare *Aeneid* iii.393, *requies ea certa laborum.*

20 f. **incluta .... arma,** compare *Aeneid* vi.479, *inclutus armis.*

21 f. **foedusque precari | pacis,** compare *Aeneid* xi.356, *pacem hanc aeterno foedere firmes,* and *Aeneid* xi.362, *pacem te poscimus omnes.*

23. **tunc Turnum super adsistens,** compare *Aeneid* x.490, *quem Turnus super adsistens.*

placido ore profatur: compare *Aeneid* i.521, *placido sic pectore coepit; Aeneid* vii.194, *placido prior edidit ore;* also Aeneid xi.251. Compare line 423, and line 488.

24. **quae tanta animo dementia crevit:** compare *Aeneid* v.465, *infelix, quae tanta animum dementia cepit?;* compare *Eclogues* ii.69, *quae te dementia cepit.* With this address to the dead compare Aeneas' words to Lausus, *Aeneid* x.825 ff.

25. **superum monitis:** compare *Aeneid* iii.715, *me digressum vestris deus appulit oris;* and *Aeneid* iv.361, *Italiam non sponte sequor; Aeneid* vii.239; and elsewhere. Compare lines 162 f., 426, 545.

26. **Daunia proles,** compare *Aeneid* xii.723, *Daunius heros.*

27. **pactis .... tectis,** compare *Aeneid* x.649, *thalamos .... pactos.*

28. **disce Iovem revereri et iussa facessere divum,** compare *Aeneid* vi.620, *discite iustitiam moniti et non temnere divos.*

iussa facessere: compare *Aeneid* iv.295, *iussa facessunt;* also *Georgics* iv.548, *praecepta facessit;* and *Aeneid* ix.45, *praecepta facessunt.*

29. **memoresque malorum,** compare *Aeneid* i.543, *deos memores fandi atque nefandi.*

33. **suprema dies:** compare *Aeneid* vi.502, *suprema nocte,* and 513, *supremam noctem.*

dies is fem. for the sake of the meter as often in Virgil, for example, *Aeneid* vi.429, and *Aeneid* ix.281.

36. **nunc armis laetare tuis,** compare *Aeneid* x.827, *arma, quibus laetatus, habe tua.*

37. **at non tibi erit Lavinia parvo**: compare *Aeneid* xi . 479 f., *Lavinia virgo,* | *causa mali tanti,* and *Aeneid* xii . 937, *Tua est Lavinia coniunx.* For the use of **parvo**, see *Aeneid* x . 494 f., *haud illi stabunt Aeneia parvo* | *hospitia; Aeneid* ii . 104, *magno mercentur Atridae.*

38. **nec dextra tamen Aeneae cecidisse pudebit**: compare *Aeneid* x . 829, *hoc tamen infelix miseram solabere mortem:* | *Aeneae magni dextra cadis;* also *Aeneid* xi . 688 f., *nomen tamen haud leve patrum* | *manibus hoc referes, telo cecidisse Camillae.*

39. **arma virumque**: *Aeneid* i . 1; ix . 777; xi . 747.

40. **largior**, compare *Aeneid* x . 493 f., *quisquis honos tumuli, quidquid solamen humandi est,* | *largior.*

41 f. **ingentia baltei | pondera**, compare *Aeneid* x . 496, *immania pondera baltei.* Vegius makes the *ei* of *baltei* one syllable by synizesis as in *Aeneid* i . 120, *Ilionei.* Virgil, *Aeneid* x . 496, shortens *baltei* by elision with the following line.

41 ff. Contrast *Aeneid* x . 500, *Quo nunc Turnus ovat spolio gaudetque potitus.*

44 f. **vos memores tamen, Ausonii, melioribus uti | discite bellorum auspiciis,** compare *Aeneid* xii . 435 f., *Disce, puer, virtutem ex me verumque laborem* | *fortunam ex aliis.*

melioribus . . . . auspiciis, *compare Aeneid* iii . 498 f., *melioribus, opto,* | *auspiciis.*

45. **ego sidera iuro**, compare *Aeneid* vi . 458, *per sidera iuro.* For **iuro** with accusative without a preposition, compare *Aeneid* xii . 197, *terram, mare, sidera, iuro.*

46. This line is probably a reminiscence of *Aeneid* vi . 460, **nunquam . . . .** **libens** echoing the *invitus* of Virgil.

in proelia movi, *Aeneid* vii . 603, *movent in proelia.*

47. **vestris actus furiis** may suggest Allecto, *Aeneid* vii . 415 ff.

50. **Troia tecta,** compare *Aeneid* vii . 157 ff., *Ipse* [Aeneas] *humili designat moenia fossa* | *moliturque locum, primasque in litore sedes* | *castrorum in morem pinnis atque aggere cingit.*

52 f. **pedum vi | quadrupedes citat: vi** metonymy for *ictus* as in *Aeneid* iii . 242. For the use of spurs see *Aeneid* xi . 714, *quadripedemque citum ferrata calce fatigat,* and *Aeneid* vi . 881, *spumantis equi foderet calcaribus armos.*

54. **Ignavos . . . . ,** epithet applied by Turnus to the Trojans in *Aeneid* xii . 12.

strepit altus plausibus aether: the same rhythm is found in *Aeneid* vi . 709, *strepit omnis murmure campus.*

55–58. **et quamvis . . . . honores,** compare *Aeneid* xi . 2–5, *Aeneas quamquam et sociis dare tempus humandis* | *praecipitant curae turbataque funere mens est,* | *vota deum primo victor solvebat Eoo.*

55. **inhumata rogis dare corpora surgat | ingens cura animo,** compare *Aeneid* xi . 22 f., *interea socios inhumataque corpora terrae* | *mandemus*

57. **sub pectore,** compare *Aeneid* iv . 67, *vivit sub pectore vulnus.*

volvens, compare *Aeneid* i . 305, *per noctem plurima volvens.*

58. **meritos superum mandabat honores,** compare *Aeneid* iii . 264, *numina magna vocat meritosque indicit honores.*

meritos . . . . honores: these words occur in *Aeneid* iii . 118 and 264; v . 652.

59. Compare *Aeneid* v . 96 ff., and *Aeneid* xi . 197.

60. in templa: often used in the plural when a single sanctuary is meant, as in *Aeneid* ix . 626, *ad tua templa;* and *Aeneid* vi . 41, *Teucros vocat alta in templa sacerdos.*

61. For the general idea see *Aeneid* v . 330.

62. viscera diripiunt: compare *Aeneid* xii . 214 f., *viscera vivis | eripiunt;* also *Aeneid* i . 211, *tergora diripiunt costis et viscera nudant.*

62. trucidant: see *Aeneid* ii . 494 and xii . 577.

64. tum vina effundunt pateris, compare *Aeneid* v . 98, *vinaque fundebat pateris.*

dona Lyaei, see *Aeneid* i . 686, *laticemque Lyaeum.*

65. accumulant, compare *Aeneid* vi . 885, *accumulem donis.*

66. tura ignes adolent: compare *Aeneid* i . 417, *ture calent arae; Georgics* iv . 379, *adolescunt ignibus arae; Aeneid* i . 704, *flammis adolere penatis; Eclogues* viii . 65, *adole . . . . tura.*

altaria fumant, compare *Eclogues* i . 43, *bis senos cui nostra dies altaria fumant.*

67. tum plausus per tecta movent, compare *Aeneid* v . 148, *tum plausu fremituque virum . . . . consonat omne nemus.*

68. Saturnia Iuno: *Aeneid* v . 606; ix . 2, 745, 802; x . 760; xii . 156.

69. iam placidam, compare *Aeneid* xii . 841.

meliorem is a reminiscence of the phrase *in melius* of *Aeneid* i . 281.

71. in medium effertur, compare *Aeneid* v . 401, *in medium.*

73. duplices mittebat ad aethera palmas: compare *Aeneid* i . 93, *duplices tendens ad sidera palmas; Aeneid* ix . 16, *duplicisque ad sidera palmas sustulit;* compare lines 543 f.

74. complexus Iulum, compare *Aeneid* xii . 433, *Ascanium . . . . complectitur.*

75. Compare Anchises' speech to Aeneas, *Aeneid* v . 724 ff., and Venus' speech to Cupid, *Aeneid* i . 664.

spes una, compare *Aeneid* xii . 57, *spes tu nunc una, senectae.*

76. quem variis actus fatis discrimina duxi, compare *Aeneid* i . 204, *per varios casus, per tot discrimina rerum.*

77. ecce inventa quies, compare *Aeneid* iii . 495, *vobis parta quies.* Contrast this line with *Aeneid* iv . 169, *ille dies primus leti primusque malorum.*

78. modum, compare *Aeneid* iv . 98, *sed quis erit modus?*

79. dura in bella, compare *Aeneid* x . 146, *duri certamina belli.*

80. dis auspicibus, compare *Aeneid* iv . 45, *dis equidem auspicibus.*

81 f. cum primum Aurora rubebit | crastina, compare *Aeneid* xii . 76 f., *cum primum crastina caelo | puniceis invecta rotis Aurora rubebit.*

83 f. alto | pectore verba trahens, compare *Aeneid* i . 371, *imoque trahens a pectore vocem.*

blando sic ore locutus, compare *Aeneid* i . 670 f., *blandis . . . . | vocibus.*

85. O socii, compare the well-known speech of Aeneas, *Aeneid* i . 198 ff.

86. bellorum aestus: compare *Aeneid* iv . 564, *irarum . . . . aestus,* and *Aeneid* viii . 19, *curarum . . . . aestu.*

87. **hiemes**, 'storms': *Aeneid* i . 120–122, *navem . . . . vicit hiems; Aeneid* i . 125, *emissamque hiemem; Aeneid* ii . 110 f., *aspera ponti | interclusit hiems; Aeneid* iii . 194–195, *imber | noctem hiememque ferens.*

quicquid acerbum, compare *Aeneid* xii . 678, *quidquid acerbi est.*

88. Compare *Aeneid* iii . 658, *monstrum horrendum, informe, ingens, cui lumen ademptum.*

89 f. **convertite mentem | in melius**: compare *Aeneid* i . 281, *consilia in melius referet;* see note on 85 above.

iam finis adest, compare *Aeneid* i . 223, *et iam finis erat.*

90. **meta malorum**, compare *Aeneid* iii . 714, *haec meta viarum.*

96. **vosmet**, compare *Aeneid* i . 207, *durate, et vosmet rebus servate secundis.*

99. **discite me**, compare *Aeneid* xii . 435, *disce, puer, virtutem ex me.*

102. **idem ego sub maiora potens vos praemia ducam**, compare *Aeneid* xii . 436 f., *nunc te mea dextera bello | defensum dabit et magna inter praemia ducet.*

idem ego, *Aeneid* x . 851, *idem ego.*

103 f. **talibus orabat**: *Aeneid* iv . 437; vi . 124; x . 96.

variosque in pectore casus | praeteritos volvens, compare line 57 and note, also line 306.

varios . . . . casus: *Aeneid* i . 204, *per varios casus; Aeneid* x . 352, *per varios sternit casus.*

104. **partam . . . . quietem**: compare *Aeneid* iii . 495, *vobis parta quies; Aeneid* vii . 598, *nam mihi parta quies.*

106 f. **gravibus tandem evasisse periclis | exsultans**, compare *Aeneid* iii . 282, *iuvat evasisse tot urbes.*

109. **stragemque minatur**, compare *Aeneid* xi . 348, *mortemque minetur.*

112. **conatibus**, compare *Aeneid* xii . 910, *in mediis conatibus aegri | succidimus.*

117 f. **Anchisa genitus**: compare *Aeneid* v . 244, *satus Anchisa;* also *Aeneid* v . 424; vi . 331; vii . 152; in *Aeneid* vi . 322, the phrase *Anchisa generate* occurs.

mulcebat . . . . | . . . . dictis: compare *Aeneid* i . 197, [Aeneas] *dictis maerentia pectora mulcet; Aeneid* v . 464, *mulcens dictis; Aeneid* v . 770, *quos bonus Aeneas dictis solatur amicis.*

118. **antiquum . . . . timorem**: compare *Aeneid* vii . 365, *cura antiqua;* and *Aeneid* v . 608, *antiquum . . . . dolorem.*

119. **agitans**, compare *Aeneid* ii . 420 f.

121. **altior**, compare *Aeneid* viii . 162, *cunctis altior ibat Anchises.*

122. **supereminet omnes**: *Aeneid* i . 501, [Diana] *supereminet omnis; Aeneid* vi . 856, [Marcellus] *supereminet omnes.*

129. **defessum**, compare *Aeneid* xii . 593, *fessis . . . . Latinis.*

130. **crebrescere**, compare *Aeneid* xii . 406 f., *horror | crebrescit.*

131. **confossum**, compare *Aeneid* ix . 444 f., *tum super exanimum sese proiecit amicum | confossus.*

133. **corripuit**, 'reprove,' 'check,' compare Ovid, *Metamorphoses* iii . 564 f., *turba suorum | corripiunt dictis.*

manibus verbisque silentia ponens, compare Ovid, *Metamorphoses* i . 205 f., *voce manuque | murmura compressit.*

134. spumantis apri, compare *Aeneid* i . 324, *aut spumantis apri cursum cla-*
more prementem.

138. pavitat, compare *Aeneid* xi . 813.

ululatu, compare *Aeneid* iv . 667, and ix . 477, which end in this cadence after
hiatus.

140. ore silet, by analogy to such a phrase as *ore locutus* comparé Georgics
iv . 444.

gemitum . . . . premit, compare *Aeneid* x . 464 f., *magnumque sub imo | corde*
premit gemitum.

141. suppressa voce quierunt, compare *Aeneid* vi . 102, and xi . 300, *ora quie-*
runt.

142 f. tunc sic illacrimans, compare *Aeneid* xi . 29, *sic ait inlacrimans.*

alto corde Latinus | verba dabat: compare *Aeneid* i . 371, *imo trahens a pec-*
tore vocem; and *Aeneid* xi . 840, *deditque has imo pectore voces.*

144. alternasque vices miscent: compare *Aeneid* xi . 426 f., *multos alterna re-*
visens | lusit et in solido rursus Fortuna locavit; and *Aeneid* ix . 164, *discurrunt*
variantque vices.

146. dominandi innata cupido, compare *Georgics* iv . 177, *innatus . . . . amor*
. . . . habendi.

147. mortales quo caeca vehis: compare *Aeneid* iii . 56 f., *quid non mortalia*
pectora cogis | auri sacra fames; Aeneid iv . 412, *improbe Amor, quid non mortalia*
pectora cogis.

152 f. tristia . . . munera, contrast *tristia dona, Aeneid* iii . 301.

159. Aeneadas turbasse in bella coactos, compare *Aeneid* xii . 580 f., *Aeneas*
. . . . testatur . . . . deos iterum se ad proelia cogi.

160 f. promissa quietis | pignora, compare *Aeneid* xi . 362, *pacem te poscimus*
omnes, | Turne, simul pacis solum inviolabile pignus.

163. nostris pellere tectis, compare *Aeneid* iii . 167, *hae nobis propriae sedes.*

164. nataeque abrumpere foedus, compare *Aeneid* xii . 31 (Latinus to Tur-
nus), *promissam eripui genero, arma impia sumpsi.* See *Aeneid* vii . 268 ff., *est*
mihi nata | . . . . opto, in which Latinus offers the hand of Lavinia to Aeneas.

165. For Aeneas' peaceful intent at the time of his arrival in Italy, see *Aeneid*
vii, 155, *pacemque exposcere Teucris;* see also *Aeneid* xi . 96, *nos alias hinc ad*
lacrimas eadem horrida belli | fata vocant, for his regret at the continuance of the
war. For Latinus' own aversion to the war, see Aeneid xii . 31, *arma impia sumpsi.*

166 f. quae tanta insania mentem | implicuit; compare *Aeneid* xii . 37, *quae*
mentem insania mutat; also *Aeneid* iv . 595, in which the same phrase occurs.

168. sublimemque in equo, compare *Aeneid* vii . 285, *Latini | sublimes in*
equis.

radiantibus armis, compare *Aeneid* viii . 616, *arma . . . . radiantia.*

172. magnique albentes ossibus agri, compare *Aeneid* xii . 36, *campique in-*
gentes ossibus albent.

174. fluviique humana caede rubentes: compare *Aeneid* xii . 35, *Tiberina*
fluenta | sanguine; compare also the prophecy in *Aeneid* vi . 87, *Thybrim multo*
spumantem sanguine.

185. lacrimisque genas implevit obortis: compare *Aeneid* vi . 686, *effusaeque* *genis lacrimae; Aeneid* iv . 30, *sinum lacrimis implevit obortis; Aeneid* vi . 867, and *Aeneid* xi . 41, *lacrimis . . . . obortis.*

186 ff. This passage is based upon *Aeneid* xi . 59 ff.

sese . . . . volvens, miserabile corpus | **attolli**, compare *Aeneid* xi . 59, *tolli miserabile corpus* | *imperat.*

187 f. Fulfillment of Turnus' dying request to Aeneas, *Aeneid* xii . 934 f., *Dauni miserere senectae* | *et me, seu corpus spoliatum lumine mavis, redde meis.*

190. feretro: compare *Aeneid* xi . 64, and *Aeneid* vi . 222, *ingenti . . . . feretro.*

191. Compare *Aeneid* xi ..78 f., *multaque praeterea Laurentis praemia pugnae* | *aggerat et longo praedam iubet ordine duci.*

194 f. equum . . . . | **rorantem**, compare *Aeneid* xi . 88 f., *bellator equus . . . .* | *it lacrimans.*

197. versa arma gerunt, *Aeneid* xi . 93, *versis Arcades armis.*

tum extera pubes, compare *Aeneid* iv . 350, *nos fas extera quaerere regna.*

200 f. caedentes sese, compare *Aeneid* xi . 86, *pectora nunc foedans pugnis, nunc unguibus ora.* Compare line 217, *pectora caedentes.*

in tecta, compare *Aeneid* vii . 170 ff.

gressum . . . . in tecta Latinus | **flexerat**, compare *Aeneid* xi . 99, *gressumque in castra ferebat.*

205. superbam | **. . . . animam:** compare *Aeneid* vi . 817, *animamque superbam; Aeneid* xi . 715, *animis . . . . superbis.*

206 f. largis . . . . | **. . . . lacrimis:** compare *Aeneid* ii . 271, *largos . . . . fletus; Aeneid* vi . 699, *largo fletu;* compare line 181.

212 f. favillae | **altivolae:** *Aeneid* ix . 76, *fert . . . .* | *commixtam Volcanus ad astra favillam; Aeneid* iii . 573, *candente favilla;* Ovid, *Metamorphoses*, xiv . 575, *tepida latuerunt tecta favilla.*

213. nec spes plus ulla salutis, compare *Aeneid* ii . 803, *nec spes opis ulla dabatur.*

215. signum, 'omen,' 'sign' : compare *Aeneid* iii . 388, *signa tibi dicam; Aeneid* ii . 171, *nec dubiis ea signa dedit Tritonia monstris.*

216 f. extemplo concussi animos, turbataque cives | **pectora caedentes**, compare *Aeneid* xi . 451, *extemplo turbati animi concussaque vulgi* | *pectora.*

217 f. miserandae sortis iniquum | **deflebant casum**, compare *Aeneid* xii . 243, *Turni sortem miserantur iniquam.*

218. longoque ex ordine: compare *Aeneid* i . 395; vi . 482; xi . 79; viii . 722; xi . 143 f., *longo ordine.*

219. totis . . . . viribus, compare *Aeneid* xii . 528, *totis in vulnera viribus itur.*

220. Compare Virgil's two insect similes, that of the bees, *Aeneid* i . 430–436 (also *Georgics* iv . 162), and that of the ants, *Aeneid* iv . 401–407.

nigra cohors, compare *Aeneid* iv . 404, *nigrum . . . . agmen.*

222. instantes operi: compare *Aeneid* i . 423, *instant ardentes Tyrii;* and *Aeneid* i . 436, *fervet opus.*

222 ff. securis | **. . . . saeva**, compare *Aeneid* vi . 819, *saevasque securis.*

incumbat, see line 108.

verso . . . . , 'destroy,' compare Ovid, *Heroides* i . 24, *versa est in cineres . . . . Troia.*

parvas | .... **casas,** compare *Eclogues* ii . 29, *humilis . . . . casas.*

232 f. senio confectus, compare *Aeneid* xi . 85, *aevo confectus.*

voces | . . . . **querulas,** compare *Culex* 151, *querulae . . . . voces.*

234–238. tum vero . . . . circumlabitur alis, compare Ovid, *Metamorphoses,* xiv . 573 ff., *cadit Ardea, Turno* | *sospite dicta potens, quam postquam Dardanus ignis* | *abstulit, et tepida latuerunt tecta favilla,* | *congerie e media, tum primum cognita, praepes* | *subvolat et cineres plausis everberat alis.*

236. indicium nomenque urbis versae Ardea servans, compare *Aeneid* vii . 411 ff., *locus Ardea quondam* | *dictus avis, et nunc magnum manet Ardea nomen,* | *sed fortuna fuit.*

243 f. volitans . . . . | **fama ruit:** compare *Aeneid* vii . 104 f., *circum late volitans iam Fama per urbes* | *Ausonias tulerat; Aeneid* ix . 473 f., *interea pavidam volitans pennata per urbem* | *nuntia Fama ruit;* also *Aeneid* xi . 139 ff., *iam Fama volans, tanti praenuntia luctus,* | *Euandrum, Euandrique domos et moenia replet,* | *quae modo victorem Latio Pallanta ferebat.*

246. letali vulnere, compare *Aeneid* ix . 579 f., *abditaque intus* | *spiramenta animae letali vulnere rupit.*

247–249. mox turbati omnes nigras duxere frequentes | **incensas ex more faces: ardentibus agri** | **collucent flammis,** compare *Aeneid* xi . 142 ff., *de more vetusto* | *funereas, rapuere faces; lucet via longo* | *ordine flammarum et late discriminat agros.*

249. dehinc se venientibus addunt, compare *Aeneid* xi . 145 f., *contra turba Phrygum veniens plangentia iungit* | *agmina.*

250. quos postquam toto videre ex agmine matres, compare *Aeneid* xi . 146 f., *quae postquam matres succedere tectis* | *viderunt, maestam incendunt clamoribus urbem.*

254. furibundus, 'frenzied with grief,' compare *Aeneid* iv . 646, [Dido] *conscendit furibunda gradus.*

255. Turnumque super prostratus et haerens, compare *Aeneid* xi . 149 f., *feretro Pallante reposto* | *procubuit super atque haeret lacrimansque gemensque.*

256. edidit ore, compare *Aeneid* vii . 194, *placido prior edidit ore.*

258 f. quo me tantis iactate periclis | **duxisti,** compare *Aeneid* ix . 490.

259. Compare *Aeneid* viii . 482, *saevis tenuit Mezentius armis,* and *Aeneid* xii . 890, *saevis certandum est comminus armis.*

260. praestans animi, *Aeneid* xii . 19, *O praestans animi iuvenis.*

261 ff. hic clarae virtutis . . . . | **nate, refers?:** compare *Aeneid* xi . 54 f., *hi nostri reditus exspectatique triumphi?* | *haec mea magna fides.*

263 f. Haec illa quies promissa parenti | **afflicto toties,** compare *Aeneid* xi . 152, *non haec, O Palla, dederas promissa parenti.*

266. quanto volvuntur fata tumultu, compare *Aeneid* i . 22, *sic volvere parcas.*

270. nunc, mi Turne, iaces, compare lines 36 f., *heu, nobile corpus,* | *Turne, iaces.*

271 f. quo pulchrior alter | **non fuit in tota Ausonia,** compare *Aeneid* vii . 54 f., *multi illam magno e Latio totaque petebant* | *Ausonia; petit ante alios pulcherrimus omnis* | *Turnus.* Compare also *Aeneid* vii . 649 f., *quo pulchrior alter* | *non fuit excepto Laurentis corpore Turni.*

273. **eloquio**, compare *Aeneid* xi . 383, *proinde tona eloquio.*

nec quis positis ingentior armis, *Aeneid* xi . 641, *ingentem corpore et armis* | .... The adjective *ingens* is applied to Turnus in *Aeneid* xii . 927.

274 f. **serenus** | **ille decor**, compare *Aeneid* ii . 285 f., *serenos* | .... *vultus.*

277 f. **tali rediture paratu** | **discedens voluisti avidis te credere bellis:** compare *Aeneid* xi . 45 f., *non haec Euandro de te promissa parenti* | *discedens dederam;* compare also *Aeneid* xi . 152, *non haec, O Palla, dederas promissa parenti.*

278. **voluisti avidis te credere bellis**, compare *Aeneid* xi . 153, *saevo velles te credere Marti.*

279. **heu mortem invisam**, contrast *Aeneid* xi . 177, *vitam* .... *invisam.*

284. **obscuram**, compare *Aeneid* vi . 268, *ibant obscuri.*

290 f. **natum rapuistis, et Ardea flammis** | **consumpta in cinerem versa est**, compare Ovid, *Metamorphoses* xiv . 573, *Turnusque cadit; cadit Ardea.*

291 f. **nunc aethera pennis** | **verberat**, compare *Aeneid* vii . 411, *locus Ardea quondam* | *dictus avis.*

293. **sors** .... **senectae**, compare *Aeneid* vi . 114, *sortem* .... *senectae.*

296. **infrendens**, *infrendere*, 'to gnash,' used only with *dentibus* by Virgil, *Aeneid* iii . 664; viii . 230; x . 718.

298. **trahens duros gemitus:** the parallel phrase *trahens* .... *vocem* occurs in *Aeneid* i . 371.

rapidos .... **dolores:** compare *Georgics* iv . 263, *rapidus* .... *ignis; Aeneid* i . 42, *rapidum* .... *ignem.*

299. **validis Iovis unguibus ales:** compare *Aeneid* xii . 247 f., *Iovis ales* .... *pedibus* .... *uncis,* and *Aeneid* xi . 752, *aquila unguibus haesit;* compare also *Aeneid* i . 394, *Iovis* .... *ales; Aeneid* ix . 564 f., *pedibus Iovis armiger uncis; Aeneid* xi . 752, *aquila implicuit* .... *pedes atque unguibus haesit.*

302 ff. **postera lux latum splendore impleverat orbem:** compare *Aeneid* vii . 148–155, *postera cum prima lustrabat lampade terras* | *orta dies* .... *tum satus Anchisa delectos ordine ab omni* | *centum oratores augusta ad moenia regis* | *ire iubet, ramis velatos Palladis omnis,* | *donaque ferre viro, pacemque exposcere Teucris;* compare also *Aeneid* v . 42, *postera cum primo stellas Oriente fugarat* | *clara dies; Aeneid* iii . 588, *postera iamque dies primo surgebat Eoo; Aeneid* xii . 113 f., *postera vix summos spargebat lumine montis* | *orta dies;* and *Ciris,* 349, *postera lux ubi laeta diem mortalibus almum.*

303 f. **tunc pater infractos fatali Marte Latinus** | **defecisse videns Italos**, compare *Aeneid* xii . 1, *Turnus* .... *infractos adverso Marte Latinos* | *defecisse videt.*

306. **ingentesque animo curas, et foedera volvens:** with *volvens,* compare lines 57, 103, and notes. With the whole line compare *Aeneid* xii . 190, *paribus se legibus ambae* | *invictae gentes aeterna in foedera mittant* (Aeneas' oath to Latinus), also *Aeneid* xii . 202, *nulla dies pacem hanc Italis nec foedera rumpet* (Latinus' oath to Aeneas).

308 f. **praestantes vocat electos ex agmine toto** | **mille viros, qui Dardanium comitentur ad urbem**, compare *Aeneid* vii . 153, *centum oratores augusta ad moenia regis* | *ire iubet,* and *Aeneid* xi . 331, *centum oratores prima de gente Latinos* | *ire placet.*

310. spectatum virtute ducem, compare *Aeneid* viii.151, *rebus spectata iuventus.*

togatos, compare *Aeneid* i.282, *gentemque togatam.*

312 ff. quando auspiciis, monitisque deorum | Troianam miscere Italo cum sanguine gentem | expediat .... intersint: compare *Aeneid* vii.271 f., *qui sanguine nostrum | nomen in astra ferant;* also *Aeneid* xii.838, *hinc genus Ausonio mixtum quod sanguine surget.*

315. Aeneadasque vehant alta intra moenia laeti, compare *Aeneid* vii.160 f., *turris ac tecta Latinorum | ardua cernebant iuvenes muroque subibant.*

316 f. interea .... pacem, Aeneid xii.596 f.

vulgus inerme, *Aeneid* xii.131, *vulgus inermum.*

321. alacris, compare *Aeneid* v.380 f., *ergo alacris .... Aeneae stetit ante pedes.*

322. pectore toto, compare *Aeneid* ix.276 f., *iam pectore toto | accipio et comitem casus complector in omnis.*

325. Teucrorum castra subibat, contrast *Aeneid* vii.161, *muro .... subibant.*

326. cincta comas ramis oleae, pacemque rogabat: compare *Aeneid* vii.154 f., *ramis velatos Palladis omnis | donaque ferre viro, pacemque exposcere Teucris;* also *Aeneid* xi.100 f., *iamque oratores aderant ex urbe Latina | velati ramis oleae veniamque rogantes.*

327 f. bonus Aeneas, *Aeneid* v.770, *quos bonus Aeneas dictis solatur amicis,* and *Aeneid* xi.106, *quos bonus Aeneas haud aspernanda precantis prosequitur venia.*

intra regia duci | tecta iubet, compare *Aeneid* ii.32, *primusque Thymoetes | [equum] duci intra muros hortatur.*

regia .... | tecta, compare *Aeneid* vii.668, *regia tecta subibat.*

328. causam .... viae, compare *Aeneid* ix.376, *quae causa viae?*

placido ore, *Aeneid* vii.194.

329 f. tunc senior sic incipiens ardentia Drances | verba movet, compare *Aeneid* xi.122f., *tum senior semperque odiis et crimine Drances | infensus iuveni Turno.*

ardentia, compare *Aeneid* ii.405, *ardentia lumina,* often so used by Virgil, who does not, however, apply it to speech.

331. O Troianae dux inclute gentis, compare *Aeneid* vi.562, *dux inclute Teucrum,* and *Aeneid* xi.124 ff., *O fama ingens, ingentior armis | vir Troiane, quibus caelo te laudibus aequam? | iustitiaene prius mirer belline laborum? | .... quaerat sibi foedera Turnus.*

336. nec .... umquam, compare *Aeneid* iv.338 f., *nec coniugis umquam | praetendi taedas;* this line has the same cadence as that of Vegius. Compare also *Aeneid* xii.918, *nec .... usquam.*

341. id rabidus Turni, et stimulis incensus iniquis: with **rabidus,** compare *Aeneid* xi.336 f., *quem gloria Turni | obliqua invidia stimulisque agitabat amaris.*

351. spumabat: The figure is that of an angry animal breathing forth fire. Virgil uses it in describing wild boars and horses, but not people. The closest parallel occurs in *Aeneid* viii.304 f., *super omnia Caci | speluncam adiciunt spirantemque ignibus ipsum.*

352 f. **at vero dignum invenit pro talibus ausis | exitium**, compare *Aeneid* ii . 535–537, *pro talibus ausis | di . . . . persolvant grates dignas.*

353 f. **momordit | . . . . prostratus humum**, compare *Aeneid* xi . 417 f., *qui . . . . procubuit moriens et humum semel ore memordit.*

358 f. **in te omnis domus, et fessi inclinata Latini | spes iacet**, compare *Aeneid* xii . 59, *in te omnis domus inclinata recumbit.*

359 f. **super aurea . . . . | sidera:** compare *Aeneid* i . 379, *super aethera notus;* also *Aeneid* ii . 488, *ferit aurea sidera clamor,* and *Aeneid* xi . 832 f., *ferit aurea clamor | sidera.*

360. **ingentem bello**, compare *Aeneid* xi . 641, *ingentem corpore et armis.*

caelestibus armis, *Aeneid* xii . 167, *pater Aeneas . . . . caelestibus armis.*

361. **extollunt**, compare *Aeneid* xi . 401 f., *extollere viris | gentis bis victae.*

362. **consultaque turba**, compare *Georgics* iii . 491, *consultus . . . . vates.*

363. **invalidique aetate senes:** compare *Aeneid* iv . 599, *confectum aetate;* and *Aeneid* xi . 85, *aevo confectus;* and *Aeneid* xii . 132, *invalidique senes.*

laeta iuventus, compare *Aeneid* ii . 394 f., *hoc . . . . omnisque iuventus | laeta facit.*

367. **Ausonia**, compare *Aeneid* vii . 54 f., *illam . . . . totaque petebant | Ausonia.*

368. **in te unum conversi oculi**, compare *Aeneid* xii . 656 f., *in te ora Latini | in te oculos referunt,* and *Aeneid* xii . 704, *et omnes | convertere oculos.*

369. For an account of the aged Latinus and his only daughter, see *Aeneid* vii . 52 f., *sola domum et tantas servebat filia sedes, | iam matura viro.*

iam senior, compare *Aeneid* vii . 45 f., *rex arva Latinus et urbes | iam senior longa placidas in pace regebat.*

371. **mittat**, compare *Aeneid* xii . 191 f., *paribus se legibus ambae | invictae gentes aeterna in foedera mittant.*

372. **ergo age, magne veni Teucrorum ductor**, compare *Aeneid* ii . 707, *ergo age, care pater.*

Teucrorum ductor, *Aeneid* viii . 470, *maxime Teucrorum ductor.*

373. **ingredere . . . . honores**, compare *Eclogues* iv . 48, *adgredere . . . . honores.*

374. **cunctique . . . . simul ore fremebant**, compare *Aeneid* i . 559, and v . 385, where the same phrase occurs.

375. **pius Aeneas:** compare line 406, also *Aeneid* i . 220, 305, 378; iv . 393; v . 26; and elsewhere.

376. **amico pectore**, compare *Aeneid* iii . 463, *ore . . . . amico.*

377. **placida solitum sub pace**, compare *Aeneid* vii . 46, *longa placidas in pace regebat.*

378. **violentia Turni**, compare *Aeneid* xi . 376, *talibus exarsit dictis violentia Turni,* and *Aeneid* xii . 45 f., *haudquaquam dictis violentia Turni | flectitur.*

379. **tanti discrimina Martis:** the cadence is the same as that of *Aeneid* i . 204, *per tot discrimina rerum.*

380. **iuvenilis . . . . laudis**, compare *Aeneid* ii . 518, *iuvenalibus armis.*

381. **quicquid id est**, *Aeneid* ii . 49, *quidquid id est, timeo Danaos.*

382 f. **et sanctam aeterno cum foedere pacem | iungere**, compare *Aeneid* xi . 356, *et pacem hanc aeterno foedere firmes.*

383 f. rex idem imperium, et veneranda tenebit | sceptra socer, compare *Aeneid* xii . 192 f., *socer arma Latinus habeto | imperium sollemne socer.*

384 f. statuentque mei mihi moenia Teucri, | et nomen natae urbis erit, compare *Aeneid* xii . 193 f., *mihi moenia Teucri | constituent urbique dabit Lavinia nomen.*

385 f. sociosque penates | adiciam: compare *Aeneid* xii . 192, *sacra deosque dabo; Aeneid* xii . 836 f., *morem ritusque sacrorum | adiciam.*

386. vos communes in saecula leges, compare *Aeneid* xii . 190 f., *paribus se legibus ambae | invictae gentes aeterna in foedera mittant.*

387. concordes . . . . amores, compare *Aeneid* vi . 827, *concordes animae.*

388. quod restat adhuc, compare *Aeneid* ii . 142, *quae restet adhuc.*

391. clara dies, compare *Aeneid* v . 42 f., *postera cum primo stellas Oriente fugarat | clara dies.*

392. dixerat, compare line 374 and note.

affatu: compare *Aeneid* iv . 283 f., *quo nunc reginam ambire furentem | audeat adfatu;* also *Aeneid* xi . 120 f., *dixerat Aeneas, illi obstipuere silentes | conversique oculos inter se atque ora tenebant.*

393. stupefacti, compare *Aeneid* vii . 119, *stupefactus numine.*

394. mox robore toto | congestas statuere pyras: compare *Aeneid* vi . 214 f., *principio pinguem taedis et robore secto | ingentem struxere pyram;* also *Aeneid* xi . 185, *iam . . . . constituere pyras;* and *Aeneid* xi . 204, *innumeras struxere pyras.*

395–398. ignemque repostis | civibus immisere: altumque sub aethera fumus | evolat, atque atris caelum sublime tenebris | conditur: with this passage compare *Aeneid* xi . 185 ff., *huc corpora quisque suorum | more tulere patrum, subiectisque ignibus atris | conditur in tenebras altum caligine caelum.*

398–400. innumeras ex omni rure bidentes | glandilegosque sues iugulant, pinguesque iuvencos | immittuntque rogis, compare *Aeneid* xi . 197, *multa bouum circa mactantur corpora morti | saetigerosque sues, raptasque ex omnibus agris | in flammam iugulant pecudes.*

400. latos . . . . campos, *Aeneid* x . 408, *per latos acies Volcania campos.*

401. fremit impulsus clamoribus aer, compare *Aeneid* xi . 192, *it caelo clamorque virum clangorque tubarum.*

403. tunc Teucri Ausoniique omnes, mixto agmine, laeti, compare *Aeneid* v . 293, *conveniunt Teucri mixtique Sicani.*

404 f. tecta . . . . | Laurenti, atque altis erectam moenibus urbem, compare *Aeneid* vii . 160 f., *tecta Latinorum | ardua cernebant iuvenes muroque subibant.* For the description of Latinus' palace see *Aeneid* vii . 170 ff.

408. animi maturus Aletes, compare *Aeneid* ix . 246, *hic annis gravis atque animi maturus Aletes.*

409. gravis Ilioneus, compare *Aeneid* ix . 246, *annis gravis;* in *Aeneid* i . 521, the phrase *maximus Ilioneus* occurs.

Mnestheusque, acerque Serestus: compare *Aeneid* ix . 171, *instat Mnestheus acerque Serestus;* also *Aeneid* ix . 779, and *Aeneid* xii . 547, *Mnestheus acerque Serestus.*

410. Sergestus . . . . fortisque Cloanthus: compare *Aeneid* i . 510, *Sergestumque vidit fortemque Cloanthum; Aeneid* iv . 288, *Mnesthea Sergestumque vocat* *fortemque Serestum; Aeneid* i . 222, and *Aeneid* i . 612, *fortemque Gyan, fortemque Cloanthum.*

412. interea effusi stabant per moenia cives, compare *Aeneid* xii . 131 ff., *tum studio effusae matres et vulgus inermum | invalidique senes turris ac tecta domorum | obsedere, alii portis sublimibus astant.*

415. laeta fronte Latinus, compare *Aeneid* xi . 238, *haud laeta fronte.*

416. magna . . . . comitante caterva. This expression occurs in *Aeneid* ii . 40; ii . 370; v . 76.

417 f. postquam . . . . venientem . . . . vidit | . . . . haud vera illusit imago, compare *Aeneid* x . 456, *haud alia est Turni venientis imago.*

420 f. late regalem oculis spargebat honorem | sidereis, compare *Aeneid* i . 591, *laetos oculis adflarat honores.*

421. data copia fandi, compare *Aeneid* i . 520; and *Aeneid* xi . 248, *coram data copia fandi.*

424 f. venisti tandem, compare *Aeneid* vi . 687, *venisti tandem.*

cupidum nec fixa fefellit | spes animum, compare *Aeneid* vi . 691, *nec me mea cura fefellit.*

425. lux Troianae clarissima gentis, compare *Aeneid* ii . 281, *O lux Dardaniae, spes O fidissima Teucrum.*

426. magnorum quem iussa deum tot casibus actum, compare *Aeneid* i . 598 f., *terraeque marisque | omnibus exhaustis iam casibus.*

434. nunc age occurs in *Georgics* iv . 149; *Aeneid* vi . 756; vii . 37.

437. sunt mihi regna, compare *Aeneid* i . 71, *sunt mihi bis septem.*

440. quem contra, compare *Aeneid* ix . 280, *contra quem* [Ascanium] *taila fatur | Euryalus.*

bonus Aeneas, *Aeneid* v . 770.

442. placidae . . . . pacis, i.e., 'old age,' compare *Aeneid* vii . 45 f., *rex arva Latinus et urbes | iam senior longa placidas in pace regebat.*

443. quaeso, compare *Aeneid* xii . 72, *ne, quaeso, ne me lacrimis . . . . prosequere.*

444. nunc adsum, compare *Aeneid* i . 595, *coram . . . . adsum.*

445 f. magni mihi surgit imago | Anchisae, compare *Aeneid* ii . 560, *subiit cari genitoris imago.*

447. talibus orabant inter se, et tecta subibant, compare *Aeneid* viii . 359, *talibus inter se dictis ad tecta subibant.*

talibus orabant: compare *Aeneid* iv . 437; vi . 124; x . 96.

448. cum studio effusae matres . . . ., compare *Aeneid* xii . 131, *tum studio effusae matres.*

matresque nurusque, compare *Aeneid* xi . 215, *matres miseraeque nurus.*

449. longaevi . . . . patres, compare *Aeneid* v . 715, *longaevosque senes.*

450. pulchra . . . . corpora, compare *Aeneid* xii . 270, *pulcherrima . . . . corpora.*

451. ante omnes, compare *Aeneid* v . 570, *formaque ante omnis pulcher Iulus.*

magnum Aenean: *Aeneid* x . 159; ix . 787; x . 830.

445. tenuit . . . . imber, *Georgics* i . 259, *frigidus agricolam si quando continet imber.*

resolutis, compare Ovid, *Metamorphoses* xi . 516, *ecce cadunt largi resolutis nubibus imbres.*

[169]

456. curvumque....**aratrum,** compare *Georgics* i.508, *curvae....falces.*

463. pulcher Iulus: compare *Aeneid* v.570, *formaque ante omnis pulcher, Iulus,* also *Aeneid* vii.107, and 477 f.

464. dehinc Itali, mixtique Phryges, compare *Aeneid* v.293, *undique conveniunt Teucri mixtique Sicani.*

468. sidereos deiecta oculos: compare *Aeneid* xi.479 f., *iuxtaque comes Lavinia virgo* | ....*oculos deiecta decoros;* compare also *Aeneid* i.561, *vultum demissa.*

470. primo aspectu stupefactus inhaesit, compare *Aeneid* i.613 f., *obstipuit primo aspectu Sidonia Dido* | *casu deinde viri tanto.*

474. iunguntur foedera, *Aeneid* xii.822, *foedera iungent,* compare *Aeneid* xi.355 f., *quin natam egregio genero dignisque hymenaeis* | *des, pater, et pacem hanc aeterno foedere firmes.*

475. canunt....**hymenaeum,** compare *Aeneid* vii.398, *canit hymenaeos.*

476 f. dehinc plausus fremitusque altum super aera mittunt, | **et laetam vocem per regia tecta volutant,** compare *Aeneid* v.148 ff., *tum plausu fremituque virum....consonat omne nemus, vocemque inclusa volutant* | *litora.*

478. fidum....**Achaten:** *Aeneid* i.188; vi.158; viii.521; viii.586; x.332. In *Aeneid* i.643, Achates is, as here, sent to bring gifts.

479 f. Andromachae quondam data munera, see *Aeneid* iii.482 ff., *nec minus Andromache....* | *fret picturatas auri subtemine vestis* | ....*textilibusque onerat donis.*

vestes | **intextas auro,** *Aeneid* i.648, *pallam signis auroque rigentem.*

480 ff. quod saepe solebat | ....**circumdare collo** | **auratum, gemmis circumseptumque monile:** compare *Aeneid* i.653, *quod gesserat olim.* With **collo** | ....**monile,** compare *Aeneid* i.654, *colloque monile* | *bacatus;* with **circumdare collo,** compare Ovid, *Metamorphoses* i.631, *circumdat vincula collo.*

481. dum res Troianae stabant, compare *Aeneid* ii.455, *dum regna manebant*

483 f. magnum cratera in pignus amoris | **quem Priamus patri Anchisae donavarat olim:** compare *Aeneid* v.535–538, *ipsius Anchisae longaevi hoc munus habebis,* | *cratera impressum signis, quem Thracius olim* | *Anchisae genitori in magno munere Cisseus* | *ferre sui dederat monumentum et pignus amoris;* compare also *Aeneid* ix.266, *dabo....cratera antiquum quem dat Sidonia Dido.*

489. variisque trahunt sermonibus horas, compare *Aeneid* i.748, *et vario noctem sermone trahebat.*

491 f. regali convivia luxu | **effundunt,** compare *Aeneid* i.637 f., *domus interior regali splendida luxu* | *instruitur.*

492. latosque alta intra tecta paratus, compare *Aeneid* i.638, *mediisque parant convivia tectis.*

493. strato discumbere in ostro, compare *Aeneid* i.700, *stratoque super discumbitur ostro.*

convenere omnes, *Aeneid* i.707 f., *frequentes* | *convenere.*

494. dapibus .... **futuris,** *Aeneid* i.210, *dapibusque futuris.*

495. dat manibus crystallus aquas, compare *Aeneid* i.701, *dant manibus famuli lymphas.*

496–499. **ministri | innumeri magno distinguunt ordine curas. | Pars dapibus
reficit mensas, pars pocula miscet, | craterasque replet,** compare *Aeneid* i . 705,
centum . . . . ministri | qui dapibus mensas onerent et pocula ponant.

499. **nunc hac, nunc volvitur illac:** compare *Aeneid* iv . 285; viii . 20, *animum
nunc huc celerem nunc dividit illuc.*

500. **turba frequens,** compare *Aeneid* i . 707, *per limina laeta frequentes.*

varios miscentque per atria motus, compare *Aeneid* xii . 217, *Rutulis . . . .
vario misceri pectora motu,* for a verbal similarity.

501 f. With Latinus' interest in Iulus compare that of Dido, *Aeneid* i . 712 ff.

immotis spectabat . . . . | luminibus, compare *Aeneid* i . 717 f., *oculis . . . . |
haeret.*

504. **maturumque animum ante annos,** compare *Aeneid* ix . 311 f., *Iulus, | ante
annos animumque gerens curamque virilem.*

506. **complexum manibus iunctumque fovebat,** compare *Aeneid* i . 687, *dabit
amplexus,* and *Aeneid* i . 718, *gremio fovet.*

509 f. **postquam epulis compressa fames:** *Aeneid* i . 216, *postquam exempta
fames,* and *Aeneid* viii . 184, *et amor compressus edendi.*

traducere longam | incipiunt fando . . . . noctem, compare *Aeneid* i . 748,
vario noctem sermone trahebat.

511. With the conversation described in this and the following line compare
Aeneid i . 750 ff., *multa super Priamo rogitans, super Hectore multa; | nunc, quibus
Aurorae venisset filius armis, | nunc, quales Diomedis equi, nunc, quantus Achilles.*

515. **ardens in equo,** compare *Aeneid* xii . 71, *ardet in arma.*

517 f. **magnorum heroum Latiique antiqua potentis | gesta recensebant:** this
conversation is based upon that of Aeneas and Evander, *Aeneid* viii . 314 ff.

518–521. **fugientemque horrida nati | arma sui Saturnum . . . . | . . . . genusque
in montibus altis | composuisse vagum, legesque et iura dedisse,** compare *Aeneid*
viii . 320 ff., *primus ab aetherio venit Saturnus Olympo | arma Iovis fugiens et
regnis exsul ademptis. | is genus indocile ac dispersum montibus altis | composuit
legesque dedit, Latiumque vocari | maluit, his quoniam latuisset tutus in oris.*

519 f. **Saturnum Italis latuisse sub oris: | hinc Latium dixisse,** compare *Ae-
neid* viii . 357, *hanc Saturnus condidit arcem | . . . . illi fuerat Saturnia nomen.*

520 f. **genus . . . . composuisse vagum,** compare *Aeneid* vii . 202 ff., *Latinos |
Saturni gentem haud vinclo nec legibus aequam, | sponte sua veterisque dei se more
tenentem.*

523 ff. **utque Electra Atlantide cretus | Iasio Idaeas caeso Phrygiae isset ad
urbes | Dardanus:** compare *Aeneid* iii . 165 ff., *nunc fama minores | Italiam dixisse
ducis de nomine gentem: | hae nobis propriae sedes; hinc Dardanus ortus | Iasius-
que pater;* also *Aeneid* viii . 134–137, *Dardanus, Iliacae primus pater urbis et auc-
tor, | Electra, ut Grai perhibent, Atlantide cretus, | advehitur Teucros; Electram
maximus Atlas | edidit.*

525. **ex Corytho,** *Aeneid* iii . 170 f., *Corythum terrasque requirat | Ausonias.*

527. **Hectoreae gentis,** compare *Aeneid* i . 273, *gente sub Hectorea.*

530 f. **tum fremitus, laetaeque per atria voces | alta volant, strepitu ingenti
tectum omne repletur,** compare *Aeneid* i . 725 f., *fit strepitus tectis vocemque per
ampla volutant | atria.*

[171]

532. dant lucem flammae, et lato splendore coruscant, compare *Aeneid* i . 727, *noctem flammis funalia vincunt.*

533. cithara, compare *Aeneid* i . 740 f., *cithara crinitus Iopas | personat.*

534. plausum ingeminant, compare *Aeneid* i . 747, *ingeminant plausu Tyrii, Troesque sequuntur.*

536. largo . . . . luxu, compare *Aeneid* i . 637, *regali . . . . luxu.*

537. celebrata: for a similar use compare *Aeneid* v . 603, *celebrata . . . . certamina.*

tum maximus heros, see *Aeneid* vi . 192, *tum maximus heros.*

538. Aeneas urbem curvo signabat aratro: compare *Aeneid* v . 755 f., *interea Aeneas urbem designat aratro | sortiturque domos;* also *Aeneid* vii . 157, *ipse humili designat moenia fossa.*

540. Compare similar prodigies in *Aeneid* ii . 680 ff., and *Aeneid* vii . 72 ff.

ecce, compare *Aeneid* ii . 682 f., *ecce levis summo de vertice visus Iuli | fundere lumen apex.* The *editio princeps* misprints *fatu* for *fatum.* Compare *Aeneid* ii . 680, *mirabile monstrum;* for the idea of ill fortune implied in *fatum* compare *Aeneid* vii . 73, *visa, nefas, longis comprendere crinibus ignem.*

diffundere flammam, *Aeneid* ii . 683, *fundere lumen;* also *Aeneid* x . 270 f., *flamma | funditur.*

542. summo . . . . vertice, *Aeneid* ii . 682, *summo de vertice.*

543 f. obstipuit pater Aeneas, compare *Aeneid* v . 90, *obstipuit visu Aeneas.*

duplicesque tetendit | ad caelum cum voce manus: compare *Aeneid* ii . 688, *caelo palmas cum voce tetendit; Aeneid* iii . 176, *tendo . . . . supinas | ad caelum cum voce manus;* x . 667, *duplicis cum voce manus ad sidera tendit.*

544. Compare *Aeneid* ii . 689 f., *Iuppiter omnipotens . . . . | aspice nos, hoc tantum, et si pietate meremur.*

545. terraque, marique, compare *Aeneid* i . 598 f., *terraeque marisque | omnibus exhaustis casibus.*

547 f. per si quid agendum est | quod restat, compare *Aeneid* ii . 142, *per, si qua est, quae restet.*

548. placidam . . . . quietem, *Ciris,* 343, *placidam . . . . quietem.*

549. augurio, compare *Aeneid* ii . 691, *da deinde augurium.*

firmate, compare *Aeneid* ii . 691, *haec omnia firma.*

malisque imponite finem, compare *Aeneid* ii . 619, *finemque impone labori.*

550. talia iactantem, compare *Aeneid* ii . 588, *talia iactabam;* lines 551–555 are imitated from *Aeneid* ii . 588–594.

aurea mater, compare *Aeneid* x . 16, *Venus aurea.*

551. se Venerem confessa, compare *Aeneid* ii . 591, *confessa deam.*

552. nate, compare *Aeneid* ii . 594, and elsewhere.

nate, animo pone hanc curam, compare *Georgics* iv . 531, *nate, licet tristis animo deponere curas.*

capesse: for a parallel form see *Aeneid* i . 77, *mihi iussa capessere fas est.*

554. nunc tibi parta quies, nunc meta extrema malorum, compare *Aeneid* vii . 598, *nam mihi parta quies.*

555. componunt saecula pacem, compare *Aeneid* vii . 339, *compositam pacem.*

556 f. e vertice, compare *Aeneid* ii . 682, *summo de vertice.*

nec .... horresce, compare *Aeneid* iii . 394, *nec tu mensarum morsus horresce futuros.*

558. celebri .... sanguine, compare *Aeneid* i . 286, *pulchra .... origine.*

559. ad sidera mittat, compare *Aeneid* i . 259, *sublimemque feres ad sidera caeli.*

561 f. egregiis totum qui laudibus orbem | complebunt, contrast *Aeneid* i . 287, *imperium Oceano, famam qui terminet astris.*

563 f. quos gloria summo | Oceanum transgressa ingens aequabit Olympo, contrast *Aeneid* i . 287, *imperium Oceano .... qui terminet.*

565 f. quos .... ardens .... | .... vehet super aethera virtus, compare *Aeneid* vi . 129 f., *quos .... ardens evexit ad aethera virtus; Aeneid* i . 287 f., quoted in note on 563 f.

super aethera, compare note on line 359.

571 f. sacros Troia ex ardente penates | ereptos: compare *Aeneid* ii . 293, *sacra suosque tibi commendat Troia penates; Aeneid* iii . 148 ff., *Phrygiique penates, | quos mecum ab Troia mediisque ex ignibus urbis | extuleram.*

573. ad aeternum mansuros tempus honores, compare *Culex*, 38, *gloria .... mansura per aevum.*

575. ad sedes alias, compare *Aeneid* i . 270 ff., *regnumque ab sede Lavini | transferet, et longam multa vi muniet Albam | .... inde | .... Romulus excipiet gentem et Mavortia condet | moenia Romanosque suo de nomine dicet.*

577 f. pace tenebis | sub placida gentem Iliacam, see *Aeneid* i . 265 ff., *tertia dum Latio regnantem viderit aestas, | ternaque transierint Rutulis hiberna subactis.*

579. Elysias .... ad umbras, compare *Georgics* i . 38, *Elysios .... campos.* Virgil, in *Aeneid* vi . 744, speaks of *amplum .... Elysium* as *laeta arva.*

580 f. Italis dominabere, leges | communes Teucrisque ferens, compare *Aeneid* i . 264, *moresque viris et moenia ponet.* See the response of the oracle of Apollo, *Aeneid* iii . 97 f., *hic domus Aeneae cunctis dominabitur oris.*

581 f. tum laetus ad altum | te mittes caelum, compare Jupiter's promise to Venus, *Aeneid* i . 259 f., *feres ad sidera caeli | magnanimum Aenean.*

sic stat sententia divum: compare *Aeneid* i . 257, *manent immota tuorum | fata tibi; Aeneid* i . 260, *neque me sententia vertit.*

583. leves .... ad auras, Ovid, *Metamorphoses* xiv . 597, *perque leves auras.*

585. divae .... parentis, compare *Aeneid* iv . 365, *diva parens.*

586. compositos felici in pace, compare *Aeneid* i . 249, *placida compostus pace.*

590 f. iam paribus Phryges atque Itali se moribus ultro, | et socia ingenti firmabant pectora amore, compare *Aeneid* xii . 190 f., *paribus se legibus ambae | invictae gentes aeterna in foedera mittant.*

593. se immisit: compare *se volvebat*, line 83 above; compare *Aeneid* vi . 262, *antro se immisit aperto.*

596. qui res hominum, compare *Aeneid* i . 229, *qui res hominumque deumque | aeternis regis imperiis.*

599. nec .... te .... sententia fallit, compare *Aeneid* i . 260, *neque me sententia vertit.*

600. tres . . . . annos, compare *Aeneid* i . 265 f., *tertia . . . . aestas,* | *ternaque . . . . hiberna.*

601. nullo discrimine: compare *Aeneid* i . 574, *Tros Tyriusque mihi nullo discrimine agetur; Aeneid* x . 108, *Tros Rutulusne fuat, nullo discrimine habebo.*

603 f. meritumque ferebas | **illaturum astris,** *Aeneid* i . 259 f., *sublimemque feres ad sidera caeli* | *magnanimum Aenean.*

604. illaturum astris, compare *Aeneid* i . 259, *feres ad sidera caeli.*

605. Aeneia virtus, Ovid, *Metamorphoses* xiv . 581, *Aeneia virtus.*

606. hominum pater atque deum, compare *Aeneid* i . 254, *hominum sator atque deorum.*

607. pectore verba ferens, compare *Aeneid* i . 371, *imoque trahens a pectore vocem.*

609. et terra et pelago et per tanta pericula vectos, compare *Aeneid* i . 3, *multum ille et terris iactatus et alto.*

611. Iunone secunda: compare *Aeneid* iv . 45, *Iunone secunda;* see *Aeneid* i . 279 f., *aspera Iuno . . . . consilia in melius referet,* and *Aeneid* xii . 841, *Iuno . . . . mentem . . . . retorsit.*

617. laude perenni, compare *Aeneid* ix . 79, *fama perennis.*

619. super aethera mittam, compare *Aeneid* i . 379, *super aethera notus.*

620 f. nec regia Iuno | **abnuit,** compare *Aeneid* vii . 438 f., *nec regia Iuno* | *immemor est.* Compare also Ovid, *Metamorphoses* xiv . 593 f.

621 f. magnum Aenean . . . . ad altum | **efferri caelum,** compare *Aeneid* i . 259 f., *feres ad sidera caeli* | *magnanimum Aenean.*

625. ubi currit in aequora harundine tectus: compare *Aeneid* viii . 34, [Tiberinum] *umbrosa tegebat harundo;* compare Ovid, *Metamorphoses* xiv . 598.

626 ff. Compare Ovid, *Metamorphoses* xiv . 603 ff.

628. super aera, compare line 476, **super aera.**

629 f. quem Iulia proles | **indigetem appellat, templisque imponit honores:** compare *Aeneid* xii . 794, *indigetem Aenean scis ipsa . . . . deberi caelo;* and Ovid, *Metamorphoses* xiv . 606 ff.; also Livy i . 2 (end), *Iovem indigetem appellant.*

INDEX

INDEX

A

Abbreviator, Vegius as, 10

Achates, 47

Acta Sanctorum, 146

"*aemulus Numae,*" 20

Aeneas: apotheosis of, 26; of Augustan Rome, 24; builds city, 53; death of, 4, 48; in illustrations, 44, 45, 46, 48; in Italy, 53; marriage of, 46, 53; slays Turnus, 53; translation of, 53; victory, 45; of Virgil, 27, 158 f.; wedding feast, *frontispiece*

Aeneas of Gaza, 23

Aeneas Silvius Piccolomini (Pope Pius II), 8, 11, 18, 20, 148, 149

Aeneid: as allegory, v, 2, 24; epitomes for twelve books, 49; incomplete, 31; interpretation, v, 25, 26; Irish, 39; Italian, 39; other supplements to, 1, 2; as a parable, 26; the Pilgrim's Progress of antiquity, 24; sequel to the, v, 37; supplement to, appeared until 1650, v, 30; symbolic expression, 25; *The XIII Bookes of Aeneidos,* 37, *facing* 50; *see* Parallel passages

Aitken, G. A., 38 n.

Alberti, Leon Battista, 24

Aldus, *see* Manutius

Alfonso, King of Naples, 19

Allegory, 25, 26, 29, 30, 32, 38; *Aeneid* as divine, v, 2

"*alter Augustus,*" 20

"*alter Maro,*" 5, 30

"*alter Parthenias,*" 5

"*ambas jungebat palmas,*" 72 f. (ll. 346 f.), 155

Allegorizers, the, 24, 25

Ambergau, Adam de, v, 29; colophon, 50; facsimile of opening lines of *Virgil* of 1471, 50

Ambrose, 13

Anachronisms, 34; *see* Description of Brant's woodcuts, 44 ff.

Anchises, 28, 47

Angelico, Fra, 12, 13, 17

Antiquities of Saint Peter's, writings on, 20

Antwerp, 29

Appian, *Civil Wars,* 19

Apollonius of Tyana, 13

Archaeology, 14, 15

Ardea, 45; article on, 154; burning of, 4; in illustrations, 45

Ardea, the "bird," 45, 155

Aretino, Carlo, 15

Argument, The (Twyne and Phaer), 53

Argumentum, 48, 49, 52

Aristotle, 18

Arundel Manuscripts, 5, 49

Ascanius, 46, 47

Ascensius, Iodocus Badius, commentary by, 1, 32, 33, 146, 154, 155, 156

Associates of Vegius, 15

Astyanax, 145, 154, 157

Atticus, 23

Augustine, Saint, 12

Aurispa, 17, 30

Authorship, 11 ff.; *see* Bibliography, 145 f.

B

"Babylonian Captivity," 5

Badius, 33; *see* Ascensius

Bährens, 49

Baillet, Adrien, 146

Barlandus, 33

Barozzi, L., and Sabbadini, R., 19 n., 146

Barzizza, Gasparino, 19

Basil, 13

Basilica of St. Peter, history of the, 14

Basle, 19 n., 29, 41, 42, 46

Bayle, Pierre, 146

Beccadelli, Antonio, 18, 19

Bellay, Cardinal du, 38

Bembo, Cardinal, 29

Bernard, 13

Bernardino, Fra, of Siena, 8, 20; canonization of, 8

Beroaldus, 33

Bible, 25; editions before 1500, v

Bibliographical Society Publications, 33 n., 38 n., 148

Bigne, de la, 147

Biography, 6, 8; of Vegius, *see* Life and work

Bisticci, Vespasiano da, 9; biographer, 23, 30, 147

Blondus, Flavius, 14, 18, 21

Block prints, 42; *see* Woodcuts

Boethius, of 1501, 42
Bologna, 10
Borinski, C., 147
Borrichius, Olaus (Borch, Olaf von), 31
Boswell, James, 39
Botticelli, 16
Boulting, William, 20 n.
Bracciolini, Poggio, 17
Bradstreet, Anne, 154
Brant, Sebastian, vi, 1, 40, 44; Columbus'
  letter, 41; *Narrenschiff,* 41; *Virgil,* 40,
  41, 43, 147; woodcuts, 30, 40, 41, 42, 46;
  see Redgrave
Brescia, 29
Brisciola, Laelius, 31
British Museum, vi, 49
British versions, 36
Bruni, Leonardo, 10, 21, 22
Bunyan, John, 24
Burchardt, Jacob, 147
Burke, Edmund, 39
Burlesque, 38
Burt, T. Seymour, 2, 39, 40
Butler, 38
Byzantium, 21

C

Calderinus, 33
Camaldulites, Order of the, 23
Canon of the Basilica of St. Peter, Vegius,
  11, 29
Capra, Bartolomeo de la, 17, 18
Carmina Illustrium Poetarum Italorum, 147
Carthage, 25
Cassian, 13
Cato, 23
Celestial City, 25
Cerda, Juan Luigi de la, 31, 147
Charles I, 38
Christian exegesis, 26
Christina, Queen, 31
Chrysostom, 13; Saint, 23
Cicero, 17, 18; manuscript of works, 17
Claudian, 18
Classics, illustrated, 42; *see* Brant
Coleman, C. B., 10 n.
Cologne, 29
Colophon, 48 f., 50; Adam de Ambergau's,
  50; Douglas', 100, 142; Twyne's, 91
Columbus, caravels of, 41, 42, 43; letter of,
  41; typical Renaissance discoverer, 41 f.

Commentary, by Ascensius, 1, 32, 33; by
  Beroaldus, 33; by Barlandus, 33; by Don-
  atus, 32; by Fabricius, 33; by Landinus,
  32; by Mancinellus, 33; by Pomponius
  Laetus, 33; by Servius, 32; by Vives, 33
Comparetti, D., 1, 14 n., 25, 147
Constantine the Great, 20
Constantinople, 16; fall of, 20
Convivium Deorum, 10 n., 17, 145
Conway, R. S., 26 n., 147
Copinger, W. A., vi, 29 n., 50, 147
Cortesius, Paulus, 30, 147
Cosimo, 23
Country life of Vegius, 7
Court poetry, 17; *see* Writings
Criticism, 30 ff.; *see* Scaliger
Crotti, Lanzaretto, 18
Crotti, Luigi, 18
Culture, 15; education the basis of, 13
Curia, 10
Cyprian, 13
Cyriaco of Ancona, 18

D

d'Adda, G., 18 n.
Dancing, 157
Dante, 24
Dardanus, 156
d'Asti, Antonio, 5, 18, 146
Datary, Vegius promoted to, 10
Date, of *editio princeps,* v, 29; of final ap-
  pearance of Thirteenth Book, v, 30; of
  Scotch translation, 93; *see* Editions
Daunus, King, 45, 53
Davidson, English translation by, 39
Davies, G. S., 12, 147
Decembrio, Pier Candido, translator of
  Appian and Plato, 1, 2; wrote supplement
  to *Aeneid,* 2, 19
Decoration, monochrome, 41
Decretals, pseudo-Isadorian, 10
De educatione liberorum, 7, 8 n., 13, 27, 145
De felicitate et miseria, 7, 17, 145
d'Este, Marquis Niccolo, 20
"*dehinc,*" 58 (l. 83), 153
De perseverantia religionis, 7, 12 n., 27, 145
*De rebus antiquis memorabilibus basilicae
  Sancti Petri,* 18, 146
"*De varietate Fortunae,*" poem by d'Asti, 18
Dialectic, 9
Dido, 27

Munro, H. A. J., 153
Muratori, L. A., 148
Mustard, W. P., 3, 148

N

Naples, 16; literary academy at, 18–19
Narrenschiff (Ship of Fools), 41
Naudé et Patin, 148
Nepos, 23
Niccolo, 23
Nicéron, J. P., 9 n., 14 n., 148
Nicholas V, 11, 14, 20
Nisiely, Udeno, 31 n., 148
Noceto, Pietro di, 11
North, 38
Novavilla, C. S. de, 2
Numicus (or Numicius), River, 48, 53
Nuremburg, 29
Nurse, Vegius', 6

O

Omens, 70 (ll. 312 ff.), 72 (ll. 346 f.), 155, 157
"O socii," 58 (l. 85), 160
Opera Vegii, 15 n.
Ostia, 12
Orpheus, 9
Ovid, 4, 7, 8, 10, 18, 39, 154, 156, 161, 164, 165, 169, 173; Brant's illustrations, 42; Marlowe's translation of, 38

P

Pagan literature, 24
Pagan poets, 15, 16; and painters of Renaissance, 16
Paganism, 24
Painters and sculptors, 16
Palingenius, Marcellus, 36
Palinurus, 28
Pallas, 44
Palmer, H., 33 n., 148
Pancilorus, Hippolitus, 148
Panormitanus, 30
Papacy, return of, to Rome, 11
Papal secretaries, Vegius and Valla, 10
Parallel passages, 158–174
Paris, publications, 29
Parody, 33, 38
"parvo numerosa iuventus," 50
Pastor, L., 148
Pater, Walter, 16, 148

Pavia, 1, 9, 10, 12, 15, 18, 19, 29; University, 18
periocha, 48, 49
Persius, 18
Petrarch, 1, 5, 24, 31
Phaer, Dr. Thomas, vi, 25, 36, 37, 38; translation by, 95–142, 148
Philalethes, 7
Piccolomini, *see* Aeneas Silvius
Piccolomini, Angelina, 19
Pippo di Gante da Pisa, Isaia di, 12
"plagosus Orbilius," 8
Plato, 18, 25
Pliny, 18, 155
Plutarch, North's, 38
Poems, Virgil's, MS, 19
"poetam haud reiiciendum," 19
Poetry, 9, 35; pagan, 11, 16
Politian, 32
Polysyndeton, 50
Pompeiana, 9, 145
Pontanus, Jovianus, 31
Pope Pius II, 8
Porphyry, 13
Priam, King, 47
Printing, art of, 43 n.; Bible before, v; European, 42; invention of, v, 14, 29, 40; 180 editions of Virgil before 1500, v; *see Incunabula Virgiliana*
Proba, 14
Procopius of Rabenstein, 20
Prologues, 48 f.
"Proloug" by Gavin Douglas, vi
Proloug of the Threttene Buik, The, vi, 35, 95–100
Prose writing, 12, 145
Publication, of Vegius' Thirteenth Book, 29
Puritanism, 24, 25

Q

Quadrio, Severio, 148
Quintus of Smyrna, 31
Quotations from classics, 13

R

Raffaele, Luigi, vi, 9 n., 11, 19, 21 n., 29, 30 n., 49 n., 145, 148
Redgrave, G. R., 40 n.
Religious training, 13
"revomentes," 31, 54 (l. 5), 153
Rho, Antonio da, 19

Robbias, the della, 17
Roman See, 5
Rome, 11, 12, 14, 15, 29; founding of, 24, 25
Rose (Ross), Alexander, 38
Rosinello, Bernardino, 22
Rossi, J. B. de, 14 n., 147, 148
Rue (Ruaeus), Charles de la, 31, 32
Rusticalia, 145
Rutili, 44, 53

S

Sallust, 18
Sandys, J. E., 24, 148
Santa Croce, church of, 22
Saxius, J. A., 2, 9 n., 10 n., 18 n., 149
Scaliger, J. C., 4, 31, 149, 154, 156, 157
Scheidels Chronik, 45
Scholars, associates of Vegius, 15
Scotch translation, vi, 33, 95–142; earliest
    publication, vi; with "proloug," vi
Scott, Sir Walter, 33
Seneca, 18, 154
Servius, 32
sesqui, 50
Settignano, Disiderio da, 23
Shackleton, Richard, 39
Shepherd story, 7
Similes, Virgil's, 163
Statius, 4, 18, 31
Strassburg, 29, 41, 42, 44, 45
Style, 30; of French translations, 38; of
    Phaer and Twyne, 37; of Vegius, 34, 36
Subiaco, 11, 29
Suetonius, 18
Sulpicius Apollinaris, 48
*Supplement to the Twelfth Book of the
    Aeneid, A*, 9, 29; see *Aeneid* and Thir-
    teenth Book
Sweynheym and Pannartz, 29
Synizesis, 153, 159

T

Terence, 18; epitomes of plays of, by Sul-
    picius Apollinaris, 48; illustrated by
    Brant, 42
Thirteenth Book of the *Aeneid*, 34, 39;
    commentary, 32, 33, 153 ff.; date, 9, 29;
    earliest MS, 29; *editio princeps*, v, 29, 50,
    51; first publisher, v; flaw in composi-
    tion, 4; of historical interest, 32; literary
    form, 4, 24; last appearance of, 1; lines

in, 4; original caption, 9; parody, 1; plot,
    4; reason for, v, 28, 29; similes in, 4;
    story of, 2–3; symbolic interpretation,
    2; translations, 1, 14, 23, 33, 53, 95; ver-
    sification, 32; wit, 7
"Threttene Buik of the Eneados, The," 30,
    95
Tiraboschi, G., 149
Title-page, 43; decoration for, 42; of
    Twyne and Phaer *Virgil, facing* 50
Tornielli, Cavaliere Giorgio, 39
Translations of Maphaeus Vegius' "Thir-
    teenth Book": Burt's, 40; Douglas', 33;
    English, 40, 51, 53; first metrical, 33;
    French, 38; in Great Britain, 33; Irish,
    39; Italian, 39; Scotch, 95–142; by Tra-
    versari, 23; by Twyne and Phaer, 38,
    53–91
Translations:
    of Latin authors, 14, 37
    of MSS, 20
    of *Virgil,* 36 f.; Davidson's, 39
Traversari, Ambrogio, 17, 21, 23, 24
Troia, 44, 45
Troy, 28
Turin, 29
Turnus, 28, 45, 154, 163; illustration, 44;
    slain, 53
Twyne, Thomas, M.D., vi, 37, 51, 157; text
    by, 53
Types of *editio princeps*, Roman, vi, 29;
    opening lines, *facing* 92

U

University life, 9

V

Valerius Maximus, 18
Valla, Lorenzo, 5, 9, 11, 19, 30; Biblical
    scholar, 10; death of, 5; life of, 5 n.
variantque pedes, 82 (l. 535), 157
Vasari, 16
Vegius, Bellortus, 6, 7, 9
Vegius, Caterina Lanteria, 6
Vegius, Eustace, 7
Vegius, Laurence, 6, 7
Vegius, Maphaeus: allegorical interpreta-
    tion, 27; born, 5; buried, 15; contempo-
    raries, 5; criticism of, 32; death, 29; as
    educationalist, 13; epigram to, 49; family
    and childhood, 6; heroic poems, 3; as a